Magnifying Mal-Development
Alternative Economic Survey, India

Magnifying Mal-Development

Alternative Economic Survey, India

Alternative Survey Group

RAINBOW PUBLISHERS

Zed Books
London and New York

Magnifying Mal-Development: Alternative Economic Survey, India was first published in India in December 2004 by Rainbow Publishers Ltd., A-19, Sector 56, NOIDA-201 301, U.P., India. e-mail: rainbow_p@vsnl.net

Magnifying Mal-Development: Alternative Economic Survey, India was first published outside South Asia in December 2004 by Zed Books Ltd., 7 Cynthia Street, London N1 9JF, London, UK and Room 400, 175 First Avenue, New York, NY 10010, USA.

Distributed in the United States exclusively by Palgrave McMillan, a division of St. Martin's Press, LLC, 175 Fifth Avenue, New York, NY 10010, USA.

Cataloguing-in-Publication Data is available from the British Library.

Library of Congress Cataloging-in-Publication Data has been applied for.

ISBN 1-84277-575-8 (UK)

ISBN 81-86962-81-6 (Hb-India)
ISBN 81-86962-82-4 (Pb-India)

Cover design: Pravin Mishra
Typeset in 10 pts. Plantin Bold Condensed and Plantin at Printways.
Printed and bound at S.P. Printech, Delhi-110 092, India Tel: 22514076

Contents

Acknowledgements

An informal group effort such as this involving a large number of persons with a commitment to some social values, incurs many debts in the process of bringing out this volume. First and foremost, the group thanks the contributors. In addition, for editing, copy-editing, and all the logistics and chores of publications we are grateful to the following: Benodini Banerjee, Dhruva Narayan, Feroze Ahmed, Kamal Nayan Kabra, Ranjana Padhi, Smitu Kothari and V. Upadhyay. We place on record our thanks to Zed Books for joining as publisher of the volume.

We are happy to report the valuable support extended by our publishers. We are grateful to our avid readers who have so enthusiastically sustained this exercise for nearly a decade. Like in the earlier years, we are hopeful of the enthusiastic response of our readers. The Alternative Survey Group may be contacted at C/o Prof. Kamal Nayan Kabra, B-202, Anandlok Apartments, Mayur Vihar Phase-I, Delhi-110 091 or C/o Prof. V. Upadhyay, IIT, Hauz Khas, New Delhi-110 016 or C/o Jaya Mehta, 20, Chandralok, Indore-452 018, Madhya Pradesh.

Alternative Survey Group

Contributors

Alpana Sagar is Assistant Professor, Centre for Social Medicine and Community Health, Jawaharlal Nehru University (JNU), New Delhi.

Arun Kumar is Professor, Centre for Economic Studies and Planning, JNU, New Delhi.

Hari Om Verma is Former Director, Institute of Technology and Management; and was Reader in Economics, Ramjas College, University of Delhi, New Delhi.

Hariharan Ramachandran is Director, Institute of Applied Manpower Research (IAMR), Delhi.

Imrana Qadeer is Professor, Centre for Social Medicine and Community Health, JNU, New Delhi.

Jaya Mehta is a senior economist and social activist, Indore, Madhya Pradesh.

K.S. Chalpati Rao is Professor, Institute for Studies in Industrial Development (ISID), New Delhi.

Kamal Nayan Kabra has recently completed his tenure as Professor of Economics, Indian Institute of Public Administration (IIPA), New Delhi.

Kumaresh Chakravarty is a leading columnist and former President, Delhi University Teachers' Association (DUTA), New Delhi.

Manmohan Krishna is Reader in Economics, Allahabad University, Allahabad, Uttar Pradesh.

Prakas Louis is Executive Director, Indian Social Institute (ISI), New Delhi.

Pranjoy Guha Thakurta is a senior journalist and Director, School of Convergence, International Management Institute, New Delhi.

Pushpa Kumari is Associate Professor, Institute of Management Technology, Nagpur, Maharashtra.

R.K. Mishra is Professor and Dean (Research), Institute of Public Enterprises, Hyderabad, Andhra Pradesh.

S.L. Arora is Senior Research Officer, IAMR, Delhi.

S.P. Singh is Associate Professor (Economics), Department of Humanities & Social Sciences, Indian Institute of Technology (IIT), Roorkee, Uttar Pradesh.

Sanjay Kapoor is Consulting Editor, *Hard News*, New Delhi.

Simrit Kaur is Reader, Faculty of Management Studies, University of Delhi, Delhi.

Surinder Kumar is Professor of Economics & Dean, Faculty of Social Sciences, Maharshi Dayanand University, Rohtak, Haryana.

T. Ravi Kumar is Reader in Economics, Kirorimal College, University of Delhi, Delhi.

T.M. Thomas is Reader in Economics, Deshbandhu College, University of Delhi, Delhi.

V. Upadhyay is Professor and Chairperson, Department of Humanities & Social Sciences, IIT, New Delhi.

Vasanthi Raman is Senior Fellow, Centre for Women's Development Studies, New Delhi.

Vaskar Nandy is Polit Bureau Member, PCC, CPI (M-L).

Vivek Kumar is Assistant Professor, Centre for the Study of Social Systems, JNU, New Delhi.

Preface

As we present to our readers the eleventh issue of the *Alternative Economic Survey*, we realise how increasingly formidable the challenges inherent in India's dominant political economy are becoming both at the level of cognition and of intervention for transformation. At the level of facts and their presentation in the official discourse, systematic recourse is made to falsification and mis-representation without looking at the linkages with the policies. The way the National Democratic Alliance (NDA) government went about playing up the GDP growth rate of over 8 per cent estimated for the year 2003–04 turning it into a 'Shining India' election campaign was not just episodic. It revealed how falsification and distortion of reality of the economy and society are effectively concealing how and why the living conditions of most Indians have deteriorated. Many more instances of this tendency can be seen. Take any aspect of the economy—inflation, unemployment, poverty, external viability of the Indian economy, rural development, food security, conditions of agriculturalists, industrial performance, state of public finance, or the operations of the monetary and banking sectors. You will find that the facts on the ground and their official level presentation and perception are diametrically different. This tendency culminates in giving a clean chit of health, positive performance and effectiveness to the current policy regime.

All over the world, including India, formidable and unassailable evidence and analyses show that in terms of the concerns and needs of the vast majority of the humanity, the situation is steadily worsening. Those claiming that 'There is no Alternative' to the imposition of a blatantly pro-G-7, pro-MNCs, pro-super rich policies, that this process is irreversible, and that it would amount to inflicting injuries on oneself if a country tries to chart a different course are even to this day labouring hard to defend 'economic' globalisation. There is also a welcome trend that concedes that special efforts would be needed to make 'globalisation' work. Interestingly, some powerful and influential sections from within the G-7 establishment seem to break rank from the dominant orthodoxy by recognising most of the limitations, failures and distortions of the neo-liberal liberalisation, privatisation and globalisation (LPG) regime. Having discovered the 'innocent fraud' perpetrated in the name of the market system, these 'Left' neo-liberals are advocating far-reaching corrective measures 'making globalisation good.'

Thanks to the indomitable democratic spirit and political maturity of the Indian people that the hard sell of its performance by the NDA regime failed to cut much ice. It was shown the door. However, the absence of any real alternative, committed to and capable of transformative politics makes people oscillate between the two almost similar faces of the phenomenon. The rhetoric of 'human face' indulged in by the successor United Progressive Alliance (UPA) government seems more oriented to selling a bitter pill than to herald any substantive change.

This is the context in which the Alternative Survey Group is presenting its latest reviews. As in the past, an objective analysis using authentic information under a theoretical framework, which recognises people's interest, has been attempted by a group of social scientists, activists, journalists etc; each responsible for one's exercise and yet contributing to a common cause. The 2004–05 budget was presented mid-year along with the review of the preceding year by the new UPA government that is dominated by earlier 'reformers'. This document is a strong indicator of the pervasive elements of continuity, with a different looking National Common Minimum Programme (NCMP), though laced with some substantive modifications and corrections. Hence, it would be interesting to watch how far the elements of continuity overpower the promises of modification.

We are grateful to the growing body of our avid readers for enabling us to sustain the exercise. As usual, their feedback would be the main source of our inspiration.

Kamal Nayan Kabra
V. Upadhyay

New Delhi

Alternative Survey Group

Liberalisation as Development Policy
Magnifying Mal-development

Kamal Nayan Kabra

Assessing the outcomes of India's development policies under the sway of liberalisation requires a careful selection of the criteria, values and indicators that crucially reflect the health of Indian society. This task requires one to disabuse oneself of the massive misinformation prevalent under the guise of reciting the mantra of growth as the *summum bonum* of progress. In the year 2003–04, it was claimed that with an 8 per cent growth of GDP, India is firmly set on the path of a global position of power!

Those who gloat over the arithmetic of growth rates manage to do so by shutting themselves into the cocoons of their exclusive 'globalised', asocial existence with a complete lack of any social empathy. As members of a 'rather homogeneous global elite'[1], they are influenced by the received wisdom of the powerful, in particular the so-called 'Washington (neo-liberal) Consensus'. (Williams 2003: 385) Accordingly, many aspects that determine the meaning and relevance of GDP are either given token lip service by invoking phrases such as 'liberalisation with a human face' or are ignored altogether. Such aspects include:

- Composition of output, price tags, inputs-intensity, proportion of domestic procurement, factor payments, especially labour-intensity and other labour relations.
- Location of production centres; physical, social and other use-value related aspects of the components of GDP, whether merit or demerit goods and services; public, quasi-public, or private goods; traditional, innovated, or mimetic goods, low-income or high-income goods, etc. The nature and character of the goods and services comprising GDP are critical to its developmental content. Demerit goods are undesirable on the basis of society's common judgment, i.e., the goods not affordable by the vast majority or goods that impose severe environmental and cultural costs on society, or which increase the trade deficit and force the country to borrow for consumption or increase the energy insecurity of the country.
- Compatibility of products with the life style, values, and cultural ethos of the nation, especially of the various sections of people in society.
- Social, environmental and other externalities, particularly with respect to sharing of the national resources. This often implies questions of ownership, control, and organisational forms of the flows of production and the production entities that form the institutional matrix.
- Impact on the future generations, social tranquillity, and cultural plurality. These do not ever seem to form part of the official conception of the economy. An exclusive market-determined, market-centric version is not only assumed to be autonomous of the rest of society but, according to the official view, also sets the pace for the rest of society.

This task requires one to disabuse oneself of the massive misinformation prevalent under the guise of reciting the mantra of growth as the *summum bonum* of progress.

Those who gloat over the arithmetic of growth rates manage to do so by shutting themselves into the cocoons of their exclusive 'globalised', asocial existence with a complete lack of any social empathy.

1. A term referring to the neo-liberal economists, policy-makers and their supporters, who stand by the Washington Consensus and with its eroding validity and legitimacy are becoming ever more virulent and desperate, as can be seen in their writings and scheming tactics.

The overwhelming concern with output often tends to overlook the steady worsening of the social balance. This is often the result of some endemic aspects of the inherited structure of the economy such as composition of output, distribution of command over resources, pattern of effective demand, place in the global economy, and marginalisation of a large part of the population. Under the pretext of taking an exclusive economy-centric and supposedly neutral view, the establishment appears to be unconcerned about various social and value-related aspects. A section of the liberal opinion, lately describing itself as committed to responsible global capitalism, recognises the serious social, economic, institutional, and technical limitations of this powerful wealth-creation system. This section also bemoans the moral and ethical bankruptcy and suboptimal performance of the system when viewed in a comprehensive socio-economic and cultural perspective. (Dunning 2003: 1–40)

A crucial neo-liberal assumption is that everything else will follow suit if the economy is right, prices are right, investment is picking up, foreign direct investment (FDI) inflows are gushing in, stock markets are booming, and trade is flowing freely. One is left to wonder when and how everything else that is socially relevant and valuable would be taken care of in a growing market economy? However, it has become obvious that under the market-led growth dispensation, the prevailing order is only strengthened. All those who are well off become better still, and the existence of those who are not privileged is condemned to a fast deterioration. Needless to say, the prevailing social order gives a new lease of life to the iniquities, anomies, and dysfunc-tionalities inherent in it. Growth as such can do precious little to undo it all. Furthermore, the neo-liberal perspective is enforced in a manner as if national boundaries do not matter.

There is enough evidence to show that the neo-liberal, GDP-centric view of national well-being, livelihood, and socio-economic performance and the economy's sector specific and structural aspects have come to be amenable to hegemony and dominance of some nations. Furthermore, the top echelons of such nations and their Third World counterparts are being accepted as just and beneficial. The state enters the picture as a mediator, facilitator, protector, and *legitimiser* of the prevailing order. Liberalisation has removed the fig leaf of its pretensions of the broader social forces being inclusive under the earlier *statist*, market economy policy. Although GDP appears to be rising, the growth is also highly volatile, unbalanced, and non-sustainable. Along with this growth, India is sliding into deepening mal-development. In the following section, we will examine this proposition and provide some telling, though limited, evidence.

A section of the liberal opinion, lately describing itself as committed to responsible global capitalism, recognises the serious social, economic, institutional, and technical limitations of this powerful wealth-creation system.

Growing Mal-development

Let us attempt to unravel how the processes referred to above have been unfolding in 2003–04 as seen in the medium-term context of the era of liberalisation. In May 2004, with the replacement of the National Democratic Alliance (NDA) government by the one of United Progressive Alliance (UPA), India entered a new political phase of going ahead with liberalisation with the acknowledgement of the need to 'reform the reforms' as spelt out in UPA's National Common Minimum Programme (NCMP). Let us examine the content, cost, and direction of the development goals under the Structural Adjustment Programme (SAP), a policy package that is a stronger version of the package implemented in 1980–81. This package redefined the development policy instruments and has been operating for thirteen years now. It is important to focus on the year 2003–04. This is because it was claimed that India achieved a real breakthrough rate of growth of over 8 per cent during this year, leading to the much-publicised as well as derided phenomenon of 'India Shining'.

...the prevailing social order gives a new lease of life to the iniquities, anomies, and dysfunctionalities inherent in it. Growth as such can do precious little to undo it all.

Those who have redesigned India's current economic and development policy regime with a view to combine 'reforms' with the concerns of the common man have made a rather positive assessment of India under liberalisation over the last two decades in the following statement:

> The economy has made significant strides over the last two decades with average annual growth rising from a low level of 2.9 per cent in the seventies to 5.8 per cent in the nineties. The improvement in growth has also been accompanied by structural change as, between the seventies and 2003–04, the share of agriculture and allied sectors in Gross Domestic Product (GDP) has declined from an average of 42.8 per cent to 22.1 per cent, the share of services has improved from an average of 34.5 per cent to 51.0 per cent, while the share of industry has improved marginally from an average of 22.8 per cent to 26.9 per cent. Inflation has remained in single digits in recent years in contrast to the double-digit inflation in the early seventies and the early nineties. Food grains production increased from 108.4 million tonnes in 1970–71 to 210.8 million tonnes in 2003–04. The external sector experienced a transformation with foreign exchange reserves touching US$113 billion at the end of 2003–04 from less than US$1 billion on July 12, 1991. The response of the economy to the East Asian crisis in 1997 and the drought in 2002, one of the severest in recent years, demonstrated its resilience.[2]

The above strong elements of continuity despite a change of government have to be seen in the context of the fact that the present policy-makers were the authors, rather the agencies that inaugurated the new policy regime in 1990–91. Incidentally, no other policy change has taken us so far away from the values and legacy of the freedom struggle. It brought about a qualitative, openly announced transformation, rather perversion, of the economy-state-society interface in India in favour of the internal and external forces upholding the banner of globalisation. Along with addressing the macro-economic balance, they portrayed the liberalisation package as a means for overcoming the 'limitations' of India's development policy. It was the non-performance of the economy in terms of its rate of growth that was held responsible for the failure to ameliorate the living conditions and prospects of the majority of Indians. The long-term perspective of the new policy package is best expressed in the Budget speech of 1990–91: 'The emergence of India as a major economic power will soon be a reality'.

The …strong elements of continuity despite a change of government have to be seen in the context of the fact that the present policy-makers were the authors, rather the agencies that inaugurated the new policy regime in 1990–91. Incidentally, no other policy change has taken us so far away from the values and legacy of the freedom struggle.

The regime that succeeded the original 'reformist' one and continued with the next phase of the SAP up to 2003–04 with far fewer reservations also placed before the nation a similar great global power vision to be attained by 2020. Given the multifarious links of the policy shift with globalisation and its choice of policy goals and instruments, it is clear that these changes sought to make India an integral part of global capitalism. Hence we need to review the results of the SAP in terms of the structure, content, inclusiveness, sustainability of development, and policy autonomy.

Global capitalism is characterised by deep-seated and far-reaching power asymmetries. Needless to say, Indian policy makers are deeply aware of these hard realities. Hence, their global power vision has been defined not in terms of the perspective of the New International Economic Order (NIEO) expounded in the early1970s or in terms of the philosophy of *swadeshi*, but simply, in the words of the person who held the finance and the foreign affairs portfolio in the NDA government at different times, 'as a status quo power that does not seek to upset the existing order through violent means' but 'has sought to change existing power equations in the global order' by criticising 'the developed world for its unfair economic policies' and 'appeal to their reason and wisdom' in the course of seeking 'to engage the North in dialogue'. (Sinha 2004)

The long list of achievements of the era of 'reforms' as quoted above is an impressive account of the claims made by liberalisers. The highly selective choice of the variables for self-congratulation by those with well-known neo-liberal predilections is pretty obvious. However, the 'structural change'— increase in the aggregate food grains output, marking of a 'transition from a food deficit economy' 'to a food

2. Macro-Economic Framework Statement laid before Parliament as required under the Fiscal Responsibility and Budget Management Act, 2003.

exporter', having huge foreign exchange reserves that make India an 'aid giving nation', (Sinha 2004) and a manageable rate of inflation—are merely some of the elements used as props for the 'India Shining' propaganda by the NDA regime. More realistically, this list of achievements indicates, as we show in the following section, a deep crisis for the Indian masses and the narrowing down of the policy options within the prevailing policy and development paradigm.

Foreign Exchange Reserves: False and Misleading Claims

Let us look at the view that foreign exchange reserves of the magnitude never seen earlier are an indicator of the success of the policy of globalisation. Clearly this tall claim ignores the rising, chronic import surplus, and huge outstanding external liabilities that exceed the total amount of borrowed and unearned accumulation of foreign exchange reserves. The involuntary investment of these reserves in the US treasury bills should be considered more seriously. Their 'value' to the Indian economy does not seem to go beyond increasing the capability to finance India's rising import bill, which has all along been moving ahead of the total export earnings. Moreover, the export earnings taken in their nominal total involve heavy direct and indirect subsidies that impose substantial social and economic costs. The main role of these reserves seems to be the maintenance of the confidence of the foreign financiers in the ability of the economic policies of India to ensure the safety of their funds and continuation of India as a borrower. These would continue to remain favourable to the interests of global finance and pose the ever-present danger of a sudden herd like flight of external finance from the country.

The involuntary investment of these reserves in the US treasury bills should be considered more seriously. Their 'value' to the Indian economy does not seem to go beyond increasing the capability to finance India's rising import bill, which has all along been moving ahead of the total export earnings.

The direct financial cost of these funds, lured in by a whole array of measures for wooing foreign short-term and long-term funds, significantly exceeds the returns made by investing most of these funds in just nominal-returns-giving US treasury bills, which makes India a loyal member of the 'US treasury bill standard'. (Hudson 2003) To be 'voluntarily' a member of the US treasury bills standard could be a shade better than the situation when we were forced to join the Sterling area by the British rulers of India. But is that what our national sovereignty is to guarantee us? The fact that such questions do not even enter the policy-making processes indicates how we have virtually lost the ownership of our policies. We are being coaxed, cajoled, and coerced into following the policies dictated by the international financial centres and their mentors. It seems to be an uncritical pursuit of an FDI-based 'development'. We have seen above how the ruling elite nonchalantly assert that India is meekly accepting the global power balance, with hardly any quid for this quo, except for occasional verbal criticism and appeal for benevolence!

The direct financial cost of these funds, lured in by a whole array of measures for wooing foreign short-term and long-term funds, significantly exceeds the returns made by investing most of these funds in just nominal-returns-giving US treasury bills, which makes India a loyal member of the 'US treasury bill standard'.

The claim regarding our escape from the contagion of the East Asian currency crisis of the late 1990s is similarly misplaced. The fact is that it was the non-acceptance of a key element of the Washington Consensus, the policy of full capital account convertibility, which saved the Indian economy from the negative and destabilising effects emanating from the East Asian meltdown. Moreover, it must be recognised that many factors contribute to making these large and costly reserves of foreign exchange a fair-weather friend. Such factors include the phenomenon of money laundering; fairly regular illegal flight of capital from India on a vast scale;[3] and the extensive use of the transfer pricing mechanism by the MNCs operating in India. In addition, there is a rather large volume of portfolio investment in the bourses of India by foreign institutional investors (FIIs), aggregating to over $27 billion over this period. It may be noted that the volatility of the FII investments is legendary and reflects, inter alia, the effect of the low interest regimes in the recession-hit G-7

3. For a telling illustration of the processes and magnitude of it, see, Zdanowicz (1966), and Petras (2003).

countries that is playing a crucial role in making India an attractive destination for parking surplus funds and the savings of the Non-resident Indians (NRIs).

To take the massive volume of unearned foreign exchange reserves as a measure of strength and resilience of the Indian economy while her asymmetrical position in the world economy remains unchanged (reflected, for instance, in India's signing the WTO treaty, which is universally acknowledged to be iniquitous) is to harbour a rather costly illusion (Williams 2003). These reserves certainly showcase the success of the policy thrust of the past thirteen years or so that has been directed at ensuring ample and regular external liquidity on a scale large enough to sustain the dependency that reinforces open door policies, give confidence to the global financiers regarding India's capacity to honour its external payments obligations, and live down the implications of signing the WTO agreement. In simple terms, the policy of opening up leads to the use of global markets as the engine and mechanism of the development amounts. It helps expand the market for the MNCs and assure external lenders and investors that their debts would be scrupulously served, irrespective of the costs imposed on the people of India.

However, this policy has been adhered to irrespective of its costs and implications for the healthy functioning of the economy. The economy has been unable to increase the weight of the manufacturing sector in GDP, increase the availability of affordable wage-good, provide livelihood security, or create an economic environment of relative price stability for sustaining the small producers and the levels of consumption of the poor, fixed income consumers. These costly foreign exchange reserves hardly make any positive impact on the lives of the ordinary people. However, they do appear to make a difference to the private corporate sector, which is increasingly connected with the economies of the G-7 countries. This seems to be the meaning of liberalised imports and vigorously pushed up exports, together amounting to about 30 per cent of India's GDP, reflecting increased globalisation of the Indian economy.

The economy has been unable to increase the weight of the manufacturing sector in GDP, increase the availability of affordable wage-good, provide livelihood security, or create an economic environment of relative price stability for sustaining the small producers and the levels of consumption of the poor, fixed income consumers.

Growth Minus Positive Content

It is clear that variables like GDP growth, food output, food grains reserves, and exports are not desirable for their own sake. This was shown by the recent Indian experience of huge food stocks sitting uneasily with endemic hunger and occasional starvation deaths accompanied by highly subsidised exports at prices not only below par but lower than those charged from some segments of the Indian buyers. (Patnaik 2003) Clearly, a kind of '*beggar thy own countrymen policy*' to globalise and attain fiscal stabilisation has been put into operation. While a little less than Rs. 3,000 crore was spent on drought relief in the last year, a subsidy amounting to nearly Rs. 5,900 crore was given to exporters of food grains supplied by Food Corporation of India (FCI). Most of that food was illegally diverted to the Indian markets, a parliamentary committee seems to suspect.

Clearly, a kind of '*beggar thy own countrymen policy*' to globalise and attain fiscal stabilisation has been put into operation.

Some argue about the great virtues of high growth rates on the basis of significant positive co-relation between high growth rates and reduction of absolute poverty as observed in the history of many present-day rich countries. However, they fail to establish whether economic growth leads to these impressive indicators or growth is made possible by the direct and independent pursuit of adequate and quality supply of education and health services, essential infrastructure facilities, and at least a modicum of livelihood. In any case the growth enthusiasts hardly ever bother to show how non-sustainable and volatile is such high growth rate.

Even a moderate inflation rate, which persists over a long period and is treated as a kind of natural corollary of liberalisation-led growth, erodes the purchasing power of the non-indexed wages of the labouring masses much more than a short-lived double-digit inflation rate. The free market seems to have given the market forces a *carte blanche* to continually push up the prices of their products and redistribute incomes in their own favour. This has been amply demonstrated by the price behaviour over the last few decades. The policy-makers appear comfortable with the steady erosion of the purchasing power available to the majority of price-takers in the economy. This is because its reverse, a steady profit inflation, firms up incentives for growth, which is their openly advocated highest policy goal. Their only concern is the political acceptance of this dispensation, which comes under a cloud when the rate of inflation approaches or crosses the double-digit level and tends to threaten their own fiscal management. 'Getting the prices right' may be a good neo-liberal theorem. In practice, however, it has become another name for the freedom of the market oligarchs to fleece the consumer and unilaterally redistribute income in their own favour, as the prices they charge are incomes for the industrialists while they are a reduction in the real incomes of the consumers.

The free market seems to have given the market forces a *carte blanche* to continually push up the prices of their products and redistribute incomes in their own favour.

Livelihood Crisis and Growing Inequalities

In a country with widespread denial of the means of adequate and secure livelihood, output growth without continually reducing the intensity of the endemic livelihood crisis is meaningless. Growth by itself cannot change its own composition and the associated processes for creating livelihood security, which is a basic prerequisite for empowerment of the people. For this purpose, specific and pointed interventions are needed. The processes of empowering the market, which is the kernel of liberalisation, cannot by itself create enough earning opportunities to be able to grant the right of economic citizenship to everyone. Notwithstanding the nature and extent of state intervention in India so far, the inclusion of a large part of the labour force in the vital and dynamic economic processes that contribute to development has been grossly inadequate while the number of persons without a secure source of regular income and livelihood is huge. The combined result of all the policy changes during the last thirteen years has been inimical to employment. The substantial evidence of the rapidly deteriorating employment situation compels the market enthusiasts to quietly admit this failure and promise 'more of the same' for tackling this festering sore. But the year 2003–04 seem to have marked not only an accentuation of this trend, owing, among other things, to greater commitment to fiscal consolidation than to public spending and other policies for ensuring the livelihood rights of the poor. As a result there has been a sharp reduction in employment in the largest and relatively more dynamic organised public sector. Ironically, this decline in public sector employment has been treated as a feather in their cap by the policy-makers in India as it is considered a step towards the high objective of fiscal consolidation. The *Economic Survey* of 2003–04 mentions 'the decline in public sector employment', but a punch line says that this decline reflected 'a conscious policy decision'! Clearly, destroying employment without providing alternatives is not a matter that concerns the neo-classical votaries of liberalisation.

The processes of empowering the market, which is the kernel of liberalisation, cannot by itself create enough earning opportunities to be able to grant the right of economic citizenship to everyone.

The *Economic Survey* of 2003–04 mentions 'the decline in public sector employment', but a punch line says that this decline reflected 'a conscious policy decision'!

A recent study, published in the *Economic and Political Weekly*, asserting the authors' faith in the 'intrinsic value of growth', lest they be branded anti-growth, which is obviously a crime in the neo-liberal religiosity, carefully analysed recent employment data and discovered that in spite of a growing economy and a declining share of agriculture, 'labour market opportunities in India appear to have stagnated'. The supply of educated individuals seems to outweigh demand in the job market so much so that 'even second tier jobs like shop keeping, petty business, small production units are not made easier owing to education'. They go on to show that during the last twenty years, the growth of both labour force and employment decreased. In aggregate terms, especially between 1993–94 and 1999–2000, the decline in the growth of employment opportunities outstripped decline in the labour force. (Desai and Das 2004)

The above study also shows that in the new economic climate, financial returns for white collar work have increased far beyond returns to other occupations. A far more unjustifiable trend has been the massive, limitless enrichment of the narrow segment represented by the country's corporate bosses, unchecked by any restraint as a result of the freedom to play with the people's money for their narrow, personal enrichment. The corporates honchos are granting themselves enormous sums by way of remuneration. During 2003–04 the total remuneration of the top ten executives of the private corporate sector totalled Rs. 3,198.67 lakh, while the remuneration of the top ten owner (promoter) CEOs during the same year was Rs. 8,383.73 lakh. On a broader horizon, we find that a group of 295 top corporate executives collected a grand sum of Rs. 40,571.65 lakh in 2003–04 by way of rewards, excluding stock option. It amounts to an average of Rs. 138 lakh for each of these executive. (Business India 2004)

These figures show at least two things. First, with per capita income during the same year at current prices being a little below Rs. 25,000, the average remuneration per top corporate executive is 552 times larger. Many more thousand such executives take salaries and other perks around this average. Second, with so few collecting such large incomes, there are millions who have to make do with much less than the national average. A telling illustration of these pitiably low incomes can be seen in the wage rate paid to the agricultural workers. As shown by S.P. Singh in this volume, in the year 1999–2000, a farm hand earned Rs. 40.14 for performing farm operations and Rs. 54.09 for non-farm operations. It is well known that the total number of days in a year these workers are able to get paid work hardly exceeds 200. The number of such workers denied their rightful living wage-rate was 107 million in the year 2001. It seems these glaring inequalities and denial of human dignity forms no part of the morality of global capitalism dominating the Indian policy scene. The beneficiaries and decision-makers of this set of arrangements do everything possible under the sun to ensure that the GDP with such a skewed pattern of distribution should continue to grow at a fast pace and in the process accentuate the inequalities. If this is their idea of development, what would retrogression consist of?

...in the new economic climate, financial returns for white collar work have increased far beyond returns to other occupations. A far more unjustifiable trend has been the massive, limitless enrichment of the narrow segment represented by the country's corporate bosses, unchecked by any restraint as a result of the freedom to play with the people's money for their narrow, personal enrichment.

It is clear that this policy regime has deregulated executive pays along with giving the market forces a free hand. The *Economic Survey* does not even report the trends in real wage rates either for industry or agriculture, not to mention the unorganised informal work. Evidently, the policy objective of equity, if not of reducing inequalities by drastic redistribution of property and assets, at least of preventing its further consolidationby ex-post measures, has been discarded.

In addition to collecting enormous amounts 'legally', the powerful are collecting untold amounts through the symbiotically inter-connected politics-business-bureaucracy nexus and by way of corporatisation of personal spending using creative and aggressive accounting. Such atrocious disparities cannot be justified on any economic, social, or moral criteria. If the astronomical, self-awarded CEO payments alone can provide incentives to the Indian private business, it is clear that the majority of the people will have to be written off from the normal economy. Given such an orientation of the powerful, the growth-oriented and market-friendly measures are shown to be highly desirable! Such measures include extracting savings at negative real rates of interest from the household sector, including the survival-granting informal sector, and making them available to the private corporate sector, which specialises in cutting jobs in order to maximise profits, and to the stock market operators for improving the share of unearned speculative gains in GDP. Such perverse pursuits do not even appear as negative traits on the mental radar of the friends of the markets, except for an emergent body of scholars and public personalities, described as the 'Left neo-liberals'.

...with per capita income during the same year at current prices being a little below Rs. 25,000, the average remuneration per top corporate executive is 552 times larger.

These massive fast growing inequalities are telling instances of the surge of the processes of mal-development in the Indian society of the early 21st century. Similarly, the cumulative effects of the long-run, uninterrupted inflation on both the erosion of the real purchasing power and redistribution of income in favour of the non-work income earners are paraded as positive policy outcomes, as they improve both the incentives and the resource availability for private investment. It is another story that high corporate investments have failed to materialise as substantial parts of the bulging profits have remained undeclared, which have either been sent to money laundering havens abroad or are converted into highly liquid assets such as bullion. The *investment strike* by the big corporate sector has remained a largely unexplored area for the policy-makers.

The dismal employment generation during the entire liberalisation era has been particularly marked in the organised sector. In February 2004, the registered unemployed numbered 4.11 crore, of those nearly seventy per cent were educated. (GOI 2004) It is futile to expect the SAP to have given a different outcome because a market-led process cannot incorporate those who are not initially a part of the game. The bystanders or deprived spectators, subsisting on the fringe of the market, are only further marginalised. The various ways in which the employment situation is assessed (see the chapter on Employment in this volume), bring out pointedly that output growth has not been able to prevent a further deterioration of the unemployment problem. Various estimates of the extent of productive absorption of labour population have adopted various criteria. However, it remains to be seen if the participation of the labour in market processes enables them to acquire secure and regular access to the wherewithal necessary for survival. As some of the perceptive studies of levels of living and poverty show, the proportion of the people without even food security, in the sense of access to the minimum acceptable level of calories, is a little above two-thirds of the population. (Mehta 2004) Clearly, the output growth acceleration of the past two decades has been bought at the cost of chronic hunger and malnutrition and mass poverty.

It is another story that high corporate investments have failed to materialise as substantial parts of the bulging profits have remained undeclared, which have either been sent to money laundering havens abroad or are converted into highly liquid assets such as bullion. The *investment strike* by the big corporate sector has remained a largely unexplored area for the policy-makers.

...the proportion of the people without even food security, in the sense of access to the minimum acceptable level of calories, is a little above two-thirds of the population.

Obviously, the pursuit of livelihood security, equity, and empowerment of the common people cannot be achieved unless the political and legal citizenship is combined with economic citizenship. Such attempts, as mounted by the neo-liberal dispensation, may create the illusion that a thirty-forty year period of some 7–8 per cent rate of growth of GDP may magically compound and bring us at par with the developed countries. Even when some additional social indicators such as the human development index popularised by the United Nations Development Programme (UNDP) are added to GDP as an indicator of development, the weight given to GDP remains substantial and there is no suggestion that GDP has to be combined with the processes of wealth generation. The structural correctives such as the extent of unemployment, sector-wise shares of output, the ratio of high-income goods and low-income wage goods, location of production facilities, and the environmental impact of the existing production facilities still remain outside the picture. Even on the basis of the truncated, incomplete correctives applied by the human development index, the latest UNDP Report (2003–04) shows that after taking into account the social indicators, India's rank on the basis of per capita GDP went down from 127 to 117 (in a group of 177 nations). This illustrates the irony that the higher the growth of GDP with increasingly higher weight of high-income goods and services, the more exclusionary such a growth becomes. (See Kumar 2004) This trait, for example, was witnessed in the 417 per cent growth in the production of passenger cars between 1990–91 and 2003–04 while the production of commercial vehicles increased only 146 per cent and the overall rate of growth of industries remained under 7 per cent over the same period. (*Economic Times* 2004) Implications of such hyper growth of vehicles of personal use do not seem to enter the so-called mainstream economic or development discourse. It impacts the diversion of scarce material and financial resources away from goods of mass consumption, and thus from broad based productive employment opportunities. Furthermore, the burgeoning production of cars is resulting in ballooning import of petroleum products, growing energy insecurity of the country besides worsening of pollution, congestion of roads, and increase in the number of deaths and injuries in road accidents.

Several other policy-led features of the recent economic change exacerbate a negative character of GDP growth for the masses of India. We have already referred to a number of dramatic instances of increasingly perverse distribution of income, wealth, and socio-economic power besides a topsy-turvy sense of priorities. The loans for buying consumer assets such as passenger cars and luxury houses are being offered with indiscriminate tax concessions and at rates lower than or comparable to those charged on occupational loans to the poor peasants and artisans. Such methods of direct income transfer from the average citizen to the more affluent and reducing the cost of production of the manufactured goods made by private companies have evidently been designed to improve corporate profitability. There have also been steep reductions in customs and excise duties, which have hardly been passed on to consumers. That explains the 80 per cent contribution of the manufacturing sector to the inflation in 2003–04.

...the higher the growth of GDP with increasingly higher weight of high-income goods and services, the more exclusionary such a growth becomes. This trait, for example, was witnessed in the 417 per cent growth in the production of passenger cars between 1990–91 and 2003–04 while the production of commercial vehicles increased only 146 per cent and the overall rate of growth of industries remained under 7 per cent over the same period.

The prevalent economic policies have reduced incentives for labour absorbing technologies and increased the indiscriminate use of capital. Thousands of crores of rupees are given by way of an assortment of tax holidays to the information technology (IT) companies and to any one for setting up industrial enterprises in the designated backward areas even with rather thin economic linkages with the local communities. Incentives are also provided to exporters, even to the exporters of state subsidised food grains (who sell some of those food stocks in the local black market). One of the worst examples of the excessively soft and liberal treatment given to the corporate capital is the total exemption of the dividend income from income tax besides from capital gains tax if shares are held for at least an year before their sale. One IT tycoon , who holds 83.7 per cent of his company's equity, recently took home tax-free Rs. 566 crore from the company by way of dividend in addition to Rs. 1.8 crore as managerial remuneration. (*Business India* 2004) This amount is many times more than the sum total of the remuneration package of the top ten CEO's at Rs.31.98 crore in 2003–04, (*Business India* 2004) not to speak of the mind boggling comparison vis-a-vis the current per capita income of about Rs. 22,000. Such bonanza for the corporate elite put a question mark on the prevalent policies and programmes for livelihood security to the masses besides highlighting the need for financial prudence and efficient use of resources. Removal of entry restrictions and freeing of investments presumed increases in market competition, but that is not visible anywhere yet. This is especially true if we take into account the losses incurred by closed and sick industrial units that have wasted thousands of crores of rupees of bank advances, loans from the public financial institutions, and investments of shareholders. They are described as non-performing assets as if it is the inanimate assets that are responsible for such a state of affairs. It is undoubtedly the result of some fraudulent machinations and some tricky vanishing acts!

The prevalent economic policies have reduced incentives for labour absorbing technologies and increased the indiscriminate use of capital.

Growing Deprivation and Inefficiencies

Clearly the widespread economic disparity and exclusion are among the congenital features of a volatile, uncertain, and inefficient growth that needs ever increasing inputs to give the same rate of growth. It is surprising indeed that the neo-liberal orthodoxy gives scant attention to the fact that the growth of the recent years has been achievedwith fluctuating returns on an increasingly large volume of financial, human, and techno-logical resources. Furthermore, land and other natural resources are being snatched from those who are declared to be their inalienable and rightful owners with paltry or no compensation. All that one sees is that there is *ex-post* reporting of the capital-output ratio rather than total inputs-output ratio.

The cumulative result of the features of the policy and growth processes discussed above manifest themselves in a growing deprivation of the majority and a totally unjust enrichment of a tiny minority. The official statistics give only some very broad information on the distributive aspects, as in the form of consumption disparities based on the periodic sample surveys or the shares of factor incomes in the National Accounts Statistics. These data, valuable as they are, are hardly able to give a vivid and detailed account of the ground reality, which reflected far better in the reports of vigilant and fast expanding media, grass roots and Dalit literature, and the growing body of micro-level socio-economic studies. They portray a disturbing scenario of hunger, food insecurity, starvation deaths, trafficking in women and children, abysmally low and sub-human standard of living for millions of people in villages and urban slums, incidents manifesting the desperation of the unemployed and the deprived, poverty-bred crimes, devaluation of human lives. Given the multiple layers of existence in India, all separated by vast and seemingly unbridgeable chasms, the official data on consumption and factor income shares disparities and their arithmetic averages can hardly prove equal to the task of capturing the growing and painful disparities in the country.

...the ground reality ...[is] reflected far better in the reports of vigilant and fast expanding media, grass-roots and Dalit literature, and the growing body of micro-level socio-economic studies. They portray a disturbing scenario of hunger, food insecurity, starvation deaths, trafficking in women and children, abysmally low and sub-human standard of living for millions of people in villages and urban slums, incidents manifesting the desperation of the unemployed and the deprived, poverty-bred crimes, devaluation of human lives.

Without indicating the disparities, deprivation, and discrimination, it may not be possible to make sense of the phenomenon of mal-development, which has made deep inroads in India of the early 21st century. The first requirement for this purpose is trying to get a sense of the huge concentration of resources, income, wealth, and power. The flip side of such concentration surely would be mass deprivation. The chapter on Agriculture in this volume shows the extent of land concentration and landlessness. An analysis of some structural features of the Indian economy can show how deep-seated the malaise is. The structural imbalance and retrogression, reflected in the shrinkage share of the farm sector in GDP without finding alternative sources of livelihood for the agriculturists (agriculture dependent persons number increased from 185 million in 1991 to 235 million in 2001) indicates some of the basic parameters for measuring the effectiveness of the country's economic management.

With the industry refusing to respond enthusiastically to the fulfilment of its dream agenda,[4] the structure of the economy becomes more unbalanced and employment growth difficult. The premature hyper growth of the services sector, 'mostly due to fast growth in communication services, financial services, business services and community services' has little to offer for the basic needs of most Indians—food, clothing, housing. The services sector relates very marginally to the rural sector owing to its concentration in urban areas. The rural masses with abysmally low levels of literacy and modern skills can find few employment opportunities in this sector. The demand for these services arises largely at rather high and secure levels of income, but the bulk of the rural population is very far from such income levels.

Thus the growth experienced by India, owing to its structure, composition, technology, and location, not to mention the institutional gridlock of the concentrated financial resources, productive assets, external economic linkages, and pro-rich bias of public policies, has very limited positive meaning and pay-off for an overwhelmingly large part of the population. The ratio of the agricultural per capita income to the non-agricultural per capita income is now about 1:8. This is a sharp reminder that without directing growth and its benefits towards the needs of all sections of society, the orthodox commitment to the magic of the high growth rates is simply *non sequitur*. When trying to interpret the ratio of the per capita incomes of the farm and non-farm sectors, one must not forget the vast inequalities within these sectors besides

4. The lacklustre performance of industry to-date is the principal cause for at most a marginal acceleration of the growth rate in the post-1991 reforms era. (Panagariya 2004)

the power of the prevailing distribution of income and wealth in determining the future rate of growth of GDP and distribution the costs and benefits of the growth.

The experience of the era of 'reforms' has clearly demonstrated that neither the processes of growth can go very far without incurring high costs of system maintenance nor can they succeed in meeting the basic objective of the economic management, viz, provide secure and adequate means of livelihood to the people. The successive electoral verdicts over the last thirteen years have forced the recognition that the 'reforms' have overlooked the needs of the common people. But it is still not recognised that the processes of the SAP have enfeebled the state and considerably constricted its freedom to accommodate any humane elements in its policies. One can see the derisive cacophony of opposition to the UPA government's promise of going in for legally guaranteed work to the poor in the so-called business press and fora. The government's own approach to the programme is quite lackadaisical. A citizenry with livelihood security is a threat to the iniquitous, immoral, and unjust world characterised by mal-development, and it is a multi-faceted mal-development, which is magnifying itself under the aegis of the SAP.

...the growth experienced by India, owing to its structure, composition, technology, and location, not to mention the institutional gridlock of the concentrated financial resources, productive assets, external economic linkages, and pro-rich bias of public policies, has very limited positive meaning and pay-off for an overwhelmingly large part of the population.

References

Business India, 2004. 2–15 August.

Desai, Sonalde and Maitreyi Das. 2004. 'Is employment driving India's Growth Surge? A Reality Check', *Economic and Political Weekly*, 3 July.

Dunning, John H. 2003. *Making Globalisation Good*. Oxford: Oxford University Press.

Government of India (GOI). 2004. *Economic Survey:2003–2004*.

Hudson, M. 2003. *Super Imperialism: The Origin and Fundamentals of US World Dominance*. London: Pluto Press.

Kumar, T. Ravi. 2004. 'Industry', in this volume.

Mehta, Jaya. 2004. 'Poverty', in this volume.

Panagariya, A. 2004. 'Economic Reforms and Growth in India', *Economic and Political Weekly*, 19 June.

Patnaik, Utsa. 2003. *Social Scientist*, November-December.

Petras, James. 2003. 'Dirty Money: The Foundation of US growth and Empire', in *The New Politics of Development: The Age of Empire Building and New Social Movements*, Ashgate: Burlington.

Sinha, Yashwant. 2004. *The Hindu*, 16 March.

The Economic Times. 2004. 27 July.

Williams, Shirley. 2003. 'Global Social Justice: The Moral Responsibilities of the rich to the Poor', in Dunning, John H. (ed.), *Making Globalisation Good*. Oxford: Oxford University Press.

Zdanowicz, John S. et.al. 1966. 'Capital Flight from India to the US through Abnormal Pricing in International Trade', *Finance India*. December.

The successive electoral verdicts over the last thirteen years have forced the recognition that the 'reforms' have overlooked the needs of the common people.

Macroeconomic Scenario

Arun Kumar

The High Growth Rate: A New Path or a Fluke?

The fiscal year 2003–04 saw the rate of growth of the economy double to 8.1 per cent from 4 per cent in 2002–03. In fact, it reached 10.4 per cent in the last quarter of the year. The government has claimed that the economy has reached a new growth path and the Planning Commission's projected annual rate of growth of 8 per cent would be achieved this year as well. Just as in 1991, a euphoria is being created that the economy has turned the corner. The international observers of the Indian scene have added to this chorus in heralding a new boom. What is not being asked is whether this indeed was the start of a new growth path or just a one-shot affair that is unlikely to be sustained.

If one looks at the sectoral growth rates, the key contributor to the substantial economic growth last year was the turnaround in agriculture, where the rate of growth moved from –5.5 per cent to 9.1 per cent. Thus, while in 2002–03 agriculture contributed –1.2 per cent to the growth of the gross domestic product, in 2003–04 it contributed 2 per cent to it. This sharp turnaround is not an unprecedented event in Indian economic history. As recently as in 1987–88, the country was hit by the biggest drought of the twentieth century and the rate of growth of the economy fell to 3.8 per cent. In 1988–89, with a normal monsoon, the rate of growth of the Primary Sector, which is mostly composed of agriculture, vaulted to 15.4 per cent, resulting in a GDP growth of 10.5 per cent. The next year the rate of growth declined to 6.7 per cent. In 1996–97 also, the rate of agricultural growth had touched 9.6 per cent, more than last year, and the GDP growth rate was 7.8 per cent, only a shade less than the last year's. The GDP growth rate fell to 4.8 per cent the following year.

The official rate of growth of the economy in the five years preceding the last one averaged about 5.3 per cent, which implies that the rate of growth is likely to drop from 8 per cent to this average rate if the monsoon is normal. The economy operates at a given capital output ratio—the amount of capital used to produce one unit of output. Since the investment rate represents the amount of new capital coming into use, this, when divided by the capital output ratio, gives the trend rate of the growth of the economy. Since the former has been hovering at around 23 per cent in the last 10 years and the latter at around 4.5, the rate of growth has averaged 5 per cent. Usually, the capital output ratio changes slowly, except for the fluctuations due to changes in capacity utilisation, which implies that unless the rate of investment shoots up to 36 per cent, the rate of growth cannot be sustained at 8 per cent.

There are no signs of a sharp rise in the rate of investments, so there is unlikely to be a sharp rise in the rate of growth of the GDP.

There are no signs of a sharp rise in the rate of investments, so there is unlikely to be a sharp rise in the rate of growth of the GDP. The entire investment is made up of foreign investment, which is still negligible and can be ignored, and the public and private investment. The public investment is being limited by the persistent rise in the fiscal deficit. The government has repeatedly cut back Plan size in the face of rising deficits. The corporate sector is facing uncertainty and recessionary conditions and has consequently reduced investments (GOI 2004: 9). In fact, it is worth mentioning that the rapid rate of growth of GDP in China, South Korea and other economies of South-East Asia has been based on a rate of investment between 32 per cent and 40 per cent. India would also have to get to these levels of investment for a sustainable high level of growth, but there is little sign of movement in that direction since 1991. Hence, India cannot be said to have transited to a new growth path.

Weakening Sectoral Interlinkages

It is surprising that industry, which had recovered from a recession, did not experience an acceleration in its rate of growth consequent to the sharp rise in the rate of growth in agriculture and additional purchasing power in the rural areas. The rate of growth of industry at 6.5 per cent hardly increased from the previous year's level of 6.4 per cent. In fact, the mining, quarrying, and construction group showed a decline in its growth rate. This puzzle needs to be resolved. In 2002–03, when agriculture suffered a sharp setback, the rate of growth of industry did not decline. Thus, it appears that the two sectors have got sufficiently decoupled. Several reasons could have contributed to this.

The contribution of the agricultural sector to the GDP has been constantly declining over the years and it is down to 22 per cent in the official statistics. However, the fraction of the population dependent on agriculture is declining gradually, which indicates that the disparities between the people dependent on agriculture and the other sectors are growing. The purchasing power of those in agriculture is getting marginalised and a rise or a fall in their fortunes is having only a small effect on the overall economy. Until the end of the 1970s, whenever there was a drought, the rate of growth of the industrial sector used to fall. Now, even if the black economy is also counted, the share of agriculture in the GDP would be about 15 per cent. This fact underscores the growing marginalisation of agriculture and the majority of the population.

Recent data do not reveal a stable relationship between growth rates in industry and agriculture. There is no clear time lag pattern either between the two. Other factors are becoming more important for the growth of industry such as globalisation, growth of the services sector, and the black economy.

Services are more or less growing at about 7 per cent, de-linked from the other sectors. This sector now constitutes more than 50 per cent of the GDP in the legitimate economy, and counting the black economy also, its share in the total economy is nearly 60 per cent. Since this is substantially concentrated in the urban areas, its links with industry are extremely important.

In 2002–03, when agriculture suffered a sharp setback, the rate of growth of industry did not decline. Thus, it appears that the two sectors have got sufficiently decoupled.

Services are more or less growing at about 7 per cent, de-linked from the other sectors.

Table 1
Growth Rates (in %)

Year	*Agriculture*	*Industry*	*Services*	*GDP (at Factor cost)*
1987–88	–1.0	7.0	–	3.8
1988–89	15.4	8.6	–	10.5
1990–91	4.6	7.4	–	5.6
1995–96	–0.3	12.3	–	7.3
1996–97	9.6	7.1	7.2	7.8
1997–98	–2.4	4.3	9.8	4.8
1998–99	6.2	3.7	8.4	6.5
1999–00	0.3	4.8	10.1	6.1
2000–01	–0.1	6.5	5.5	4.4
2001–02	6.5	3.4	6.8	5.8
2002–03	–5.2	6.4	7.1	4.0
2003–04	9.1	6.5	8.4	8.1

Note: 1. For the first four rows the growth rate under Agriculture is for the Primary sector.
2. The figures for 2001–02 are provisional estimates, those for 2002–03 are quick estimates, and the ones for 2003–04 are advance estimates.

Source: *Economic Survey 2003–04*, p. 3 and p. S–10.

What is driving growth in the services sector? Globalisation and the black economy are clearly the critical factors. Not only a large part of the black economy is composed of services, but the demand for services from the black economy is also substantial. So, it fuels its own growth. Globalisation is also resulting in a rapid growth of services in the areas of software, telecommunications, financial sector, and trade.

Are globalisation and the black economy, which are fuelling the growth of the services sector, having an impact on the other two sectors? Actually, they are disrupting the linkage between the sectors. Opening up of the economy is having an adverse impact on agriculture due to the regime of subsidies in the advanced nations. Agriculture's situation is becoming increasingly precarious (Kumar, 2004). Industry is also not faring much better due to lowering of customs duties. Clearly, the small scale sector, with little access to capital and technology, is in trouble. Even the large and the medium scale enterprises are not doing too well given that the weak base of indigenous technology and inadequate capital.

Thus, globalisation and the black economy are causing the linkage between industry, services, and agriculture to diminish, with adverse consequences for large sections of the population. The 'India Shining' campaign failed to get votes precisely for this reason.

Fluctuations in the Economy

Since 1991, because of the retreat of the state and the globalisation process, counter-cyclical intervention by the government has declined. Further, due to an increase in the international influences in an increasingly open economy, fluctuations in the economy have grown and uncertainty has increased (Kumar 1996).

The cyclical tendencies in an economy get accentuated by growing disparities. When a tendency for deficiency of demand is aggravated, spare capacity in industry builds up quickly.

With the retreat of the state, cyclical behaviour seems to have become an important aspect of the economy. As theory suggests, the down-turns seem to be longer than the up-turns resulting in short booms followed by long depressions. The Keynesian policy options are not available to the government because of the kind of globalisation we are undergoing at the initiative of the International Monetary Fund (IMF) and the World Bank.

The cyclical tendencies in an economy get accentuated by growing disparities. When a tendency for deficiency of demand is aggravated, spare capacity in industry builds up quickly. Rising unemployment and under-employment also accentuate the trend. Demand for mass consumption items is slow to rise due to these two factors. Thus, growth is not stable and fluctuations abound.

With globalisation and opening up of the economy, Indian industry is forced to produce similar products as are produced internationally.... Consequently, fewer jobs per unit of investment are being created.

The problems are further aggravated by the growing uncertainty in the economy that results from the globalisation process. With markets more open than earlier and the flow of goods and capital easier, local industries face greater uncertainty and investments in them becomes riskier. For instance, Indian edible oil producers could not anticipate the flow of palm oil into Indian markets and that resulted in problems for them. The milk producers are currently complaining of the adverse impact of imports on their livelihood. The small scale producers in various sectors face the onslaught of cheap Chinese goods. Even if imports do not take place, there is a threat of imports and even if capital is not coming in today, it can come and take over industries at a later date. All this results in stagnant levels of Investment and unchanged rates of growth. Even stock markets are becoming more and more dependent on inflows from the foreign institutional investors (FIIs) and the fluctuations in the international stock markets.

With globalisation and opening up of the economy, Indian industry is forced to produce similar products as are produced internationally. The technology for producing these goods is the same all over the world. Indian industry also has to go in for the same technology, as the prevailing technology is not compatible, and this is capital intensive (K/L rises). Consequently, fewer jobs per unit of investment are being created. Moreover, this trend in investment is resulting in emergence of high-wage islands, which are further aggravating economic disparities in the population.

The 'golden quadrangle project' is an example of the higher K/L compared to the earlier, more labour intensive way of making roads. The conception of this project is based on elitist thinking—making a highway system that is comparable to international highways; that too when many villages are not even connected by roads. The project is being constructed in a highly mechanised way. Where the earlier construction projects of this magnitude might have provided work to millions of people, now only thousands are working. Also, it would benefit road transportation and adversely affect the railways, which the poor use. It is also causing enormous displacement of people whose homes and farms fall in the path of the project. None of these things are being considered.

Given the global mobility of capital, the government is forced to welcome any capital that comes in on terms dictated to it. Otherwise, capital threatens to go elsewhere. This forces industry to go in for further modernisation and the accompanying greater capital intensity.

The economic trends emanating from globalisation and the government's change in perspective are causing a jobless growth in India. It is not that India is alone in this regard; even Europe has experienced jobless growth. Today, even in the USA there is concern about jobless growth and there is a clamour against outsourcing of services. The problem of unemployment will worsen as the rate of growth of the economy slows down normally, which may be aggravated in case of a poor monsoon this year. In brief, the macro difficulties will worsen in 2004–05.

The social and political impact of these macro trends will be significant. The macro difficulties are resulting in a rise in disparities—nationally, regionally, and locally—in income and wealth. The overall investment is stagnating and much of it is getting concentrated in a few pockets, which is resulting suffering for the backward parts of the country. Uncertainty has a greater effect on the poor and the more backward parts as they are the least equipped to take care of themselves. Thus, the crisis reflects more strongly on the less privileged sections and regions and the growing disparities are resulting in a more volatile situation and are making governance difficult. The recent elections point to this. Neither the slogans of 'India Shining' and the 'feel-good factor' nor high growth, and large foreign exchange reserves could come to the aid of the ruling coalition, as these factors have been narrowly confined. Worse still, they are turning into a vicious circle.

Uncertainty has a greater effect on the poor and the more backward parts as they are the least equipped to take care of themselves. Thus, the crisis reflects more strongly on the less privileged sections and regions and the growing disparities are resulting in a more volatile situation and are making governance difficult.

Rising Liquidity, Falling Interest Rates and their Macroeconomic Impact

Foreign exchange reserves have been building up strongly through the last year, which has led to a proliferation of liquidity in the economy. Once again reflecting the bias of the ruling classes, the foreign exchange reserves are sought to be used by liberalising foreign exchange transactions such as investments and holding of bank accounts abroad. How these reserves can be used to accelerate investments in the country and to help the poor is hardly being considered. Why should the public sector investment programme not be accelerated? Why should the private sector be allowed to liberally borrow abroad when funds are available in the Indian financial system?

The excess liquidity, represented by a rise in money supply much in excess of the nominal growth rate of the economy, has led to the softening of interest rates. The financial entities are flush with funds that they are unable to deploy because of lack of demand from viable and secure borrowers. A large part of these funds are being parked in government securities leading to a softening of interest rates.

Unfortunately, the falling interest rates are not resulting in a rising level of investment in the economy. In fact, the rate of capital formation of the corporate

...the falling interest rates are not resulting in a rising level of investment in the economy. In fact, the rate of capital formation of the corporate sector has fallen over the last five years.

sector has fallen over the last five years. Why this paradox? The corporate sector has been distributing large sums of profits as dividends to boost the price of their stocks so that the savings of the corporate sector are adversely affected. Further, due to uncertainty, the corporate sector is not investing enough, preferring to remain liquid and earning interest on government securities. Facing uncertainty, corporate groups are trying to consolidate their holdings in their companies by buying back significant amounts of the companies' public stocks (Kumar 1996).

The unintended effect of all this is that the labour is getting hurt. If lower interest rates had led to a higher level of investment and higher employment, the decline in incomes from savings would not have pinched workers. However, employment in the organised sector is falling due to retrenchment and voluntary retirement, which makes interest income more important for a class of people. While the organised labour is more concerned about interest rates and is actively speaking about it, the unorganised labour is more affected by the lack of employment opportunities. The problem is even more serious since social security is linked to the interest earned on provident funds and the pension to be paid.

...employment in the organised sector is falling due to retrenchment and voluntary retirement, which makes interest income more important for a class of people.

The interest rates and social security need to be dealt with differently. Social security has to be provided to all and this requires a complete package. Interest rates have to be kept low to boost investments, growth, and employment. If employment generation were buoyant, then nobody would mind the raising of the retirement age, or retrenchment, as other jobs would be available. A decline in interest rates would be acceptable, as interest on retail deposits will not be too crucial for the labour. Further, if one could work till a later age, as a part of the social security package, one could also save more for one's old age. In the last sixty years, longevity has increased from fourty-four years to sixty-four years but the retirement age has hardly changed, which means that people need more funds for their old age. This will change if the retirement age is raised.

Uncertainty has aggravated the insecurity of old age. All kind of assets have proved to be unsafe. Real estate has shown uncertain returns. Share market is volatile and many companies have simply disappeared. The Unit Trust of India (UTI) and other such government agencies providing safe returns have proved to be risky. The cost of medical treatment is skyrocketing because medical treatment is getting privatised and insurance agencies are unwilling to provide cover to the elderly, particularly those above seventy. When one is most vulnerable, one has no coverage. Moreover, the government is withdrawing from public healthcare. A package covering all these aspects needs to be put in place along with soft interest rates.

Credit card companies are trying to ensnare the lower-middle and middle classes to go in for high cost borrowings to increase their consumption. These classes are being sucked into consumerism by the lure of advertising and the easy availability of credit. Many of the borrowers have been unable to even pay the interest and have had to default and alienate assets. Those caught in the pincers of consumption and credit are being squeezed to give the finance companies a higher profit. This is adding to the uncertainty faced by the middle classes.

...the high rate of growth of the economy last year is not a unique event. The rate of growth is likely to drop this year, as it has done in past after a boom year, because the Indian economy is not on a new growth path.

Conclusion: Likely Scenario in 2004–05 and the Alternative

As argued in the beginning, the high rate of growth of the economy last year is not a unique event. The rate of growth is likely to drop this year, as it has done in past after a boom year, because the Indian economy is not on a new growth path. Further, given the emerging difficulties in agriculture due to the delayed monsoon in large parts and the floods in some parts of the country, the farm output is likely to fall the cost of production is likely to rise. Thus, the macroeconomic scenario is looks less promising as compared with 2003–04. Unless the other sectors perform much better than the last year, the economy is unlikely to grow at the projected 8 per cent. The linkages between different sectors of the economy has weakened and the majority of the population has been economically marginalised because of globalisation and the rising share of the black economy.

The assumed budgetary mathematics of the Union Budget for 2004–05 will not hold for a variety of reasons, spelt out earlier, and the government is likely to cut back on its proposed expenditures, especially on social sectors and the Plan. This will affect growth. The steep rise in price of crude oil will add to inflation and create more difficulties for the government and the citizens. The slow down in the world economy due to rising energy prices will also have a negative impact on India. Thus, there are many uncertainties ahead, which will impact growth. According to current reports, business confidence has already plummeted.

The only lasting method for achieving a high growth rate could be the adoption of the philosophy of 'last person first', propounded by M.K. 'Mahatma' Gandhi. There can be no higher democratising principle than this. This would shift the focus of economic policy onto the poor. Since they are concentrated in agriculture or in the small, cottage sectors, policy making would have to concentrate on these sectors. Attention would have to be paid to employment generation and development of social and physical infrastructure.

Public investments would rise and private investments would follow. Affected by uncertainty, the latter has hardly risen in spite of declining interest rates and overflowing liquidity with banks. The steps suggested here would lead to a lowering of the capital to labour ratio and a higher GDP growth rate. This strategy of shift in focus should neither result in technological backwardness nor in flight of capital, as the more advanced sectors would continue to grow rapidly. The vested interests use this kind of argument to get more concessions from society.

The linkages between different sectors of the economy has weakened and the majority of the population has been economically marginalised because of globalisation and the rising share of the black economy.

Focus on the poor will lead to a more stable growth path than the one the economy is currently on, which is based on the market mechanism and the marginalisation of the poor and results in growing inequities and greater fluctuations.

References

GOI, Ministry of Finance. 2004. *Economic Survey 2003–04*.

Kumar, A. 2004. 'Globalization and India's Food Security: Issues and Challenges'. *Bhartiya Samajik Chintan*. January, II(4).

Kumar, A. 1996. 'New Economic Policies, Instability and Policy Ineffectiveness'. *Economic and Political Weekly*.

Focus on the poor will lead to a more stable growth path than the one the economy is currently on, which is based on the market mechanism and the marginalisation of the poor and results in growing inequities and greater fluctuations.

Poverty

Jaya Mehta

When the government violates the people's rights, insurrection is, for the people and for each portion of the people, the most sacred of rights and the most indispensable of duties.

— Marquis De Lafayette

Poverty estimates in our country are derived from the household consumer expenditure data collected by National Sample Survey Organisation (NSSO) every fifth year. Although household consumer expenditure surveys are also conducted annually, the sample size is much smaller. The Planning Commission does not take cognizance of these annual surveys. Everyone eagerly awaited the quinquennial survey results for the year 1999–2000 (55th round) for an authentic picture of the poverty trend during the decade of economic reforms. The quinquennial survey of 1993–94 and the annual surveys through out the 90s indicated that the declining trend in poverty ratio achieved during 1980s, was halted (or reversed?) in the reform era. The reform lobby was uncomfortable with the annual surveys and insisted that rigorous poverty estimates could only be obtained from the quinquennial surveys of large sample size.

The 55th round survey results (1999–2000) took everyone by surprise. The poverty ratio came down from 36 per cent in 1993–94 to 26 per cent in 1999–2000 —a 10 per cent decline in just 5 years. The reform programme of the government seemed like a magic wand! Did it actually physically annihilate the poor and the marginalised in such large numbers? The reported numbers on farmers' suicides, the starvation deaths, victims of communal riots, dalits killed by the upper castes and the tribals killed in police firing are indeed alarming for any civilised society.

The poverty estimates obtained from the 55th round survey created a serious controversy with respect to the reference period. Since 1950s, NSSO has collected consumer expenditure data on the basis of a uniform 30-day recall period. Of late the reform advocates insisted that one-month recall period was too long and especially the expenditure on food was underreported. NSSO responded by changing the reference period. In the 55th round, the consumer expenditure for food, pan, tobacco, etc. was recorded for two reference periods, one-week recall and one-month recall. The reference period for clothes, consumer durable etc. was 365 days and for other items it was one month.

The reported numbers on farmers' suicides, the starvation deaths, victims of communal riots, dalits killed by the upper castes and the tribals killed in police firing are indeed alarming for any civilised society.

The changed reference period increased the expenditure estimates and reduced poverty figures in one stroke. Such a drastic reduction in poverty raised a big uproar in the anti- reform lobby. The headcount poverty ratio of 26.7 per cent was completely at variance with the rising poverty trend shown by the annual surveys and supplementary evidence obtained from other variables closely related to poverty. The experts (pro- and anti-globalisation) argued about the rigour of monthly and weekly recall period and ultimately agreed on one point. *The 1999–2000 poverty estimates were not comparable with 1993–94 estimates. Hence, no inference could be drawn regarding impact of reforms on poverty.*

Experts are civilised people. In this world fraught with violent conflicts, they have learnt to live in harmony with 'notes of dissents' to protect their honour. However, if they were to face a group of Class 10 or B.A. first year students, who are particularly encouraged to ask questions, then their exchange may read as follows:

Q. What exactly is the meaning of 36 per cent or 26 per cent poverty in the country?

A. It is the percentage of population that lives below the poverty line.

Q. What is the poverty line?

A. It is Rs. 327 per month per capita for rural India and Rs. 454 per month per capita for urban India for the year 1999–2000.

Q. How are these figures obtained?

A. The Planning Commission updates the poverty lines for the year 1973–74 according to relevant price indices.

Q. How were the poverty lines for the year 1973–74 computed?

A. The planning commission identified the expenditure group from the NSSO consumer expenditure data, whose expenditure on food fulfilled the calorie norms. The average per capita per month expenditure of this group was fixed as the 'poverty line'. The poverty line was Rs. 49 for rural areas and Rs. 56.60 was for urban areas.

Q. What were the calorie norms?

A. For rural India, it was 2,400 Kcal per capita per diem and for urban India it was 2,100 Kcal per capita per diem.

Q. What were the poverty ratios in 1973–74?

A. The poverty was 56.4 per cent in rural areas, and 49 per cent in urban areas.

Q. Does it mean that in 1973–74, 56.4 per cent population in rural areas did not have sufficient purchasing power to afford 2,400 Kcal and 49 per cent population in urban areas could not afford 2,100 Kcal?

A. That is correct.

Q. Does it mean that we have made considerable progress in 25 years and in 1999–2000 only 27 per cent of rural population and 23.5 per cent of urban population cannot afford 2,400 Kcal and 2,100 Kcal respectively?

If the expert is bothered about rigour and truth, he or she cannot answer this question in affirmative. According to the 55th round of NSSO data the rural poverty line of Rs. 327 in 1999–2000 corresponds not to 2,400 Kcal but to 1,868 Kcal. The rural poverty line, which would correspond to 2,400 Kcal, is Rs. 567 and the

...the 1999–2000 poverty estimates were not comparable with the 1993–94 estimates. Hence, no inference could be drawn regarding the impact of reforms on poverty.

Table 1
Calorie Intake at Different Expenditure Level

(1999–2000)

Rural				*Urban*			
Expenditure class	*Proportion of persons %*	*Calorie intake*	*Expenditure on food %*	*Expenditure class*	*Proportion of persons %*	*Calorie intake*	*Expenditure on food %*
0–225	5.1	1383	67	0–300	5.0	1398	64
225–255	5.0	1609	67	300–350	5.1	1654	64
255–300	10.1	1733	66	350–425	9.6	1729	62
300–340	10.0	1868	65	425–500	10.1	1912	60
340–380	10.3	1957	65	500–575	9.9	1968	58
380–420	9.7	2054	64	575–665	10.0	2091	56
420–470	10.2	2173	63	665–775	10.1	2187	54
470–525	9.3	2289	62	775–915	10.0	2297	52
525–615	10.3	2403	60	915–1120	10.0	2467	49
615–775	9.9	2581	58	1120–1500	10.1	2536	45
775–950	5.0	2735	55	1500–1925	5.0	2736	41
950–more	5.0	3778	46	1925–more	5.0	2938	32
All	99.9			All	99.9		

Source: Nutritional intake in India NSS 55th round. Report No. 471.

30

Alternative Economic Survey, India

corresponding poverty ratio is 74.9 per cent. Thus in 1999–2000, 74.9 per cent of our rural population cannot afford 2,400 Kcal.

The expert may find this statistics too uncomfortable and may like to end the conversation. However, if these figures are given to the student, he or she will easily infer that either the definition of poverty should be revised or the poverty figures should be revised.

Official Poverty Estimates and the Reality

We present below the state-wise poverty lines and poverty ratios obtained according to the planning commission's definition of fulfilling 2,400 Kcal and 2,100 Kcal norms. These are juxtaposed against the official figures. Our estimates are only approximate. We neither had the requisite data nor did we attempt finer statistical adjustments to get more accurate estimates. Our intention here is only to bring home the wide divergence between the two sets of figures and thus point at the absurdity of official estimates.

Table 2
Poverty in India

	Rural				*Urban*			
	Official Estimates		*Our Estimates*		*Official Estimates*		*Our Estimates*	
States	*Poverty line*	*Poverty ratio*	*Poverty line*	*Poverty ratio*	*Poverty line*	*Poverty ratio*	*Poverty line*	*Poverty ratio*
A.P.	262.94	10.5	565	89.4	457.40	27.2	775	62.8
Assam	365.43	40.3	675	92.9	343.99	7.5	775	60.0
Bihar	333.07	44.0	470	79.8	379.78	33.5	535	60.2
Gujarat	318.94	12.4	775	86.5	474.41	14.8	775	53.6
Haryana	362.81	7.4	615	47.5	420.20	10.0	847	54.7
H.P.	367.45	7.5	560	44.75	420.20	4.6	575	11.3
Karnataka	309.59	16.8	681	84.6	511.44	24.6	838	58.5
Kerala	374.79	9.4	950	79.6	477.06	19.8	1014	68.6
M.P.	311.34	37.3	497	79.25	481.65	38.5	665	62.1
Maharashtra	318.63	23.2	950	94.9	593.71	26.7	915	62.2
Orissa	323.92	47.8	498	82.9	473.12	43.5	425	34.3
Punjab	362.68	6.0	775	66.6	388.15	5.5	717	46.2
Rajasthan	344.03	13.5	525	55.8	465.92	19.4	620	46.8
Tamil Nadu	307.64	20.0	950	94.5	475.60	22.5	840	58.8
U.P.	336.88	31.1	496	68.5	416.29	30.8	616	59.7
W.Bengal	350.17	31.7	615	85.6	409.22	14.7	621	45.3
Delhi					505.45	9.2	1120	53.6
All India	327.56	27.0	567	74.95	454.11	23.5	718	54.9

Note: We identified the expenditure groups where the per capita per diem calorie consumption was closest to 2,400 Kcal in rural areas and closest to 2,100 Kcal in urban areas. The average calorie consumption in the identified group was not exactly equal to 2,400 or 2,100. Sometimes it was more and sometimes less. Our estimates are based on the following approximations and adjustments. Accordingly, there could be slight overestimation or underestimation in the poverty figures computed by us.

(a) In the cases where identified group's average calorie consumption was less than 2,400 Kcal or 2,100 Kcal, the upper end-point of the identified expenditure range was taken as the poverty line. The cases where average calorie consumption was slightly more than 2,400 Kcal or 2,100 Kcal, the poverty line was taken as the average aggregate expenditure of the identified expenditure group.

(b) The poverty ratio was computed by adding the per centage population of all the expenditure groups below the poverty line. The cases where the identified group had calorie consumption below 2,400 or 2,100 Kcal, the entire population of this group was included in the poverty group. If the calorie consumption of the identified group was above 2,400 or 2,100Kcal, then half the population of this group was included in the poverty group.

Sources: 1. *Household Consumer Expenditure in India 1999–2000,* Key Results, NSS 55th Round, Report No. 454.
2. *Nutritional Intake in India 1999–2000.* NSS 55th Round, Report No. 471.

Thus in 1999–2000, 74 per cent of our rural population cannot afford 2,400 Kcal.

As can be seen from Table 2, the per capita monthly expenditure, which corresponds to the required calorie norms, is much higher than the official poverty lines in all the states. Correspondingly, in the rural areas of most of the major states, more than 80 per cent of the population is not able to afford the food, which would fulfill their calorie requirements. The case of Andhra Pradesh is glaring. The official poverty line there is the lowest and consequently poverty ratio estimated by the Planning Commission is only 10 per cent. However, as per our computation 89.4 per cent of population in Andhra Pradesh is not able to afford 2,400 Kcal per capita per diem. Similarly in Gujarat, the official poverty line is low and the poverty ratio is 12.4 per cent. The calorie norms, however, require the poverty line to be very much higher and the corresponding poverty ratio turns out to be 86 per cent. In Tamil Nadu again the poverty line is very high and poverty ratio is 94 per cent.

The inconsistency in the government determined poverty lines and nutritional norms arise because the poverty lines computed in 1973–74 have been adjusted only for the changes in price indices. Computing state level poverty lines according to state price indices has also accommodated the differing price trends in different states. However, the pattern of consumer expenditure is assumed to be constant. Neither inter state nor inter temporal differences in consumption pattern have been accounted for.

The expenditure pattern of the population has changed significantly both in rural and urban India. There is a shift in expenditure from food to non-food items. In the food basket, a shift is observed from cereals to non-cereals. This shift is observed over all expenditure groups even those at poverty line and below it. Thus, in 1973–74 the expenditure group at poverty line in rural areas spent 80 per cent of its total expenditure on food. In 1999–2000, the expenditure group at official poverty line in rural areas spends only 65 per cent of its total expenditure on food. The expenditure group at the rural poverty line conforming to nutritional norms spends only 60 per cent of its total expenditure on food (Table 1). Obviously the poverty line updated for price changes alone will be unable to meet the calorie requirements.

Relative Poverty vs Absolute Poverty

There are two ways in which researchers define poverty: relative poverty and absolute poverty. Relative poverty is defined in terms of bottom 10, 20 or 30 per cent of the population, which cannot participate in the desirable patterns of life that exist in a given society at a given time. Absolute poverty, however, refers to a situation in which a person lacks those things that help to sustain human life. It refers to the basic human needs, such as food, shelter and clothing. Generally relative poverty is considered relevant for societies where everyone has attained a certain minimum level of living and people have higher aspirations from life. For a poor country absolute poverty is more relevant.

...in the rural areas of most of the major states, more than 80 per cent of the population is not able to afford food that can fulfil their calorie requirements.

If our experts have decided that poverty in India is to be viewed in relative terms i.e. to consider only bottom 30 per cent or less as poor, then the official estimates are, of course, right and there is no need to bother about definition of poverty in terms of absolute norms.

However, if we accept that people have not yet got the basic minimum means required for a dignified human life, then we must set explicit norms for the basic minimum. In 1978, the task force appointed by the Planning Commission defined poverty line as the actual expenditure of the expenditure group, which spends enough on food to fulfill the normative calorie requirements. Norms were thus fixed only for the food component of the basic needs. No norms were fixed for the non-food items like clothes, housing, education, and health etc. Many of us have argued time and

...dignified living standards must include norms with respect to all these items and more.

1. The consumption in quantity terms is obtained from NSSO report no. 461.

Table 3
Consumption Pattern in Rural India

(Per capita Monthly Expenditure in Rs.)

Item	*Expenditure Groups*	
	300–340	*525–615*
Cereals	99.25	117.77
Gram	0.35	0.79
Cereal substitutes	0.17	0.41
Pulses & their products	14.18	22.12
Milk & Milk products	16.29	57.68
Edible Oils	13.48	21.93
Meat, Fish and eggs	9.54	20.14
Vegetables	23.12	35.43
Fruits (Fresh)	2.75	8.32
Fruits (dry)	0.67	1.65
Sugar	7.33	14.52
Salt	0.93	1.19
Spices	9.86	15.28
Beverages, refreshment	10.02	24.55
All food	**207.94**	**341.79**
Pan	1.57	3.47
Tobacco	5.57	9.01
Intoxicant	2.65	4.23
Fuel & Light	26.23	43.65
Clothing	23.92	39.22
Footwear	2.97	6.30
Misc. Consumer Goods	15.71	30.03
Misc. Consumer Service	12.69	31.66
Rent	0.24	1.58
Taxes and Cesses	0.29	0.91
Education	3.69	10.74
Medical (Institutional)	.65	7.35
Medical (Non-Instt.)	11.07	25.76
Durable Goods	4.61	10.83
All Non-Food	**112.85**	**224.74**

Source: *Household Consumer Expenditure in India 1999–2000.* Key Results. NSS 55th Round. Report No. 454.

again that dignified living standards must include norms with respect to all the above items and more.

In this context, we look at the consumption patterns in rural India at the official poverty line and also at the actual poverty line, which corresponds to the calorie norms.

The official poverty line corresponds to the monthly expenditure group Rs. 300–340. The average per capita per diem calorie intake of this group is only 1,868 Kcal i.e. 77 per cent of the accepted norm. The expenditure on all the food and nonfood items is absurdly small. The major amount of expenditure on food is incurred on cereals. In Rs. 99.25, the group procures 12.27 Kg. of grain. Out of 6.85 kg of rice and 3.9 kg of wheat the amount bought from PDS is only 0.78 kg and 0.18 kg. Its daily per capita grain consumption is 400 grams while consumption of pulses is 22 grams per day per person. The group spends Rs 16.29 on milk and milk products and procures 1.61 litres of milk per person in the whole month. Similarly, the consumption of fruits and eggs is abysmal—1.32 bananas and 0.61 eggs per person in the entire month. These figures show how fallacious is the argument that the calorie intake has reduced because even at poverty group people prefer to get their calories from more expensive food.

...fallacious is the argument that the calorie intake has reduced because even those at the poverty line prefer to get their calories from more expensive food.

The expenditure on non-food items is also ridiculously low. The two major non-food heads of expenditure for this group are fuel and light, and clothing. On fuel and light per capita monthly expenditure is Rs. 26.23. A household of 5 then spends around Rs. 130 on fuel and light. Around Rs. 70 is spent on firewood and chips. The household consumes only 10 units of electricity in the entire month. The amount spent on clothing per person per month is Rs. 23.92, which amounts to Rs. 290 in a year. Rs. 290 include expenditure on bedding, woolens and every day clothes. The expenditure on education is Rs. 3.69 per capita per month. Again if it is a household of five with two school going children the amount spent per month per child is only Rs. 10. Can these be the norms for dignified living in any society?

The expenditure at actual poverty line corresponding to calorie norms is only slightly better. It enables a monthly consumption of 13.45 kgs of grain, 5.15 litres of milk, 1.41 eggs and 3 bananas. The households at actual poverty line spend Rs. 218 on fuel and light which includes a little expenditure on kerosene. The consumption of electricity is around 28 units per month. The annual per capita expenditure on clothing is around Rs. 470, which allows a little amount to be spent on bedding, towels and woolens. Similarly expenditure on education is slightly more respectable. It amounts to Rs. 25 per school going child. Thus, even the expenditure group conforming to the calorie norms does not conform to other norms of dignified living and does not ensure fulfillment of the basic minimum. Therefore, there can be no justification for lowering the poverty line below the average expenditure of this expenditure group. (The consumption figures in quantity terms are obtained from NSSO report no. 461).

Such pervasive rural poverty demands major restructuring of land ownership and land use pattern.

Conclusion

The recognition that rural poverty in India is nearly 75 per cent and urban poverty 55 per cent changes the policy perspective drastically. When 75 per cent of the rural population belongs to the poverty group, poverty cannot be alleviated through targeted PDS or mid-day meal programme or Rozgar Guarantee Act. Such pervasive rural poverty demands major restructuring of land ownership and land use pattern. According to the same 55th round NSSO data on employment & unemployment, 40.9 per cent of the rural households are landless. Another 22.3 per cent cultivate 0.01 to 0.4 hectares of land and 16.8 per cent cultivate 0.41 to 1.00 hectares of land. Thus effectively 80 per cent of the rural households do not have access to adequate livelihood resource base. The 55th round data also tells us about a drastic squeeze on employment possibilities in agriculture. The growth rate of agricultural employment fell from 2.08 per cent between 1987–88 to1993–94 to 0.80 per cent during the period 1993–94 to 1999–2000. People debouched out of agriculture have no working or living space outside. They migrate in huge numbers from one village to another or from village to the town in search of food and work. The 75 per cent rural poverty originates from a deep-rooted crisis in Indian agriculture. Similarly 55 per cent urban poverty results from a crisis in Indian industry.

...effectively, 80 per cent of the rural households do not have access to an adequate livelihood resource base.

The 75 per cent rural poverty originates from a deep-rooted crisis in Indian agriculture; similarly, the 55 per cent urban poverty results from a crisis in Indian industry.

According to Ralph Miliband, the poor are an integral part of the working class and therefore poverty alleviation demands an economic restructuring where the share of working class in the national wealth is expanded and the share of capital is constrained. The present economic reform programme (with or without a human face) cannot and will not admit such a restructuring. What then remains the option with the people? The poor in villages and the poor in town have to reassert their primary identity as working class identity and wage a united and forceful struggle for their rightful share in the Nation's wealth.

Prices and the PDS

V. Upadhyay

After two years of low price rise, 2003–04 witnessed reemergence of inflationary pressure in the economy. The point-to-point average annual rate of inflation as measured by the Wholesale Price Index (WPI) in 2003–04 was 5.5 per cent compared to 3.6 and 3.4 per cent in 2001–02 and 2002–03, respectively. The price rise in 2003–04 was largely due to rise in the prices of edible oils, leather and leather products, basic metals and alloys, iron and steel, and mineral oils. The increase in international prices of imported commodities like crude oil, steel and edible oils has played a significant role in raising inflation rate in the country.

In recent past, compared to demand side factors, supply side factors have become more crucial in determining the extent of price rise in the economy. This is quite evident from the sudden surge in the inflation rate witnessed in the early months of 2004–05. The point-to-point inflation rate for the week ended August 28, 2004 stood at 8.33 per cent, which was the highest level reached since February 2001. Both global and domestic factors have played a significant role in the recent surge in the inflation. Whereas rapid increase in international oil prices has provided 'imported price shock' component, high food and vegetable prices caused by delayed rains have been the domestic contributory factors fueling the inflation. Rising prices of edible oils, iron ore and steel and sugar are other major contributors. If the international oil prices harden further in future, the inflation situation could easily become more menacing.

Rising prices of edible oils, iron ore and steel and sugar are other major contributors. If the international oil prices harden further in future, the inflation situation could easily become more menacing.

The WPI, however, can at times be a misleading indicator of price rise affecting the common people for several reasons. The WPI is based on wholesale prices, which are not the prices at which consumers buy products. The WPI measures the prices of both inputs and outputs. The commodity basket used in WPI includes many intermediate products, which are not the final consumption items. But most importantly, the WPI altogether leaves out the service sector, which accounts for more than half of our GDP. The impact of changes in retail prices can be better studied with the help of consumer price indices for different social groups: the Consumer Price Index for Industrial Workers (CPI-IW), the Consumer Price Index for Urban Non Manual Employees (CPI-UNME), and the Consumer Price Index for Agricultural Workers (CPI-AL). These indices, however, all suffer from one important shortcoming. The base years used in all these indices are too old rendering them meaningless. CPI-IW, which is the most commonly used index among the three CPIs, has 1982 as the base year, which is over two decades old. CPI-UNME and CPI-AL use 1984–85 and 1986–87 as the base year, respectively. The choice of base year is very important in construction of a price index because different commodities are assigned weights according to their share in total expenditure prevailing in that year. The weights derived from a base year, which is very old, bear no resemblance with the current consumption pattern. This severely limits the ability of the calculated price index to monitor price changes taking place in the economy. This shows that neither the WPI nor the three CPIs as they are constructed today are able to measure the changes in prices affecting the households properly. There is thus an urgent need to revise the price indices to make them suitable measure of inflation in the economy. The government's decision making process will also improve qualitatively if proper inflation database is available.

In the last few years, food production situation has been much worse.

High inflation rate all through the decade of 1990s has led to a sharp rise in absolute price levels of most essential commodities, especially of food articles. In March 2004, the Wholesale Price Index of food articles stood at 179 in comparison to 161 of manufactured products. Growth of agriculture slowed down considerably in the 1990s as compared to the earlier decade. Compared to 3.2 per cent per year in the 1980s, food production in the 1990s has grown only at 1.2 per cent, which is far below population growth. In the last few years, food production situation has been much worse. In 1999–00, foodgrains production was 209.8 million tonnes. Since then, this level has crossed only marginally twice: 212.9 million tonnes in 2001–02 and 210.38 million tonnes in 2003–04. In 2002–03, which was one of the worst drought years the country has faced, foodgrains production fell to 174.2 million tonnes.

Compared to 510.1 grams in 1991, per capita net availability of foodgrains per day was 416.2 grams in 2001. With the exception of two years (1975 and 1980), the country has never had such low per capita net availability of foodgrains in the post-green revolution period. The estimate for 2003 was 438.2 grams. As a result of stagnant food production, increasing dominance of market forces in the food sector, and anti-poor policies pursued by the government, food prices remain far too high and this has put the food security of millions of households in the country at risk.

As a result of stagnant food production, increasing dominance of market forces in the food sector, and anti-poor policies pursued by the government, food prices remain far too high and this has put the food security of millions of households in the country at risk.

Even high production of foodgrains does not automatically solve the problem of food security. Food security basically means that all households have both physical and economic access to adequate food for all members and they are not at risk of losing such access. High production alone does not guarantee that food is available to those who need it. When poor people cannot afford to buy adequate quantities of high cost foodgrain, there could be a highly deceptive situation with the food sector showing a surplus. It is estimated that about 300 million Indians do not have food security.

The public distribution system (PDS) is supposed to insulate the poor from the impact of rising prices of essential commodities and maintains their minimum nutritional status. The PDS has, however, completely failed in providing food security to the poor. In the past few years, the importance of the PDS as an outlet for foodgrains at controlled prices has diminished greatly as a result of steep and frequent increases in procurement prices followed by more than proportionate increases in the central issue prices of foodgrains. The current minimum support price (MSP) of the wheat is Rs. 630 per quintal.

The real beneficiaries of the large increase in procurement prices have been the surplus farmers of wheat and rice in three or four states that account for nearly 90 per cent of the procurement. The huge outlay in the name of food subsidy (Rs. 25,160 crore in 2003–04), which is a misnomer for all the losses incurred by the Food Corporation of India (FCI), helps in sustaining food prices at very high levels.

The real beneficiaries of the large increase in procurement prices have been the surplus farmers of wheat and rice in three or four states that account for nearly 90 per cent of the procurement.

In June 1997, Targeted Public Distribution System (TPDS) was introduced, under which two sets of PDS prices were announced, one each for Above Poverty Line (APL) and Below Poverty Line (BPL) households. Since the inception of the TPDS, both the APL and BPL prices have been revised several times.

In order to cut food subsidies, the Union Budget for 2000–01 proposed drastic revisions in the PDS with far reaching implications for the food security of the poor. The government fixed the final price of foodgrains to below poverty line (BPL) families at Rs. 415 per quintal (i.e at 50 per cent of the economic cost) and to above poverty line (APL) families at Rs. 830 per quintal (i.e. at the economic cost). Consequently, the selling price of wheat under PDS to BPL and APL families increased drastically. In fact, this was the largest ever increase in PDS prices. The PDS, instead of insulating the poor from rising open market prices, has become an instrument for pushing up prices. Faced with the problem of massive stocks, the government lowered the APL prices to Rs. 610 per quintal in 2001–02. The

The PDS, instead of insulating the poor from rising open market prices, has become an instrument for pushing up prices.

government further lowered the APL prices to Rs. 510 per quintal in April 2002 but raised again to Rs. 610 per quintal in July 2002.

As a result of the hike in PDS prices of foodgrains, the difference between the free market and the PDS prices has narrowed significantly. Market prices are often lower than APL prices for wheat and rice supplied thorough the PDS. This is because of massive inefficiencies in the Food Corporation of India (FCI) operations that have made 'the FCI's economic cost' (incurred for procurement, storage and transportation) more than the open market price. The FCI's charges for handling and storage of wheat are absurdly high.

FCI's economic cost of wheat was Rs. 914.71 per quintal (against MSP of Rs. 620 per quintal) in 2002–03, and it increased to Rs. 952.51 in 2003–04 as per revised estimate. High PDS prices also exert upward pressure on the market prices of foodgrains. High issue prices help keep the open market prices above levels that the market would otherwise determine. The poor are thus unable to purchase food in adequate quantities either from the PDS or from the open market.

A market price of foodgains being lower than PDS prices is an anomaly. Ideally speaking, market prices should be higher than the PDs prices. In the present situation, trades are receiving subsidised foodgrains from FCI through open market sales at very low prices, which they are reported to be reselling to FCI (illegally) at high prices, thanks to high procurement prices.

The offtake of foodgrains under the PDS has been declining for several years.

The offtake of foodgrains under the PDS has been declining for several years (Table 1). Only during the last two years it has shown increase due to the effect of drought. Whenever the offtake is less than procurement, these operations reduce overall market supply and push up prices. Procurement of foodgrains, on the other hand, has been witnessing an increasing trend. As a result, stocks of foodgrains at FCI reached unmanageable levels in 2002 when, in spite of massive selling of foodgrains in the open market at half the economic cost, the stocks of foodgrains stood at 63 million tonnes in July 2002. The country did not need a buffer stock of more than 24.3 million tonnes of foodgrains in the month of July to tide over any problem caused by unforeseen factors. Extra stocks were being maintained at an enormous cost to the nation. Even though the problem of malnutrition and semi-starvation is widespread in the country, food stocks at FCI have been increasing primarily because the people's purchasing power has declined in recent years. Huge stocks give a false impression of abundance. The stock of foodgrains stood at 24.40 million tonnes in January 2004. This reduction in stocks, however, does not indicate a reversal in the long-term trend as it has been due to increased offtake thanks to drought and very high levels of foodgrain exports during the last two years.

As a result, stocks of foodgrains at FCI reached unmanageable levels in 2002 when, in spite of massive selling of foodgrains in the open market at half the economic cost, the stocks of foodgrains stood at 63 million tonnes in July 2002.

With the frequently announced hike in the issue prices, the offtake of foodgrains from the PDS has fallen significantly over the past several years. Purchases in APL

The BJP-led government's policy has, in effect, eliminated the APL population completely from the PDS network.

Table 1
Foodgrains Procurement, Offtake under PDS and Central Stocks

(million tonnes)

Year	*Procurement (Central Pool)*	*Offtake (under PDS)*	*Central Stocks (as on January 1)*
1996–97	20.38	19.66	20.00
1997–98	23.63	16.98	18.30
1998–99	24.49	18.69	24.40
1999–00	31.41	17.07	31.40
2000–01	35.45	12.04*	45.70
2001–02	41.91	13.84*	58.00
2002–03	35.46	20.14*	48.20
2003–04	37.29	22.79*	24.40

Note: *including Antyodaya

category have stopped altogether because of the government policy of selling foodgrains to APL families at prices close to the economic cost. The BJP-led government's policy has, in effect, eliminated the APL population completely from the PDS network.

The government in December 2000 launched a scheme, the Antyodaya Anna Yojana, with an aim to provide 25 kg of foodgrains each month to one crore of the poorest families (out of the total 6.52 crore BPL families) at subsidised rate of Rs. 2 per kg. of wheat and Rs. 3 per kg. of rice. The scheme was, however, too limited in scope to make any dent on poverty. Its coverage included only a small fraction of the poor in the country. Given that a typical family's foodgrains requirement is above 60 kg per month, 25 kg does not meet even half of the monthly requirement. Under pressure from various quarters, the BJP-led government in budget 2003–04 increased the number of beneficiaries under this scheme to 1.50 crore of the poorest families. The amount of foodgrains provided was also raised to 35 kg. per month per family. The UPA government raised the coverage of the Antyoday scheme from 1 April 2004 by another 50 lakh, thus raising the number of beneficiaries to 2 crore of the poorest of the poor families.

Advocating a significant change in policy, the BJP-led government had proposed a considerably reduced role for the centre in the management of the food economy. Instead of providing subsidised foodgrains, financial assistance is to be provided to the state governments to enable them to procure and distribute foodgrains to BPL families at subsidised rates. FCI's responsibility will be limited to procurement of foodgrains for maintaining food security reserves and for such state governments who will assign it the task on their behalf. However, given the poor financial condition of most states, it is difficult to imagine state governments adequately discharging this important responsibility.

For various reasons, it has proved quite difficult to implement this policy change towards decentralisation of procurement of foodgrains. Decentralised procurement has stared in a limited way only in a few states (Bihar, Madhya Pradesh, Rajasthan and Uttar Pradesh). State governments of Punjab, Haryana and Andhra Pradesh, which are surplus states, and Kerala, a deficit state, are strongly opposed to the very basic philosophy of decentralised procurement. They point out the lack of necessary infrastructure and financial resources at the disposal of the states. Without taking steps to remove these deficiencies, decentralised procurement would increase the likelihood of less procurement or even non-procurement. This would go against the interests of farmers who would be compelled to resort to distress sales. Trades may be the only beneficiaries of such a system.

With the aim of liberalising trade in agriculture, the government removed quantitative restrictions in April 2001. As a result, India exported large quantities of wheat and rice during the last couple of years, even while a large portion of the country's population goes hungry. The country exported 12.2 million tonnes of foodgrains in 2001–02. The export price of wheat during this period was pegged at Rs. 4310 per tonnes. In spite of a drought, net cereals exports by India in 2003 were 6.1 million tonnes. The government was selling grain (wheat and rice) to foreign nationals at the price at which it is sold to the BPL families i.e., at half of FCI's economic cost. The government refused to cut issue price for the BPL families on the contention that it would further increase the subsidy burden. At the same time, it continued to provide heavy subsidies to foodgrain exports. This way, benefits of the food subsidy that are paid for by the Indian taxpayer were being enjoyed more by foreign nationals than the poor Indian families it was intended for.

It is not too difficult to find an explanation for this favoured treatment to foreign nationals by this 'nationalist' government. This action of the government, which amounts to dumping of foodgrains in the international market, was basically to

India exported large quantities of wheat and rice during the last couple of years, even while a large portion of the country's population goes hungry. The country exported 12.2 million tonnes of foodgrains in 2001–02.

In spite of a drought, net cereals exports by India in 2003 were 6.1 million tonnes. The government was selling grain (wheat and rice) to foreign nationals at the price at which it is sold to the BPL families i.e., at half of FCI's economic cost.

protect the interests of the trading community, the backbone of BJP's political support.

The UPA government has taken several steps to discourage export of foodgrains. Foodgrains (wheat and ordinary rice) exports are not to be allowed at least for one year. The NDA government's proposal to open up direct export of foodgrains by traders without any reference to food security and buffer stock norms has not been approved by the UPA government. Steps have also been taken to prevent diversion of foodgrains meant for food-for-work programmes into the export market.

Providing food subsidy is not a populist measure: this cannot be called untargeted expenditure. Such assistance to weaker sections is necessary as it helps them in sustaining themselves. Given the fact that a large segment of the population in the country is still below the poverty line, a pro-people policy framework demands continuation of food subsidy. The cut in food subsidy is against the interest of the poor.

It is true that the present PDS is beset with many serious problems. There is widespread leakage of PDS grains to the open market through bogus ration cards. It would not be an exaggeration to say that the real beneficiaries of the PDS subsidy are unscrupulous traders. Studies show that corruption in the PDS is responsible for more than one-third of foodgrains and sugar not reaching the poor. PDS definitely needs reforms. But a subsidised PDS for the well-targeted groups still remains the best from of food security for the poor.

There is widespread leakage of PDS grains to the open market through bogus ration cards. It would not be an exaggeration to say that the real beneficiaries of the PDS subsidy are unscrupulous traders. Studies show that corruption in the PDS is responsible for more than one-third of foodgrains and sugar not reaching the poor.

Considering the fact that the poor are ill equipped to face and absorb the shocks of pro-market policies, what is required is the institution of a comprehensive structure of safety nets. Notwithstanding many economic, political and administrative factors discussed above that prevent the full realisation of its potential, the PDS still remains a highly relevant scheme, which needs to be further strengthened. In order to effectively achieve its basic purpose of providing food security to the poor, the prices of foodgrains sold through the PDS should be kept at very low levels. The government has at its disposal huge stocks of foodgrains, which could be utilised to alleviate people's misery by undertaking food-for-work schemes at a large scale.

A High Level Committee, known as Abhijit Sen Committee on Long Term Grain Policy, constituted by the Department of Food and Public Distribution, has in its report submitted in July 2002, recommended that the existing Antyodaya Scheme should be expanded to become a food security for the entire destitute population. The committee also recommended that in place of the TPDS, a system of universal PDS be introduced throughout the country. These recommendations, if accepted by the government, will go a long way in enabling the PDS to fulfill the aim of providing food security to the millions of those poor Indians who suffer from malnutrition and hunger.

Employment

Hariharan Ramachandran and *S.L. Arora*

The Tenth Five Year Plan had stated that one of the most daunting challenges facing the planners is to ensure adequate growth in employment opportunities to absorb the increasing labour force and to reduce the backlog of unemployment accumulated from the past. The Plan had emphasised its concern over the acceleration in the growth of the labour force on the one hand and the downward pressure on the employment intensity of the growth process, on the other. It has been noted that the acceleration in Gross Domestic Product (GDP) growth in the 'reforms' period has not been accompanied by a commensurate expansion in employment, particularly in the organised sector.

...the acceleration in Gross Domestic Product (GDP) growth in the 'reforms' period has not been accompanied by a commensurate expansion in employment, particularly in the organised sector.

Prevalent Approaches to Understanding Employment

National Sample Survey Organisation (NSSO) collects detailed information on the employment status (using different criteria) of the population through large scale, nation-wide sample surveys in which individuals are categorised as employed or available for work but not employed. Since the late 1980s NSSO has been conducting these surveys annually, along with the quinquennial surveys. Prior to that only quinquennial surveys were conducted by the organisation. Quinquennial surveys, which were initiated in 1972–73, are more exhaustive and the sample selected for these surveys is larger in comparison to the annual surveys. Till now, NSSO has conducted six quinquennial surveys in its different rounds.[1]

The surveys conducted by NSSO take into consideration the seasonal variations in employment and also identify the magnitude of underemployment through different types of measures of employment such as Usual Principal Status (UPS), Usual Principal and Subsidiary Status (UPSS), Current Weekly Status (CWS), and Current Daily Status (CDS).[2]

1. *Usual Principal Status (UPS)*: Under this criterion, people are counted as being in the labour force on 'principal-usual activity basis' if they were either engaged in economic activities (work) or reported seeking/being available for work for the major part of the preceding 365 days. Those classified as being in the labour force on this basis are further classified as being employed or unemployed, depending on whether the majority of their days in the labour force were spent engaged in economic activity or in seeking/being available for work.
2. *Usual Principal and Subsidiary Status (UPSS)*:This criterion provides a more inclusive measure that also the participation in economic activity on a more or less regular basis of those classified as unemployed on the Usual Principal Status, as well as those classified as being outside the labour force by the same criterion. This results in a larger proportion of the population as being

1. 27th (1972–73), 32nd (1977–78), 38th (1983), 43rd (1987–88), 50th (1993–94) and 55th (1999–2000).
2. It has been A observe that these allternative measures of employment present a different picture of the employment scenario, but the broad trend is similar in all the measures.

in the labour force and lower unemployment rates relative to the UPS criterion.

3. *Current Weekly Status (CWS)*: The reference period under this criterion is the week preceding the interview. People are counted as employed if they were engaged in economic activity for at least one hour on any day during the reference week. Those not engaged in economic activity even for an hour on any day, but reporting seeking/being available for work during the reference week are classified as unemployed. To the extent that employment varies seasonally over the year, the labour force participation rates by this yardstick tend to be lower. However, the CWS unemployment rates tend to be higher when the UPS and UPSS based unemployment rates for the week are factored in. The difference between the unemployment rates based on the CWS and the UPS provide one measure of seasonal unemployment.
4. *Current Daily Status (CDS)*: Based on the reported time-disposition of the interviewed people on each day of the reference week (in units of half day where needed by the presence of multiple activities within a day), person-days in employment/unemployment are aggregated to generate estimates of person-days in employment/unemployment. The person-day unemployment rate is derived as the ratio of person-days in unemployment to the person-days in the labour force (i.e. person-days in employment plus person-days in unemploy-ment). This measure captures the 'within-week' unemployment of those classified as employed on theCWS basis.

Conceptually, the data on employment provided by the population censuses conducted by the Registrar General of India is close to the concept of UPS. However, the population census does not provide data on unemployment. By including even those who are not principal workers but work in a subsidiary capacity, e.g., students, pensioners, etc., the usual status concept comprehensively covers all those engaged in economic activities or seeking employment. In a situation where social security, in the form of a reasonable and assured support as allowance for unemployment, is not guaranteed, those who undertake economic activities in a subsidiary capacity do so generally out of economic compulsions.

In contrast to the other two concepts, which have shorter reference periods of a week or an average day of the week, the usual status concept yields more stable estimates of employment given its one year reference period over which disposition of time to activities is seen in classifying people as being in or out of the labour force, and those in the labour force as being employed or seeking work. Taking the usual status concept as the reference, it is possible to study the nature and characteristics of those employed, using the information available from the data compiled on current weekly and current daily status basis. UPSS has some limitations though, particularly when it is used for the sectors where casual workers are very large, such as the agricultural sector. This paper is based on the UPSS concept and is supplemented, wherever necessary, by the other two concepts. Since quinquennial surveys are more exhaustive as compared with the thin sample surveys, the analysis here is mainly based on the quinquennial surveys. Although some of the tables include data from the latest thin sample survey (58th round of NSSO), conducted in 2002, it must be noted that the results from the full sample differs significantly from the thin samples, the latter being found not robust enough to analyse the trend in employment even at the aggregate national level.

The total labour force stood at 430 million in 2002, of which about 71 per cent were male. The proportion of male in the labour force in 1983 was 66 per cent. The urban segment of the labour force, which was 20 per cent of the total in 1983, increased to 25 per cent by 2002.

Labour Force, Employment, and Unemployment

The total labour force stood at 430 million in 2002, of which about 71 per cent were male (Table 1). The proportion of male in the labour force in 1983 was 66 per cent.

Table 1
Growth of Labour Force (in 000's) as per Usual Status

Year	*Rural*			*Urban*			*Total*		
	Male	*Female*	*Person*	*Male*	*Female*	*Person*	*Male*	*Female*	*Person*
1983	156110	91189	247299	49260	12792	62052	205371	103981	309352
1987–88	167868	95396	263264	55781	15042	70823	223649	110437	334086
1993–94	190460	105697	296157	67183	18319	85502	257643	124016	381659
1999–2000	201976	106747	308724	78875	19249	98124	280851	125996	406848
2002	217009	104799	321808	87556	20762	108318	304565	125561	430126

Notes: Estimates for the year 1983 are as on 1 July 1983, for the years 1993–94 and 1999–2000 are as on 1 January 1994 and 2000, for the year 2002 are as on 1 October 2002.

The urban segment of the labour force, which was 20 per cent of the total in 1983, increased to 25 per cent by 2002.

The annual average growth rate of the labour force is seen to be fluctuating from about 1 to over 2 per cent between various rounds of the NSSO survey from 1983 to 2002 (Table 2). The main features of the growth in the labour force are: (a) markedly low rates of growth of the female labour force and (b) high rates of growth of the urban labour force in comparison to the rural labour force.

The trend of growth in employment is found to be similar to that of labour force throughout the reference period, although the magnitudes differ. Between 1993–94 and 1999–2000, the increase in the number of the employed was less than that in the number of employable people. As a result, unemployment, both in absolute terms and as a proportion of the labour force increased. During this period, the growth of employment was much higher in the case of males (1.39 per cent per annum) as compared with females (0.26 per cent per annum) as shown in Table 3.

Table 2
Average Annual Growth Rate of Labour Force (Usual Status)

Year	*Rural*			*Urban*			*Total*		
	Male	*Female*	*Total*	*Male*	*Female*	*Total*	*Male*	*Female*	*Total*
1983 to 1987–88	1.63	1.01	1.4	2.8	3.67	2.98	1.91	1.35	1.72
1987–88 to 1993–94	2.13	1.72	1.98	3.15	3.34	3.19	2.39	1.95	2.24
1993–94 to 1999–00	0.98	0.16	0.70	2.71	0.83	2.32	1.45	0.26	1.07
1999–00 to 2002	2.64	−0.67	1.52	3.87	2.79	3.66	2.99	−0.13	2.04

Notes: 1. Estimates for the year 1983 are as on 1 July 1983, for the years 1993–94 and 1999–00 are as on 1 January 1994 and 2000, for the year 2002 are as on 1 October 2002.
2. AAGR Stands for Average Annual Growth Rate.

Table 3
Average Annual Growth in Employment as per Usual Status

Year	*Rural*			*Urban*			*Total*		
	Male	*Female*	*Person*	*Male*	*Female*	*Person*	*Male*	*Female*	*Person*
1983 to 1987–88	1.54	0.59	1.19	2.79	3.39	2.91	1.83	0.94	1.53
1987–88 to 1993–94	2.2	1.98	2.12	3.36	3.36	3.36	2.48	2.17	2.38
1993–94 to 1999–00	0.94	0.15	0.66	2.64	0.94	2.30	1.39	0.26	1.03
1999–00 to 2002	2.66	−0.56	1.56	3.85	3.06	3.7	2.99	−0.02	2.07

Note: Same as for Table 1.

The trend of growth in employment is found to be similar to that of labour force throughout the reference period, although the magnitudes differ.

Similarly, the growth of employment was much higher in the urban areas (2.30 per cent per annum) as compared to the rural areas (0.66 per cent per annum).

The growth in unemployment during the last two quinquennial rounds was almost three times (3 per cent per annum) the growth of total employment (1.03 per cent during the period). This is the reason that the unemployment rate has increased from 1.97 per cent to 2.20 per cent (Table 4). If we compare the unemployment rates among males and females, it was higher for males (2.44 per cent) than for females (1.67 per cent). If we compare the unemployment among the rural and urban areas, it was more in the urban areas (4.63 per cent) as compared with the rural areas (1.43 per cent).

Underemployment

The unemployed, particularly those with low and medium level skills, cannot afford to remain in that status for long and tend to accept work with low wages and poor working conditions. Consequently, the number of people below the poverty line is much larger than the number of persons with open unemployment. Under the usual status concept of unemployment, a large number of the underemployed labour force is categorised as employed. In the case of rural males, out of 1000 usually employed

Table 4
Growth of Unemployed Persons (in 000's) as per Usual Status

Year	*Rural*			*Urban*			*Total*		
	Male	*Female*	*Person*	*Male*	*Female*	*Person*	*Male*	*Female*	*Person*
1983	2250	533	2784	2554	644	3198	4804	1177	5981
	(1.44)	(0.58)	(1.13)	(5.19)	(5.03)	(5.15)	(2.34)	(1.13)	(1.93)
1987–88	3058	2306	5363	2925	929	3853	5983	3234	9217
	(1.82)	(2.42)	(2.04)	(5.24)	(6.17)	(5.44)	(2.67)	(2.93)	(2.76)
1993–94	2716	958	3674	2727	1110	3837	5443	2068	7511
	(1.43)	(0.91)	(1.24)	(4.06)	(6.06)	(4.49)	(2.11)	(1.67)	(1.97)
1999–00	3366	1060	4427	3493	1048	4540	6859	2108	8967
	(1.67)	(0.99)	(1.43)	(4.43)	(5.44)	(4.63)	(2.44)	(1.67)	(2.20)
2002	3128	741	3869	3916	989	4904	7044	1730	8773
	(1.44)	(071)	(1.20)	(4.47)	(4.76)	(4.53)	(2.31)	(1.38)	(2.04)
AAGR									
1983 to 1987–88	7.05	38.45	15.69	3.06	8.48	4.23	4.99	25.19	10.08
1987–88 to 1993–94	–1.96	–13.62	–6.11	–1.16	3.02	–0.07	–1.56	–7.18	–3.35
1993–94 to 1999–2000	3.64	1.70	3.16	4.21	–0.96	2.84	3.93	0.32	3.00
1999–2000 to 2002	–2.63	–12.24	–478	4.25	–2.08	2.85	0.97	–6.93	–0.79

Notes: Figures in brackets are the unemployment rates (i.e. percentage of unemployed w.r.t. labour force).
Source: Same as for Table 1.

The growth in unemployment during the last two quinquennial rounds was almost three times (3 per cent per annum) the growth of total employment (1.03 per cent during the period).

Table 5
Distribution of Per 1000 of Usually Employed Persons (Principal and Subsidiary Status taken together) by Their Current Daily Status

Current Weekly Status	*Rural*				*Urban*			
	Male 1993–94	*Male 1999–00*	*Female 1993–94*	*Female 1999–00*	*Male 1993–94*	*Male 1999–00*	*Female 1993–94*	*Female 1999–00*
Employed	909	897	663	676	949	942	766	791
Unemployed	40	53	30	41	27	27	24	22
Not in Labour Force	51	51	306	283	25	31	210	187
All	1000	1000	1000	1000	1000	1000	1000	1000

workers, 40 were unemployed as per the CDS criterion in 1993–94, but in 1999–2000, the number of unemployed increased to 53. In the case of rural females, this number increased from 30 to 41 (Table 5).

An alternative estimate of underemployment can be made using the difference between the unemployment rates by the usual status and the current daily status criteria. In the rural areas, the unemployment rates derived from CDS are much higher than the values derived from UPSS—for males, it was 1.7 per cent by UPSS and 7.2 per cent by CDS and for females it was 1 per cent by UPSS and 7 per cent by CDS. A similar pattern can be observed in the previous three rounds of NSS (Table 6).

While in the urban areas also the unemployment rates derived using CDS were higher than those derived through UPSS, the differences were not as high as in the rural areas—for males, the unemployment rate by UPSS was 4.5 per cent and by CDS it was 7.3 per cent whereas for females the unemployment rate by UPSS was 5.7 per cent and by CDS it was 9.4 per cent. A similar pattern can be observed in the earlier three rounds also (Table 6).

Employment in the Organised and the Unorganised Sectors

The share of the organised sector employment in the total employment of the country is very small (only 7 per cent). In absolute terms, there was a marginal increase in it from 26.7 million in 1991 to 28.2 million in 1997. It declined to 28 million by 2000. Even when there was an acceleration in the rate of growth of GDP, there was not much increase in employment in the organised segment of the economy. However, the growth–lobby does not seem to appreciate the serious economic, social, and human welfare implications of growth-oriented policies and of treating employment as a secondary and uncertain by-product of their primary concern.

Because of the small share of the organised sector in the total employment, even if the growth in GDP increases further, there is little possibility of a significant increase in the share of the formal sector in so far as employment is concerned. The prospect of employment growth in the formal sector is further undermined by the increasing outsourcing of non-core work from the informal sector by the government as well as the private sector.

If we compare the employment increase in the public and the private sectors within the organised segment, the performance of the private sector was slightly better. Apparently, this was mainly due to the policy thrust of the Structural Adjustment Programme (SAP) to downsize government and reduce public spending and public employment. But, the share of the private sector in the organised sector is only 31 per cent as compared with 69 per cent in the public sector (Table 7). Even if the organised private sector grows at a higher rate, it will focus on increasing

The share of the organised sector employment in the total employment of the country is very small (only 7 per cent).

Because of the small share of the organised sector in the total employment, even if the growth in GDP increases further, there is little possibility of a significant increase in the share of the formal sector in so far as employment is concerned.

Table 6
Unemployment Rates During 1983 to 1999–2000 by Different Definitions

Year	*Male*				*Female*			
	US	*UPSS*	*CWS*	*CDS*	*US*	*UPSS*	*CWS*	*CDS*
Rural Areas								
1983	2.1	1.4	3.7	7.5	1.4	0.7	4.3	9.0
1987–88	2.8	1.8	4.2	4.6	3.5	2.4	4.4	6.7
1993–94	2.0	1.4	3.1	5.6	1.3	0.9	2.9	5.6
1999–00	2.1	1.7	3.9	7.2	1.5	1.0	3.7	7.0
Urban Areas								
1983	5.9	5.1	6.7	9.2	6.9	4.9	7.5	11.0
1987–88	6.1	5.2	6.6	8.8	8.5	6.2	9.2	12.0
1993–94	5.4	4.1	5.2	6.7	8.3	6.1	7.9	10.4
1999–00	4.8	4.5	5.6	7.3	7.1	5.7	7.3	9.4

Table 7
Employment in Organised (Public and Private) Sector

(in lakh)

Year	*Public*	*Private*	*Organised*
1991	190.57	76.76	267.3
1992	192.10	78.46	270.6
1993	193.26	78.51	271.8
1994	194.45	79.30	273.8
1995	194.66	80.59	275.3
1996	194.29	85.12	279.4
1997	195.59	86.86	282.5
1998	194.18	87.48	281.7
1999	194.15	86.98	281.1
2000	193.14	86.46	279.6

productivity by replacing labour with capital, wherever possible. There are a number of micro level studies that have observed such a trend.

The majority of the total workforce belongs to the unorganised sector, but it has little social security. The government has enacted a number of legislations during the last fifty years, which are directly or indirectly applicable to workers of this sector. In addition to this, the government has constituted cess-based welfare funds for specific groups of unorganised sector workers, i.e. beedi workers, cine workers, and certain mine workers. Apart from this, a few states such as Kerala and Tamil Nadu have taken some steps to provide social security and welfare measures to the workers of this sector. In spite of these efforts, only a small share of workers in the unorganised sector is covered under the social security schemes. Out of about 370 million workers in the unorganised sector, only about 10 million workers are covered under such schemes.

The majority of the total workforce belongs to the unorganised sector, but it has little social security.

Employment by Broad Economic Sectors

During the last two major surveys, the growth of employment in the tertiary sector at 2.83 per cent per annum was higher as compared with the primary and the secondary sectors, which showed annual employment growth of 0.06 and 2.40 per cent respectively, as shown in Figure 1. In the rural areas, the highest growth was in the secondary sector (2.48 per cent per annum) followed by the tertiary sector (2.11

Figure 1
Sector-wise Growth of Employment from 38th to 58th Round of NSSO

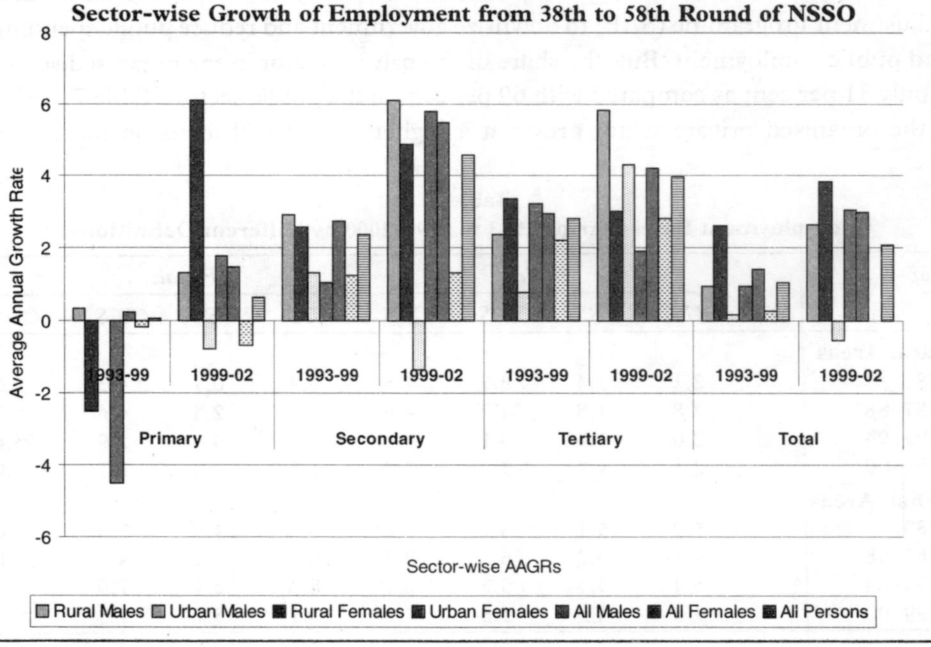

per cent per annum) and the primary sector (0.19 per cent per annum). In the urban areas, the trend was similar to that of the total economy, though the growth in the primary sector was negative (–3.34 per cent per annum).

During the last two decades, a major shift has taken place in agriculture, construction, trade, and transport industries. The share of employment in agriculture in the total economy has decreased and the share of employment in construction, trade and, transport has increased. The shift away from agriculture, however, is rather small in magnitude. More importantly, the manufacturing sector has shown an unwelcome declining trend (Table 8).

The share of employment in agriculture in the total economy has decreased and the share of employment in construction, trade and, transport has increased. The shift away from agriculture, however, is rather small in magnitude. More importantly, the manufacturing sector has shown an unwelcome declining trend.

Youth Segment of Labour Force

Between the last two major surveys (1993–94 and 1999–2000), the annual growth rate in the youth labour force was 0.51 per cent—much higher than the growth rate of 0.36 per cent in their employment (Tables 9 and 10). During this period, the growth in youth employment was only one-third (0.36 per cent per annum) of the growth in the total employment in the country (1.03 per cent). Thus the proportion of the unemployed among the youth has increased at a higher rate (3.38 per cent per annum) as compared with the growth in the total unemployed persons in the

Thus the proportion of the unemployed among the youth has increased at a higher rate (3.38 per cent per annum) as compared with the growth in the total unemployed persons in the country (3.00 per cent per annum).

Table 8
Distribution of Working Force by Rural/Urban and Industry Division by Usual Status (Primary and Subsidiary)

Industry Division	*Rural*				*Urban*			
	1983	*1987–88*	*1993–94*	*1999–00*	*1983*	*1987–88*	*1993–94*	*1999–00*
Agriculture Forestry, Fishing & Hunting	81.2	78.3	78.4	76.3	14.6	13.4	12.3	8.6
Mining and Quarrying	0.5	0.6	0.6	0.5	1.0	1.2	1.2	0.8
Manufacturing	6.7	7.2	7.0	7.3	26.7	26.0	23.6	22.7
Electricity, Gas and Water	0.1	0.2	0.2	0.2	0.9	1.0	1.0	0.7
Construction	1.7	3.3	2.4	3.3	4.7	5.4	6.3	8.0
Wholesale & Retail trade and Restaurants & Hotels	3.5	4.0	4.3	5.1	18.4	19.0	19.4	26.9
Transport, Storage and Communication	1.1	1.3	1.4	2.1	8.1	7.8	8.0	8.7
Services	4.9	5.0	5.7	5.2	25.0	25.7	28.2	23.6
Activities not Classified	0.3	0.1	–	–	0.6	0.5	0.5	–
Total	100.0	100.0	100.0	100.0	100.0	100.0	100.0	100.0

Table 9
Growth of Youth Labour Force (in 000's) As per Usual Status

Year	*Rural*			*Urban*			*Total*		
	Male	*Female*	*Person*	*Male*	*Female*	*Person*	*Male*	*Female*	*Person*
Labour Force									
1993–94	70236	38690	108926	24773	6587	31360	95009	45277	140286
1999–00	72454	37474	109928	28163	6504	34667	100617	43978	144595
2002	76975	32060	109035	33165	7508	40673	110140	39568	149708
AAGR									
1993–94 to 1999–00	0.52	-0.53	0.15	2.16	-0.21	1.68	0.96	-0.48	0.51
1999–00 to 2002	2.23	-5.52	-0.30	6.13	5.35	5.98	3.34	-3.77	1.27

Note: Same as Table 1

Table 10

Growth of Youth Employment (in 000's) as per Usual Status

Year	*Rural*			*Urban*			*Total*		
	Male	*Female*	*Person*	*Male*	*Female*	*Person*	*Male*	*Female*	*Person*
Employment									
1993–94	67746	37975	105721	22382	5598	27980	90128	43573	133701
1999–00	69392	36466	105858	25135	5610	30745	94527	42076	136603
2000	74188	31558	105746	29840	6636	36476	104028	38194	142222
AAGR									
1993–94 to 1999–00	0.40	–0.67	0.02	1.95	0.04	1.58	0.8	–0.58	0.36
1999–00 to 2002	2.46	–5.12	–0.04	6.44	6.3	6.41	3.54	–3.46	1.48

Note: Same as Table 1.

Table 11

Growth of Youth Unemployed (in 000's) as per the Usual Status

Year	*Rural*			*Urban*			*Total*		
	Male	*Female*	*Person*	*Male*	*Female*	*Person*	*Male*	*Female*	*Person*
1993-94	2483	714	3197	2392	990	3382	4875	1704	6579
	(3.54)	(1.85)	(2.94)	(9.66)	(15.03)	(10.78)	(5.13)	(3.76)	(4.69)
1999-00	3091	1006	4097	3028	906	3934	6119	1912	8031
	(4.27)	(2.68)	(3.73)	(10.75)	(13.93)	(11.35)	(6.08)	(4.35)	(5.55)
2002	2787	5.35	3322	3309	871	4180	6096	1406	7502
	(3.62)	(1.67)	(3.05)	(9.98)	(11.60)	(10.28)	(5.53)	(3.55)	(5.01)
AAGR									
1993-94 to 1999–00	3.72	5.88	4.22	4.01	–1.47	2.55	3.86	1.94	3.38
1999–00 to 2002	–3.7	–20.54	–7.34	3.28	–1.43	2.23	–0.14	–10.58	–2.45

Note: Same as in Table 1.

country (3.00 per cent per annum). Further, the unemployment rate among the youth has increased to 5.55 per cent as compared with 2.20 per cent unemployment rate for the total economy.

If we take into consideration the results of the thin sample survey conducted in the year 2002, the growth rate of youth employment appears to have increased significantly during the period 1999–00 to 2002, for males as well as females, though more severely in the case of females than males (Table 10).

Table 12

Unemployment Rates for Persons of Age 15 Years and Above with Different Educational Attainments.

Year	*General Education Level*						
	Not Literate	*Literate up to Primary*	*Middle*	*Secondary*	*Higher Secondary*	*Graduate and above*	*Secondary and above*
Rural Males							
1993–94	0.2	0.4	2.2	5.0	7.3	9.8	6.5
1999–00	0.3	0.9	2.3	4.3	6.1	8.2	5.6
Rural Females							
1993–94	0.2	0.5	3.0	11.3	19.9	27.4	16.0
1999–00	0.1	0.6	3.2	9.8	14.3	29.8	14.6
Urban Males							
1993–94	0.9	2.3	5.4	5.6	7.5	5.6	6.0
1999–00	1.3	2.8	5.2	5.1	7.7	6.3	6.2
Urban Females							
1993–94	0.3	2.9	10.9	15.7	19.2	18.9	18.2
1999–00	0.5	1.9	7.9	12.0	16.7	14.7	14.3

Unemployment by Level of Education

The unemployment rate is positively related to the educational attainments for all segments of the labour force—rural males, rural females, urban males and urban females (Table12). Unemployment of the educated section of the labour force in the rural areas is higher than that of the urban areas. Similarly, the unemployment rate of the educated females is higher than that of the educated males.

Employment Elasticity

Employment elasticity with respect to net domestic product (NDP) in a year is the ratio of 'percentage change in employment' to the 'percentage change in NDP' over the year.[3] In a recent study conducted by Institute of Applied Manpower Research (IAMR) titled '*Sector-wise Trends of Productivity in India*', sector-wise average annual employment elasticity of different periods has been compared (Table 13). During the last two decades, the employment elasticity of the total economy has decreased. The average annual employment elasticity of the five-year period from 1980–81 to 1985–86 was 0.46, but it decreased to about 0.16 during the period 1995–96 to 1999–2000.

The agriculture sector had almost zero employment elasticity because there was no growth of employment in this sector during this period. The mining and quarrying sector had negative employment elasticity (–5.27) because of the decrease in the value of NDP for this sector during this period, although employment in this sector increased during this period. Other sectors having lower percentage increases in employment as compared to that of NDP during this period were: manufacturing (0.43); services (0.49); trade (0.64), and 'electricity, gas and water supply' (0.94).

If we compare the employment elasticity during the pre-reform decade (1980–81 to 1990–91) and immediate post-reform period (1992–93 to 1999–2000), there has been a reduction of about 50 per cent (0.41 to 0.23) in it. All the sectors, except agriculture, have lower elasticity in the post-reform period as compared with the pre-reform period.

Concluding Observations

The forces of globalisation and internal economic liberalisation that have swept the world in the last decade and a half have brought in their wake significant changes in the labour market of India. They have unleashed a new level of competition in the

The agriculture sector had almost zero employment elasticity because there was no growth of employment in this sector during this period.

Table 13
Sector-wise Average Annual Employment Elasticity for the Period 1980–81 to 1999–2000

Sector	*Period*					
	1980–81 to 1985–86	*1985–86 to 1990–91*	*1980–81 to 1990–91*	*1992–93 to 1995–96*	*1995–96 to 1999–00*	*1992–93 to 1999–00*
Total	0.46	0.37	0.41	0.31	0.16	0.23
Agriculture	–0.03	0.20	0.09	0.25	0.03	0.13
Mining & Quarrying	–2.54	0.86	–0.84	–2.97	–5.27	–4.28
Manufacturing	0.43	0.27	0.35	0.24	0.42	0.34
elect. Gas &water	0.94	0.63	0.79	–0.01	–0.28	–0.16
Const.	1.71	1.72	1.71	0.20	1.47	0.93
Trade	0.64	0.73	0.69	0.48	0.80	0.66
Transport & Storage	1.14	0.65	0.89	0.57	0.59	0.58
Services	0.49	0.46	0.48	0.44	–0.09	0.13

Source: IAMR (2004), Sector-wise Trends of productivity in India.

3. NSSO's Report No. 409 on Results of 50th Round (1993–94) Survey on Employment and Unemployment quoted in the Report of the Task Force on Employment Opportunities, Planning Commission, 2001.

manufacturing and the services sectors, which had led to innovation in methods of cost-efficient production and work organisation. India's labour market has been transformed by the opening up to global buyers and sellers and the accompanying international competition, new business strategies and management practices, new forms of decentralised work-organisation like outsourcing, greater use of capital intensive technology, and changes in financial markets. The key characteristic of this transformation is minimisation of labour, particularly in the organised sector. As a result, there has been a shift of employment opportunities out of the secure and high wage jobs to the less secure and often poorly paying jobs in the informal/unorganised sector. Even the public sector, which till the 1980s had been a generous source of stable employment, has more or less stopped incremental hiring as a result of the pro-privatisation thrust of the SAP.

Even the public sector, which till the 1980s had been a generous source of stable employment, has more or less stopped incremental hiring as a result of the pro-privatisation thrust of the SAP.

The changes have not just been quantitative; they have been qualitative as well. Accompanying the reduction in the overall labour intensity of the economic growth, there has been a significant change in the skill structure of the manpower demand, with opportunities in certain highly skilled occupations increasing rapidly. The boom in the services sector has spurred growth of new employment opportunities, particularly those involving application of information technology or multiple skills. In the process, the relatively less skilled and the unskilled persons, who happen to be the most numerous and most livelihood-insecure segment of the labour force, have been adversely affected.

The changes have not just been quantitative; they have been qualitative as well.

The emerging labour market, thus, offers scope for employment and income to those with skill, often with more than one skill. However, with low and declining numbers of workers employed in response to a unit increase in output, the absolute size of this source of employment can not keep pace with the growth in the labour force. This is not only true of the organised sector, but even large areas of the unorganised sector that are either connected to the organised sector or are involved in export-oriented production or in service activities. Unfortunately, the educational and skill content of a large proportion of the Indian labour force is extremely low. The educational structure of the workforce is such that about 44 per cent of the workforce is illiterate. Another 23 per cent is either just literate or has education only up to the primary level. Thus, only a third of the work force is educated up to the upper primary level or beyond. These overall proportions conceal wide variations between the rural and urban areas and between women and men, the former being substantially disadvantaged compared with the latter., Though the situation has been improving with the youth, who comprise the fresh entrants to the labour force, being better educated, yet the pace of change is too slow to have a significant impact on the overall educational attainments of the labour force, for some years to come.

Further, in a situation where the demand for a workforce with high quality skills, and even multiple skills, is increasing, only 20 per cent of the Indian population has some marketable skills even among the urban males, according to the NSSO's 1993–94 survey.

Further, in a situation where the demand for a workforce with high quality skills, and even multiple skills, is increasing, only 20 per cent of the Indian population has some marketable skills even among the urban males, according to the NSSO's 1993–94 survey. In the case of rural males and urban females, such skills are found only in about 10 per cent of them, while only 6 per cent of the rural females possess any such skill. In many cases, the skills are traditional in nature, being in the areas of weaving, cutting and tailoring, construction activities, and motor vehicle driving[3]. Only the urban males exhibited some diversity in their skill endowments. As the state, under the compulsive logic of liberalisation, is deliberately yielding its role in education to the private entrepreneurs who treat higher and technical education as a rather lucrative business, the prospects of a real breakthrough in improving the skill profile of the new entrants to the labour force are fast receding.

Raising the employability of the nation's youth is as important as employment generation to meet their employment needs. Successive Five Year Plans and various committees and commissions have underscored the prevailing low skill levels among the Indian labour force and the need for establishing comprehensive but flexible systems of skill development to enhance its employability and increase its productivity and incomes.

The bulk of the production activity takes place in the informal sector. It is this sector that is likely to absorb increasingly large proportions of the labour force to whom the benefits of skill development and the consequent augmentation of productivity should increasingly be extended. There is enough evidence to show that even a little increase in skills brings in more than a proportionate increase in incomes. In a globalising economy, the Indian work force, particularly that engaged in the informal sector activities, will have to contend increasingly with internal and external competition from products and services coming from relatively better skilled workers. Mere survival in the market demands retention of one's competitive edge through acquisition of skills. The spectre of a worsened unemployment situation is unlikely to disappear from our midst unless a much higher priority is given to the employment objective, that too not indirectly through the ineffective route of higher rates of output growth without regard to the labour-intensity of the output-mix and a commensurate increase in the proportion of wage-goods.

The bulk of the production activity takes place in the informal sector. It is this sector that is likely to absorb increasingly large proportions of the labour force to whom the benefits of skill development and the consequent augmentation of productivity should increasingly be extended.

While the rate of unemployment may be low in the case of a workforce with low levels of education, the numbers are large. There is, therefore, no escape from the publicly funded wage employment programmes. At the same time, the problem of increasing unemployment among the educated segment of the labour force also needs to be dealt with urgently. A combination of access to credit, so as to promote self employment opportunities for the educated youth, and policy changes at various levels of government, would be needed to address the problem of unemployment of the educated youth. Some of the ongoing programmes could be strengthened to achieve greater impact.

> Projects developed under Pradhan Mantri Rozgar Yojna (PMRY) over the period of 1996–1999 have been evaluated rigorously by the financial establishments, which provided credit for these ventures ... A study of 16,0000 units by the Programme Evaluation Organisation of the Planning Commission showed that 80 per cent of the units were functioning, of which 83 per cent were reporting profits and 34 per cent of them were able to fulfil their obligations of repayment of their loans and interest on a regular basis. ... independent assessment by Reserve Bank of India (RBI)) has also established that the recovery rate of the units set up under PMRY is around 45 per cent. (Planning Commission 2002).

However, ultimately, the strengthening of the unorganised sector, both absolutely and relatively, is an inescapable option, if the people in general and the youth in particular, have to be provided adequate and secure means of livelihood. This is a policy objective no real democracy can afford to ignore. What has been done over the past so many years, calls for a serious review and rethink in order to accord employment and livelihood security the pride of place it so richly deserves.

...the strengthening of the unorganised sector, both absolutely and relatively, is an inescapable option, if the people in general and the youth in particular, have to be provided adequate and secure means of livelihood.

References

IAMR. 2004. *Sector-wise Trends of Productivity in India*, Delhi: IAMR.

Planning Commission. 2001. NSSO's Report No. 409 on Results of 50th Round (1993–94), Survey on Employment and Unemployment quoted in the *Report of the Task Force on Employment Opportunities*. New Delhi: Planning Commission.

Privatisation

Pranjoy Guha Thakurta

The 23 December 2003 meeting of the Cabinet Committee on Disinvestment (CCD) turned out to be rather disappointing for Arun Shourie. As Union Minister for Disinvestment in the Atal Bihari Vajpayee government, Shourie was hopeful that he would be able to convince his Cabinet colleagues of the need to embark on a major privatisation programme for the country's petroleum sector. But that was not to be.

When Shourie met newspersons after the CCD meeting, he put up a brave front. He announced to them that 10 per cent of the government's shares of Oil & Natural Gas Corporation (ONGC) and GAIL India Limited (formerly Gas Authority of India Limited) will be sold to the Indian public at large to raise the budgetary resources. ONGC is the country's largest explorer and producer of crude oil, while GAIL is the biggest supplier of natural gas.

What may have appeared a routine pronouncement to some, actually had an interesting background. For Shourie, it represented a version of the history of what he would consider missed opportunities. For those who were not exactly excited about the minister's zeal to push through privatisation against all odds, the CCD decision marked a watershed in the government's programme of selling off its controlling stake in the profit-making public sector undertakings, especially the professionally-managed PSUs in the petroleum industry. It was evident that Shourie had failed to convince other ministers in the Vajpayee government—including the Union Minister for Petroleum & Natural Gas, Ram Naik—that Indian Oil Corporation (IOC), the largest oil refining and marketing company in the country, should be privatised after it was split and its marketing operations were made into a separate corporate entity.

Earlier, on 3 October, 2003, the CCD had considered the move to split IOC. Many interpreted this decision as a knee-jerk reaction to the 16 September judgment of the Supreme Court restraining the Union government from going ahead with the privatisation of Hindustan Petroleum Corporation Limited (HPCL), the second largest oil refining and marketing company in the country, without obtaining prior approval of Parliament. After the country's highest court and his own colleagues scuttled Shourie's grandiose plans to privatise India's petroleum sector, IOC and HPCL in particular, he had no choice but to follow a path of least resistance, a road many believe he should have traversed in the first place. There was a perception that many of Shourie's policy prescriptions would favour certain corporate groups, notably the Reliance group controlled by the Ambani family. This perception spread after Shourie's decision in May 2002 to allow the Reliance group to acquire managerial control over the erstwhile public sector unit (PSU), Indian Petrochemicals Corporation Limited (IPCL).

By exercising control over IPCL, the Reliance group was able to hog more than three-fourths of the country's market for a wide variety of petrochemical products. This move resulted in a once competitive industry becoming the monopoly of a family-dominated group.

By exercising control over IPCL, the Reliance group was able to hog more than three-fourths of the country's market for a wide variety of petrochemical products. This move resulted in a once competitive industry becoming the monopoly of a family-dominated group. Then onwards, Shourie's privatisation methodology started encountering stiff opposition from within the Bharatiya Janata Party (BJP) as well as the National Democratic Alliance (NDA) coalition. It was not merely Naik (whose vast empire as Minister for Petroleum and Natural Gas was in danger of shrinking) who opposed him, but the Defence Minister and NDA convener George Fernandes as well, who wrote to the Prime Minister protesting against Shourie's decision that had created a private monopoly.

Even if one puts on ideological blinkers and believes that everything about the public sector is necessarily bad and the private corporate entities are invariably more efficient, and even if one is convinced that the petroleum industry is not 'strategic' in nature in a country that currently imports close to three-fourths of its requirements of crude oil and petroleum products, the moves to split IOC and privatise HPCL without seeking Parliamentary approval were clearly short-sighted. The attempt to break the Rs. 1,20,000 crore IOC into separate refining and marketing entities was difficult to justify, especially at a time when internationally the large petroleum companies are coming together to become bigger still. Besides, IOC is the only Indian company to find a place in the *Fortune* 500 list of largest companies outside the USA.

In refining, IOC currently vies with the Reliance group, which has set up one of the largest oil refineries in India and Asia but is yet to set up a commensurate marketing infrastructure. Private companies like Reliance Petroleum are reportedly eyeing IOC and HPCL's retail outlets since many of these are at prime urban locations. After IOC successfully acquired managerial control over IBP Limited (formerly Indo-Burma Petroleum) in January 2002, the government 'clarified' that one PSU should not be allowed to acquire the shares of another PSU, as this would not amount to 'real' privatisation. It may be recalled that the former Chairman and Managing Director of IOC, M.A. Pathan had argued that it would be clearly discriminatory on the part of the government if a private corporate group like Reliance was allowed to bid for IPCL while denying IOC the opportunity to bid for HPCL and Bharat Petroleum Corporation Ltd. (BPCL). His words were, of course, ignored.

The attempt to break the Rs. 1,20,000 crore IOC into separate refining and marketing entities was difficult to justify, especially at a time when internationally the large petroleum companies are coming together to become bigger still.

After the move to dismantle IOC was suggested, the company's management made a smart move. It said that if the government was indeed serious about raising resources for the Budget, it should seriously consider the offer made by the IOC management to acquire the shares of HPCL for a sum of Rs. 10,000 crore. Such an amount would cover the anticipated shortfall in receipts from divestment during the current financial year. (This is now being attempted by selling 10 per cent of the shares of ONGC and GAIL.)

Shourie was not exactly overjoyed by the suggestion made by the IOC management. Since he was evidently unhappy that the Supreme Court had disallowed the government from privatising HPCL without seeking the prior approval of Parliament, as the company had been set up by an Act of Parliament that had allowed the government to take over the assets of foreign oil companies in the 1970s, it seems he turned his sights towards IOC, which does not have any legal restraints on its privatisation. He did not succeed.

...Shourie in particular and the Vajpayee government in general were unable to forge a national consensus on privatisation.

There are various reasons why Shourie in particular and the Vajpayee government in general were unable to forge a national consensus on privatisation. Such reasons include the fact that the proceeds from the sale of equity shares of PSUs have not been put to productive use. Instead, they have been used primarily to bridge the deficit of the government. Equally contentious has been the policy of privatising the profit-making PSUs before tackling the problems of the loss-making PSUs. Questions have also been raised about the manner in which the assets of the privatised PSUs were valued.

There are 236 central PSUs in the country—130 of these earn profits while the remaining 106 incur losses.

There are 236 central PSUs in the country—130 of these earn profits while the remaining 106 incur losses. According to statistics compiled by the Department of Public Enterprises, between 1991–92 and 2000–01, the total profit after tax of all the PSUs put together went up 6.6 times. While a few large PSUs such as ONGC and IOC earned huge profits, most earned relatively modest profits. Still, the profits of all the 130 profit-making PSUs put together went up 4.6 times in this period, during which aggregate losses of all the 106 loss-making PSUs went up by a smaller proportion, by 3.4 times.

If indeed the public sector is such a drain on the exchequer, why should the government first be selling the shares of the best run, most-profitable *navaratnas* (nine jewels) before rehabilitating, shutting down or privatising precisely those loss-making PSUs that are draining the exchequer? Is it only because there are ready buyers for the assets of the first category of PSUs whereas it is a far more difficult task to improve the working of the second lot of PSUs?

Tucked away in the bunch of documents made public on 3 February 2003, the day the Finance Minister Jaswant Singh, presented his vote-on-account and the interim budget for 2004–05 in Parliament, on page 12 of a thin (16-page) document entitled 'Implementation of Budget Announcements (2003–04)' were the following two sentences: 'Disinvestment Proceeds Fund: The modalities for setting up the Fund have been worked out. The Fund is expected to be operational from 1 July 2004.'

Earlier, on 9 December 2002, Shourie had told the Lok Sabha:

> In order to provide complete visibility to the government's continued commitment of utilisation of disinvestment proceeds for social and infrastructure sectors, the government would set up a Disinvestment Proceeds Fund. This Fund will be used for financing fresh employment opportunities and investment and for retirement of public debt.

Thereafter, on the last working day of February 2003, Finance Minister stated: 'Details about the already announced Disinvestment Fund … shall be finalised early in 2003–04'.

Twelve years earlier, the present Prime Minister, Manmohan Singh, was the finance minister in the P.V. Narasimha Rao government and he had stated in his first budget speech, delivered on 29 February 1992, that he had taken credit for Rs. 2,500 crore as receipts of disinvestment. He had added that the government would 'consider a further sale of equity of Rs. 1,000 crore to provide resources for the National Renewal Fund during 1992–93, which can be used for various schemes of assistance to workers in the unorganised sector, including women workers, who may be adversely affected by the process of economic restructuring'. Manmohan Singh had further stated that such 'non-inflationary resources' would 'also be used to fund… special employment creating schemes in backward areas'.

...then Finance Minister, Yashwant Sinha had said that he hoped to raise Rs. 10,000 crore during 1999–2000 through disinvestment.

In 1997, the first report of the Disinvestment Commission headed by G.V. Ramakrishna had suggested that the proceeds of disinvestment should not be used to reduce the budget deficit but instead be placed in a separate fund to be used for the following four purposes:

(a) retiring public debt;

(b) restructuring public sector undertakings;

(c) developing the social infrastructure; and

(d) voluntary retirement schemes.

...the government's policies of privatisation have been perceived as a means through which precious family silver has been sold to pay the butler...

Two years and nine reports later, the Commission suggested that the entire disinvestment process be delinked from the budget. The Reserve Bank of India (RBI) had earlier suggested that the proceeds of disinvestment be used to bring down the public debt.

In his budget speech delivered on 27 February 1999, the then Finance Minister, Yashwant Sinha had said that he hoped to raise Rs. 10,000 crore during 1999–2000 through disinvestment. 'This will help the government … fund the requirements of social and infrastructure sectors,' he had said. It was, of course, a separate matter altogether that the actual amount raised that year from disinvestment was under Rs. 1,600 crore.

Three years later, once again during his budget speech, Sinha remarked that he was 'emboldened' to take credit for Rs. 12,000 crore as receipts from disinvestment during 2001–02. This time he was more specific. He said that Rs. 7,000 crore would be used to provide 'restructuring assistance to PSUs, (a) safety net to workers and reduction of (the public) debt burden' while the remaining Rs. 5,000 crore would be 'used to provide additional budgetary support to the Plan, primarily in the social and infrastructure sectors'. Sinha added that the additional allocation for the Plan would 'be contingent upon realisation of the anticipated receipts'. Once again, the anticipated receipts did not materialise—actual receipts were under Rs. 3,700 crore that year.

Ever since the Union government began disinvesting its shares of PSUs 1991–92 onwards, in all but three years (1991–92, 1994–95 and 1998–99) the actual proceeds have been substantially lower than the budgetary targets. For instance, in 2001–02, against the budget target of Rs. 12,000 crore, disinvestments receipts were only Rs. 3,645 crore. During the two earlier years, the position was much worse. During 1999–2000 and 2000–01, the targets were set at Rs. 10,000 crore but receipts were Rs. 1,584 crore and Rs. 1,868 crore, respectively. Against the 2003–04 budget target for proceeds of disinvestment at Rs. 13,200 crore, the actual amount raised was Rs. 14,500 crore. The current year's (that is 2004–05) budget estimate for disinvestment receipts is a modest Rs. 4,000 crore.

The total amount raised by the government through sale of equity shares of PSUs since 1992, when the disinvestment process began, is in the region of Rs. 30,000 crore. Despite the pious statements of intent issued by successive finance ministers that have been detailed, this entire sum (representing the proceeds of the sale of assets that used to belong to the people of this country) has disappeared into a big black hole called the Consolidated Fund of India. The story will be repeated this financial year as well so that the present finance minister's glowing fiscal deficit numbers don't get tarnished.

As Ramakrishna has pointed out time and again, the proceeds of disinvestment could have been used to build more than four million houses and one million schools. Even after that, the government would still have been left with enough money to voluntarily retire surplus employees of PSUs. (The same amount, on the other hand, would have reduced the government's fiscal deficit by a negligible 0.02 per cent, he has calculated.) If the proceeds of disinvestment were indeed used for socially useful purposes instead of bridging the budget deficit, the government could have built goodwill for itself among voters. It could then have justifiably pointed out that the beneficiaries of its disinvestment programme were ordinary people.

Instead, the government's policies of privatisation have been perceived as a means through which precious family silver has been sold to pay the butler—to use British Labour leader Jim Callaghan's colourful analogy while speaking against Margaret Thatcher. Most people would agree that if heirlooms have to be hawked, the funds thus raised should be used to pay for the daughter's education or to build an extra room in the house and certainly not to settle the monthly grocery bill or the salary of the domestic help.

An important reason why there was considerable opposition to privatisation was the perception that the shares of PSUs have not been properly valued. In certain instances, the under-valuation was so obvious that even the NDA government's single largest constituent after the BJP, the Shiv Sena, attacked Shourie. A case in point was the re-sale of Centaur Hotel near Mumbai's Santa Cruz airport within four months of the property being picked up by a company called Batra Hospitality. The re-sale took place at a price that was 35 per cent higher than the original purchase price—Rs. 147 crore against Rs. 115 crore.

An important reason why there was considerable opposition to privatisation was the perception that the shares of PSUs have not been properly valued.

...a clutch of multinational consultancy firms have dominated the valuation process—barely half-a-dozen of these 'global advisors' have been valuing the shares of the PSUs to be privatised and it is claimed that such firms have a vested interest in keeping share values low.

What has caused more than a few eyebrows to be raised is the fact that a clutch of multinational consultancy firms have dominated the valuation process—barely half-a-dozen of these 'global advisors' have been valuing the shares of the PSUs to be privatised and it is claimed that such firms have a vested interest in keeping share values low. What is also surprising is that no government body is involved in the valuation process on the plea that such organisations lack the necessary expertise. On paper, the privatisation process is long drawn-out as it involves meetings with various committees of bureaucrats and ministers. Still, the process is not without its limitations and certainly not half as transparent as it is in many countries. Otherwise, why would the government have to repay almost the entire amount it obtained from Zuari Maroc Phosphates for its stake in Paradeep Phosphates on account of a 'post-closure agreement' and why would Himachal Futuristic Communications ask the government to pay it a sum of Rs 1.5 crore for the 'honour' of purchasing the shares of Hindustan Teleprinters?

That's not all. The biggest limitation of the asset valuation procedure is that the land owned by PSUs has been left out of the valuation exercise on the specious plea that the land does not yield 'income'. In April 2002, the Standing Committee on Finance (comprising Members of Parliament belonging to all political parties) stated: '... the asset valuation guidelines are inadequate and vague especially on the issue of land valuation'. It added that although 'the government has taken the position that land value...is computed as part of the assets, the actual land value is not considered in most of the cases when the PSU concerned is disinvested/sold to another party.'

The timing of privatisation also appears to have been inappropriate in certain cases. World zinc prices touched their lowest level in 65 years on the London Metal Exchange the day the Ministry of Disinvestment called for financial bids for the shares of Hindustan Zinc. The government's privatisation programme was stepped up precisely at a time when the country's stock markets were in deep doldrums. Instead of adopting the strategic sale route involving a change in management, the government would have gained public confidence and achieved greater political consensus if it had gone in for more public offers, as it did in the case of Maruti Udyog and ONGC.

The biggest limitation of the asset valuation procedure is that the land owned by PSUs has been left out of the valuation exercise on the specious plea that the land does not yield 'income'.

Shourie's intransigent position on privatising petroleum companies had, at one stage, threatened to derail the entire disinvestment programme of the Union government. His mentors, former Prime Minister Vajpayee and the then Deputy Prime Minister L.K. Advani, realised this. For Shourie's actions had not merely antagonised his political opponents and given them a stick with which to beat the government, he had also upset members of his own ideological fraternity. At a particular juncture, he was willing to rush headlong into a confrontation with the judiciary that could have created a Constitutional crisis. Vajpayee and Advani had no choice but to restrain Shourie.

Prime Minister Manmohan Singh said that privatisation would not be pursued as an ideological commitment but as a measure of economic reform. He said cases like the privatisation of Centaur Hotel would not be repeated.

One of the first decisions of the newly elected United Progressive Alliance (UPA) government was do away with the Ministry of Disinvestment, convert it into a department and place it under the Ministry of Finance. While releasing the common minimum programme (CMP) on 27 May 2004, Prime Minister Manmohan Singh said that privatisation would not be pursued as an ideological commitment but as a measure of economic reform. He said cases like the privatisation of Centaur Hotel would not be repeated. Subsequently, Finance Minister Palaniappan Chidambaram said that the BJP-led NDA government had looked on privatisation as a dogma.

The CMP of the UPA government has stated that privatisation of PSUs would be considered on a 'transparent and consultative case-by-case basis'. The existing *navaratna* companies would be retained in the public sector and these companies would raise resources from the capital market. The CMP added that while every effort would be made to modernise, restructure and revive the sick PSUs, the chronically loss-making companies would either be sold off or closed after all workers had received their legitimate compensation. The UPA would induct private companies to turnaround the PSUs that have potential for revival.

Significantly, the CMP stated that the UPA government believed that privatisation should increase competition, not decrease it by leading to emergence of monopolies—a clear if unstated reference to the IPCL-Reliance deal. Moreover, the CMP said that there must be a direct link between privatisation and social needs. In other words, the privatisation revenues should be used for designated social sector schemes.

The UPA government is dependent on the Left for its survival and since the communist parties had been—and remain—dead opposed to the kind of disinvestment programme initiated by the Vajpayee government, Arun Shourie style privatisation would become a thing of the past during the tenure of the present government. As a matter of fact, one would go further and argue that because of his ideological blinkers, Shourie was almost single-handedly responsible for giving privatisation a bad name in India.

...the CMP said that there must be a direct link between privatisation and social needs. In other words, the privatisation revenues should be used for designated social sector schemes.

Regulation

Simrit Kaur and *Kamal N. Kabra*

Top-down policy changes are hardly able to go beyond cosmetic changes where the basic problems affecting people at the grass root level are concerned. The liberalisers made much of the massive misuse of the discretionary powers enjoyed by the political-bureaucratic oligarchy under the statist policy framework of India during the 1950–1990 period. Under the compulsion of external payments and fiscal deficits crises, large-scale deregulation of private sector and privatisation of many public sector enterprises (PSEs) were carried out. However, no amount of faith in the miraculous power of the 'invisible hand' could enable them to close their eyes to the need for some kind of regulatory arrangements in the form of some institutionalised 'visible hands' from the public domain to prevent the 'freed' and empowered private enterprise, especially the large enterprises and the just created private monopolies (which replaced the public monopolies in the infrastructure, public goods and some strategic sectors) from becoming a law unto themselves and hold the economy, particularly the atomistic consumers, to ransom. Evidently, the forces of market competition were not considered adequate to ensure reasonable curbs on undue profiteering at the cost of the economy as a whole. Many public enterprises were divested in favour of some strategic investors who were given management control. With the government continuing to be a stakeholder, it was natural that there should be an independent and outside regulator remaining, ideally speaking, equidistant from all the service providers and stakeholders, including the government, to discharge the following responsibilities in a judicious, impartial and transparent manner:

- Protecting consumer interests by acting as a surrogate for the marketplace.
- Providing a level playing field and fair returns to new investors.
- Developing a framework for private and public partnership, enabling efficient delivery of infrastructure services.
- Rationalising tariff according to the cost of service, but without underwriting inefficiency, so that overtime the cash inflows match cash outflows.
- Creating a credible, transparent regulatory framework that promotes efficiency and credibility and responds to socio-economic imperatives.

These objectives show only a limited amount of concern with the possibility that a combined emergence of state and market failures may make the emergent situation worse than the malaise the new arrangements were supposed to tackle. Not only the disregard of larger social objectives and responsiveness to the macro economic imperatives, including those arising from fiscal needs and external payments compulsions, may make it difficult and costly to reap the expected payoff from privatisation and deregulation, but the processes of cronyism and supply of and demand for rent of authority may continue to breed distortions. It has been argued that the huge black economy generated during an ineffective and aborted statist regime does not simply disappear on its own the moment a 'free market' policy frame is put in place. Unless an effective cleansing operation is carried out, the hordes of accumulated black income and wealth will continue to distort the operation of the economy and the processes of structural adjustment (Kabra and Upadhyay 1999). Thus it may well be treated as a necessary pre-condition of effective de-

...the forces of market competition were not considered adequate to ensure reasonable curbs on undue profiteering at the cost of the economy as a whole.

statisation that the illegal concentration of wealth in the hands of the triumvirate of businessmen, bureaucracy and politicians is significantly reduced and accountability procedures are effectively instituted. The processes of privatisation, deregulation and liberalisation have attracted charges of subjective, discretionary and non-transparent use of decision-making authority, giving credence to the view that 'a reduction of state controls may be accompanied by increased corruption' (Harriss-White 1996). The chapter on 'Privatisation' in this volume again shows how cronyism and sacrifice of public interest may flourish under a liberalised, privatised and globalised economy. If the excesses inherent in large-scale privatisation and deregulation have to be nipped in the bud, a regulatory institutional mechanism, not as a law unto itself, but with safeguards, cross-checks and accountability, has to be instituted before the processes of dismantling state enterprises and regulations are undertaken. It is common knowledge that the hurriedly introduced Structural Adjustment Programme (SAP) package at the behest of the international financial institutions did not even permit India enough time to devise her own trajectory and strategy of so-called reforms. It was basically the handiwork of international, unaccountable, economic bureaucracy with dozens of cheerleader economists in tow. Little wonder that the Indian chapter of the SAP opened without any mechanism of regulating the unregulated markets and the newly created private monopolies.

...the hurriedly introduced Structural Adjustment Programme (SAP) package at the behest of the international financial institutions did not even permit India enough time to devise her own trajectory and strategy of so-called reforms.

For the major infrastructure sectors handed over to the private companies, the government has to set up regulatory agencies. To meet these regulatory challenges, the regulatory regime must have the following attributes:

- Independence, both financial and functional, secured through transparent appointment and removal processes besides security of tenure and conditions of service.
- Transparent, predictable and objective functioning of the regulator.
- Accountability and justifiability of the decisions of regulators.
- A set of socially-determined objectives, for the attainment of which these privatised services and facilities must work and the criteria on the basis of which decisions by the regulatory agencies can go to serve these social goals.

India has seen the fiasco of social control of private sector commercial banking during the 1960s and hence should have taken pre-emptive measures to ensure that the privatisation wave does not extract an unconscionable price from the community. However, the ideological opposition of the public sector as inherently undesirable and similar acceptance of the private sector as the only wealth-creating holy cow, even with its thousand faults, normally tends to preclude many such questions.

The India Infrastructure Report (Rakesh Mohan Committee 1996) highlights the importance of autonomous regulatory bodies as an institutional framework for promoting private sector participation in infrastructure. These investors need a regulatory environment that is independent, transparent, consistent, and predictable (Rao, 1999). Independence is supposed to lie both in relation to the persons chosen as regulators and the institution once it comes into operation. In the case of the personnel, it would require an objective, open, and fair selection process; in the terms of independent appointment being similarly done so as to ensure that the best regulatory expertise is obtained. Further it must be ensured that the terms of office are specified and the members of the regulatory body cannot be removed without an adequate cause and without the due process of law. Clearly, if the political authority over the economy was held responsible for all the ills which necessitated privatisation, there should be an institutional, transparent and impartial arrangement for the selection of the personnel of the regulatory agencies and the qualifications needed for eligibility for such appointments should be carefully laid down similar to the process of selection, say, of the Vigilance Commission members.

...if the political authority over the economy was held responsible for all the ills which necessitated privatisation, there should be an institutional, transparent and impartial arrangement for the selection of the personnel of the regulatory agencies and the qualifications needed for eligibility for such appointments should be carefully laid down.

A number of instances have been pointed out in the press to show the arbitrariness as well as outright misuse of the authority vested in some of the members of these regulatory agencies. Gajendra Haldea (*Times of India*, January 2004) has pointed out that 'Warning signals suggest the possible exploitation of consumers at the hands of the regulatory commissions that now play a dominant role in several critical sectors of the economy. Often the regulators are not effective, and are not seen as honest and credible. They have vast authority with little accountability; their selection process inspires little confidence; and redressal from their actions is elusive. As a result they are a law unto themselves.' The author goes on to give several shocking examples of the less than upright behaviour of some of the regulators. It is disturbing that a close and underhand relationship is developing between the regulators and the objects of regulation. Just like the case under the much derided quota-permit-licence raj, no mechanism has been devised to ensure that the regulators do not, in effect, become pawns in the hands of the private monopolies for gaining some filthy lucre. The author, as cited above, has given some shocking instances of some such shenanigans. Even the reports of the Comptroller and Auditor General of India (CAGI) have shown some unbecoming instances of the regulators straying from the straight and upright path. Well founded criticisms of the actions of power and telecom regulators have often been editorialised by the national press. There can be no improvement with the government assuming the power to hire and fire the regulators. This has been brought out by the symbiotic relations between the politicians and the business leaders spawning India's vast black economy (Kabra 1982). In short, nearly all the features that have come in for trenchant criticism by the votaries of free markets, of the system of government control over micro decision-making by the businessmen, have become applicable to the regulators of the decontrolled regime.

Often the regulators are not effective, and are not seen as honest and credible. They have vast authority with little accountability; their selection process inspires little confidence; and redressal from their actions is elusive. As a result they are a law unto themselves.'

While on the issue of the actual experience of the regulatory agencies, in addition to the human and systemic aspects mentioned above, the conception of the regulatory agencies endowed with enormous, unregulated, unaccountable powers itself may be the genesis of their undoing along with the experiment of headlong de-regulation. It has been pointed out that,

> In the power sector for example, the regulator will make regulations having the force of law; he will have powers of search and seizure; he will adjudicate and impose heavy penalties; he will issue licences and have powers to suspend or revoke them; he may issue directions that will be binding on all, he will levy his own fees; and he will pass his own budget. (Haldea 2004)

All these powers are those of a political appointee with little guarantee that the process of transitivity will not ultimately pass on these unaccountable and invisible powers to the political appointing authority! The 1990s witnessed how old and established regulatory agencies like the Reserve Bank of India (RBI) and the Securities and Exchange Board of India (SEBI) became ineffective in the face of the massive shenanigans by the big financial operators in India's deregulated and free financial markets, leading to investigation by some joint parliamentary committees. Such massive misuse of the financial markets and defrauding of the small investor was never seen during the denigrated controls regime, which, of course, had its own complement of scams like the infamous Mundhra one. So deep seem to be the roots of these processes that the regulators themselves stand in a great need of regulation.

The 1990s witnessed how old and established regulatory agencies like the Reserve Bank of India (RBI) and the Securities and Exchange Board of India (SEBI) became ineffective in the face of the massive shenanigans by the big financial operators in India's deregulated and free financial markets, leading to investigation by some joint parliamentary committees.

When even regulatory processes go haywire, what great expectations can be entertained from the standard, simplistic propositions concerning the financial independence of the regulators at the institutional level? The scope of independence of the regulators has been extended to make them free from government or even legislative accountability, going to the extent of freedom to prepare their budget, authorise their expenses, and decide on the type of staff they need and recruit them, and use consultants as required. Such powers can hardly be expected to make

Figure 1
Regulatory Governance, Incentives & Performance

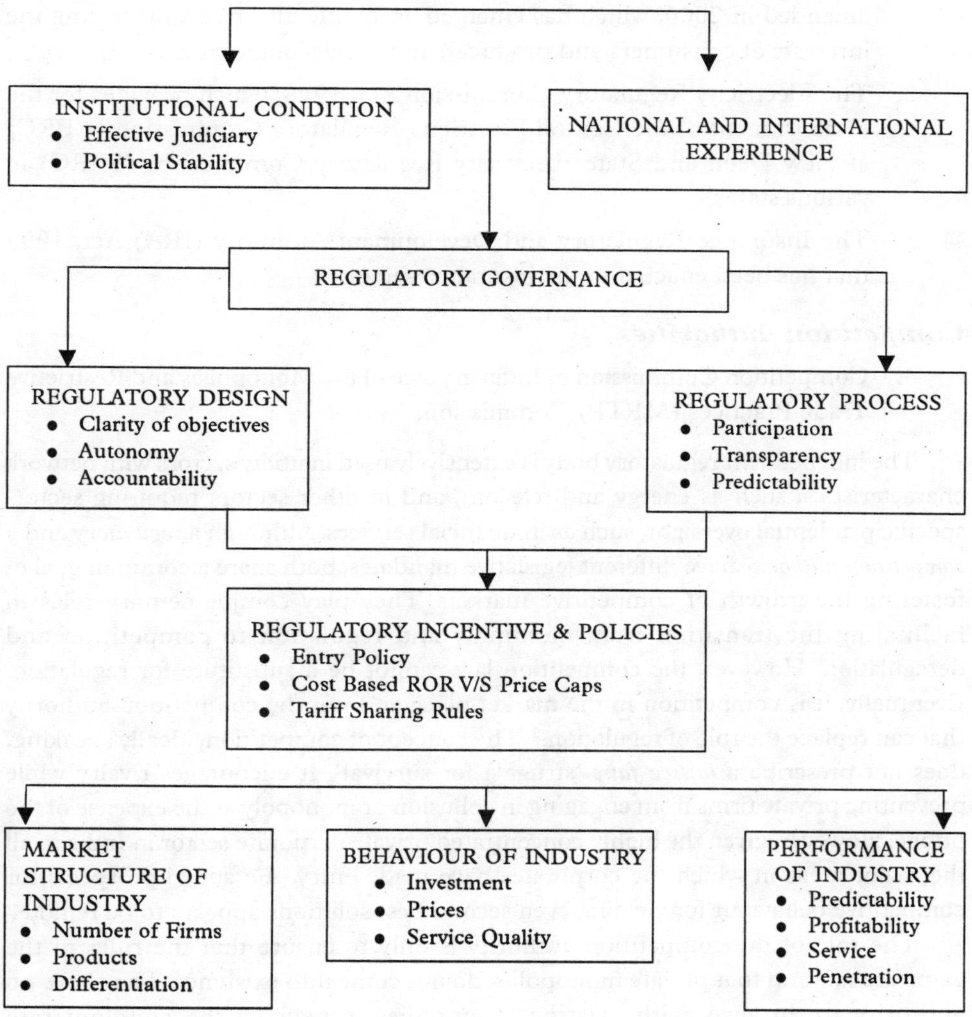

deregulation serve anything but narrow, personal objectives. True, a strong and public spirited, incorruptible media, public opinion and watchdog civil society institutions can make some difference, but given their failure to cleanse the augean stable of our political processes, how much can one expect from these well-meaning but non-coercive agencies?

The task of assessing the merits of infrastructure regulatory policies is complicated by the intricate relationships among key variables, as shown in Figure 1. The *institutional conditions box* (such as the strength and independence of a country's judicial system and the nature and stability of the country's political system) along with the *experience box* affect directly the kind of regulatory governance system of any country (Sanford 2002). A set of well-defined checks and balances regarding the regulators roles, its autonomy and accountability, represent the foundation elements of the regulatory system. Similarly, a regulatory process that emphasises stakeholder participation, transparency, and predictability will be more credible than one without these features.

Regulatory issues are not new to India. However, they have taken a different form since the inception of the SAP in 1991. With the advent of privatisation and liberalisation (Kaur 2003), the setting up of sound and fair regulatory and aompetition authorities became essential. Some of the independent regulatory and competition bodies that have been set up since 1991 are:

Although a *regulatory* and a *competition authority* have different legislative mandates, both share a common goal of fostering the growth of competitive markets.

Independent Regulators

1. Telecommunications Regulatory Authority of India (TRAI) Act, 1997, amended in 2000, which has emerged as an effective body, protecting the interests of consumers and producers in the telecom sector.
2. The Electricity Regulatory Commission Act, 1998, which provides for the establishment of the Central Electricity Regulatory Commission (CERC) at New Delhi and State Electricity Regulatory Commissions (SERC) in various states.
3. The Insurance Regulatory and Development Authority (IRA) Act, 1999 that has been enacted in the insurance sector.

Competition Authorities

4. Competition Commission of India in place of the Monopolies and Restrictive Trade Practices (MRTP) Commission.

The independent regulatory body is extensively used in utility sectors with network characteristics, such as energy and telecom, and in other sectors requiring sectof-specific prudential oversight, such as in financial services. Although a *regulatory* and a *competition authority* have different legislative mandates, both share a common goal of fostering the growth of competitive markets. They play complementary roles in facilitating the transition from monopoly and regulation to competition and deregulation. However, the competition law cannot be a substitute for regulation. Eventually, it is competition in the market place and not the competition authority that can replace the role of regulation.[1] The concept of competition, ideally speaking, does not prescribe a *laissez faire* 'struggle for survival'. It encourages rivalry while preventing private firms from engaging in collusion or monopoly at the expense of the public. However, given the highly concentrated private corporate sector in India in all the major areas in which the corporates have made entry, the actual prospects for competitive behaviour for yielding even second best solutions appears to be remote.

However, given the highly concentrated private corporate sector in India in all the major areas in which the corporates have made entry, the actual prospects for competitive behaviour for yielding even second best solutions appears to be remote.

The role of the competition authority is only to ensure that the rules of the game are fair and that private monopolies do not come into existence. They have no authority to do away with existing monopolies, especially the conglomerate concentration of economic power. Nor have such bodies anywhere in the world been successful in applying the brakes to the juggernaut of concentration and centralisation of economic resources. Nevertheless, the struggle between regulatory bodies and competition authorities is common to all countries. It is therefore necessary that the legislative mandates of the two bodies be clearly spelt out. Ambiguity in the law on the role of the regulator and the competition authorities can lead to conflicting decisions and overall confusion. In areas where *suo moto* action has to be taken by the authority, power struggles may result between the two authorities for jurisdiction.

Ambiguity in the law on the role of the regulator and the competition authorities can lead to conflicting decisions and overall confusion.

Selection of Regulators

Usually, a selection committee prepares a panel of names of regulators, which is finally considered by the Executive. For instance, the Electricity Regulatory Commission (ERC) Act, 1998, provides for a search committee for selecting members of the Regulatory Committee (RC) at the central as well as state levels. Typically, the selection committee writes to various institutions/experts asking for nominations, which are then screened by the committee to arrive at a final selection of two candidates put up for consideration of the government. One of the drawbacks of such a procedure is that the institution /expert would normally look only within its circle of associates/friends for suitable candidates. In fact, a public interest litigation (PIL) was put up in Orissa

1. For details on India's competition policy see Bhattacharjea (2003).

Table 1

Comparative Provisions Of Regulatory Legislations In India

Sl No.	*Subject*	*TRAI ACT 1997 and TRAI Ordinance, 2000*	*CERC Act 1998*
1.	Selection process	Selection of Chairman\ members by government	Selection of Chairman/ members by government on advice by selection committee
2.	Removal criteria	Criteria laid down. Removal after giving an opportunity to be heard	Criteria laid down. Removal with advice from Supreme Court
3.	Tenure	Five years	Five years. Not eligible for re-appointment
4.	Staff Appointment	Can appoint staff/officers only with government's approval	Can appoint secretary, and determine the number, nature, and categories of other staff, but with government's approval
5.	Staff salary	Staff salary determined by government	Staff salary to be determined with the approval of government by regulations
6.	Finances	TRAI to have general Funds with grants, fees, charges, etc. received by it. Salaries/expense to be met from this Fund.	Expenses to be charged on Consolidated Fund of India. Budget to be approved by government
7.	Relationship with Govt.	Statutory body, but subject to policy directions by government	Quasi-judicial body, but subject to policy directions by government
8.	Dispute Settlement Power	Has no powers for arbitrations or adjudication. Separate authority set up for adjudication	Arbitrate matters involving generating companies, transmission companies
9.	Appellate bodies	Telecom disputes settlement and Appellate Tribunal. Appeal against the orders lie with the Supreme Court	High Court
10.	Decision making process	Consultative	Hearings

that questioned the adequacy of the government's consultation process to select a new Chairman for the Orissa ERC. This resulted in a delay of over half a year before a new Chairman could be selected.

Further, the age limit for members in a regulatory committee has also been set. For example, it is 65 years for the Chairman of CERC and 62 years for other members. While the age limit as well as the tenure of members is fixed, no minimum tenure has been prescribed. As a result, there are instances of RC members retiring after serving for less than one year. Since a short tenure can preclude significant contributions to the regulatory process, a minimum tenure should be prescribed for the members. While there is a provision for a second term of three years, it is not specified that this would also be subject to an independent search committee's recommendation. Hence, the second term might well be subject to the will of the Government and become a way of capturing regulators who could be subservient to the will of the government.

Moreover, the membership and staff of the regulatory committee are dominated by government and ex-government officers because of the government limits on wages. They bring in the same culture of administration and procedure instead of initiating innovative and imaginative ways of tackling the issues. Low salaries deter qualified professionals like professional managers, economists, chartered accountants and industrial engineers from joining the regulatory committees. (Rao 2003)

...the membership and staff of the regulatory committee are dominated by government and ex-government officers because of the government limits on wages. They bring in the same culture of administration and procedure instead of initiating innovative and imaginative ways of tackling the issues.

...the Telecom Regulatory Authority of India (TRAI) had not received approval from the government for operating this fund even after four years of its functioning.

The constitution of the competition commission has also not been smooth. The Constitution Bench of the Supreme Court had earlier laid down that those tribunals with judicial powers equivalent to High Courts should be headed by a person with judicial experience. The rule was made in the context of administrative tribunals. The government had been largely following this rule. The MRTPC, which is to be replaced by the Competition Commission, was always headed by a retired High Court judge. On this basis, it was argued in a public interest litigation that the appointment of the Commerce Secretary Deepak Chatterjee as the Chairman of the Commission was giving precedence to bureaucrats. Further, in the Competition Act, one of the sections allows for the possibility of a retired High Court judge to serve under a civil servant who is appointed as Chairperson of the Commission.

The above analysis raises two crucial issues for discussion:

- Should the selection of regulators be an open and transparent process after advertising for the post?
- Should the regulatory committee be allowed to hire professional expertise at market rates?

The comparative provisions of regulatory legislations for TRAI and CERC are given in Table 1. The analysis is done for criteria such as selection process, tenure of members, staff salary and financial autonomy.

...the Indian legislature mandates that the annual reports of the activities of the regulatory commissions should be laid before the Parliament/legislature through the concerned ministries/ departments, none of the reports has so far been placed in the public domain.

Appointment of Members in a Stipulated Time Frame

There should be accountability of government functionaries to adhere to a timetable laid down by the law for appointing chairmen/members to the regulatory committee. For example, even though the 1998 ERC Act lays down a timetable for search, selection, and appointment of the chairman and members, it is not adhered to in practice. For instance, the appointment of the Chairman of Tamil Nadu ERC was delayed by over three years, and the second Chairman of CERC was appointed over 15 months after the first one demitted office. Perhaps, there should at least be a report with suitable explanations on the table of the House when the scheduled date has passed and the appointments are not made.

Financial Autonomy

In the case of the telecom regulators, the establishment of a Telecom Regulatory Fund is mandated in legislation. However, the Telecom Regulatory Authority of India (TRAI) had not received approval from the government for operating this fund even after four years of its functioning. The telecom regulator was wholly dependent on budgetary grants from the Department of Telecommunication.

The government can considerer providing greater financial autonomy to the RCs in one of these two ways:

- Making budgetary allocations to them on the basis of broad heads of expenditure and leaving the expenditure against specific line items to be determined by the commission itself.
- Allowing RCs to generate their own revenues through regulatory fees, penalties etc.

Of the 13 electricity regulators covered by that study, five have not brought out even a single annual report. About half a dozen of them had failed to conduct the minimum number of Advisory Committee meetings statutorily stipulated.

Accountability Issues

Although financial autonomy is desired, financial accountability becomes the flip side of the same coin. In the ERC and TRAI Acts, it has been mandated that the regulators shall ensure transparency while exercising their powers and discharging their functions. However, in the case of IRA (Insurance Regulatory Authority) and TAMP (Tariff Authority for Major Ports), no such specifications regarding transparency exist. Where financial accountability is concerned, the RC maintains its account subject to the scrutiny of the Comptroller and Auditor General (CAG) of India. For any other matter, these commissions are neither answerable to the government nor to the Parliament or the state legislatures. Interestingly, the minister in charge of the sector is accountable. An important issue that emerges is whether there should there be Parliament/legislative committees as in the U.K. to oversee the regulatory activities at a macro level. Though the Indian legislature mandates that the annual reports of the activities of the regulatory commissions should be laid before the Parliament/legislature through the concerned ministries/departments, none of the reports has so far been placed in the public domain.

Powers of the Regulator

While TRAI is a civil court, the CERC is a quasi-judicial body with powers of the civil court for certain limited purposes. The IRA and TAMP have not been given any such powers. As regards penal provisions for non-compliance of orders, the provisions in the TRAI Act are more rigorous than those in the ERC Act while there are no such provisions in the case of TAMP and IRA. There has been no uniformity in thinking or in the approach to regulation in the various sectors. Each regulatory authority is the result of the wisdom and genius of the concerned ministry and not of any cohesive thinking in the government as a whole. Although a commission was set up to advise the government on the process of disinvestment, there is no such body to advise the government in the introduction of a regulatory process.

Regulating the Regulator

Independent regulation of the infrastructure sectors in India is over six years old. This has been a very comfortable period with the public willing to believe the best about the regulators. However, there are clear indications that we cannot afford to be complacent. Prayas' 2003 report lists several things that should cause concern. Of the 13 electricity regulators covered by that study, five have not brought out even a single annual report. About half a dozen of them had failed to conduct the minimum number of Advisory Committee meetings statutorily stipulated. The report has also brought up the matter of the tenuous logic behind some of the orders of the Electricity Regulatory Commissions (ERCs) and their tardiness in reviewing tariffs. However, the Prayas report does not specify why the legislatures of the concerned states have not yet done anything in this matter (Bajaj 2004).

Another interesting instance could be when collusion occurs between the regulator and the firm (Stigler 1971).Generally, producers are well organised and at times the trade unions may also align themselves with the management on the issue of say pricing, to appropriate some of the monopoly returns in the form of higher wages or better working conditions. On the other hand, consumers tend to be less well organised as a lobby group than either management or labour. Further, greater frequency of contact between management and regulators could, over a period, make the latter more receptive to the firm's arguments. Regulators may also be influenced by the prospect of remunerative employment in the industry once their public days are over. When the interests of the members of the regulatory agency do not coincide with public interest, it needs to be debated whether there is a need for regulating the activities of the regulator.

...greater frequency of contact between management and regulators could, over a period, make the latter more receptive to the firm's arguments. Regulators may also be influenced by the prospect of remunerative employment in the industry once their public days are over.

Regulation and Consumer Welfare

Though one of the objectives for setting up regulatory bodies is to enhance consumer welfare, it is not necessarily adhered to. For instance, the selection and appointment of the members of the TRAI continues to be totally non-transparent. It is a purely political decision. Although there are eminent persons in the consumer movement whose contributions to advancing the cause of consumers are there, no such person

...the selection and appointment of the members of the TRAI continues to be totally non-transparent. It is a purely political decision.

is in the TRAI. There has been some progress in the TRAI responding to the representation of various consumer bodies demanding information about the costs and expenses of telecom companies in three or four cities. Many bodies are not able to participate in these meetings because of the distance and expense involved. The bodies have represented that the TRAI must have regional offices in the capital cities of all the major States (15 out of 28). This is yet to be implemented. Telecommunications services are being consumed more and more in the rural areas (Chowdary 2002). For example, in Andhra Pradesh, 35 per cent are rural consumers as against the all India average of about 25 per cent. They have many more problems than metropolitan consumers, but have the least access and capacity to represent to and participate in the TRAI's consultation meetings. Therefore, as time passes, the need for the TRAI to have regional offices increases.

...in Andhra Pradesh, 35 per cent are rural consumers as against the all India average of about 25 per cent. They have many more problems than metropolitan consumers, but have the least access and capacity to represent to and participate in the TRAI's consultation meetings.

Further, section 11 of the TRAI Act, 1997, states that the Authority is to lay down standards of quality of service to be provided by the service providers. To ensure that the prescribed quality of service is maintained, it has to conduct periodical surveys of each service provider. Indian Market Research Bureau (IMRB) did the first quarterly survey for Oct-Dec 2001. The findings of the survey confirm that the eight basic operators (including Bharat Sanchar Nigam Ltd (BSNL), Mahanagar Telephone Nigam Ltd. (MTNL) and six private licensees in 25 basic circles) have so far been unable to meet the norms laid down in the regulation. Except in trunk call services, the existing quality of service standards are below TRAI standards in fault repair services, network performance, operator services and customer care.

To conclude, the field of regulation and regulatory economics are still under evolution in India. It is critical to ensure accountability, transparency, expertise and credibility of the new regulatory regime if the process of regulatory reforms is to succeed. However, there is no substitute for direct empowerment of the people through a powerful consumer rights movement and a supporting judiciary. Basically, the nature and direction of macro and micro economic policies, which are not bound by ideological fixation for the private sector but go by the track record of various entities in terms of broader social objectives, while ensuring that they adhere to the norms of effective and accountable micro level functioning, are among the ingredients of the framework which can deliver and maintain a fair and just balance among various stakeholders.

It is critical to ensure accountability, transparency, expertise and credibility of the new regulatory regime if the process of regulatory reforms is to succeed. However, there is no substitute for direct empowerment of the people through a powerful consumer rights movement and a supporting judiciary.

References

Averch, H. and L. Johnson. 1962. Behavior of the Firm under Regulatory Constraint. *American Economic Review* 52

Bajaj J.L. 2004. 'Power Sector Reforms in India: Regulatory Issues', *IIM-B Management Review,* March.

Bhattarcharjea, A. 2003. 'India's Competition Policy: An Assessment', *Economic and Political Weekly,* 23 August.

Choudhary, T.H. 2003. 'Telecom Regulation and Consumer Welfare', *Economic and Political Weekly,* 26 October.

Haldea, Gajendra. 2004. 'Crisis of Credibility: Law Must regulate the regulators', *Times of India,* 22 January.

Kabra, Kamal Nayan. 1982. *Black Economy in India: Problem and Policies.* Delhi: Chanakya.

Kabra, Kamal Nayan and V. Upadhyay. 1999. 'Crony Capitalism and Era of Scams', in *Alternative Economic Survey, 1991–98.* Delhi: Rainbow Publishers, Lokayan and Azadi Bachao Andolan.

Harriss, Barbara-White. 1996. 'Liberalization and Corruption: Resolving the Paradox', *IDS Bulletin,* 27(2).

Kaur, S. 2003. *Privatization and Public Regulation: The Indian Experience.* New Delhi: Macmillan India.

Mohan, R. 1996. *The India Infrastructure Report: Policy Imperatives for Growth and Welfare,* Government of India, Ministry of Finance.

Rao, S.L. 2003. 'Electricity Bill, 2001: Many shortcomings, But a Step Forward', *Economic and Political Weekly,* 1 February.

Rao, S.L. 1999. 'Policy & Legal Framework for Regulation' in Srivastava, L and S. Sarkar (eds), *Transition to a Liberalized Environment: Experiences and Issues in Regulation.* New Delhi: TERI.

Sanford, B. 2002. 'Summary of the US Team' in Tsuji, M., S. Berg and M. Pollite (eds), *Private Initiatives in_Infrastructure: Priorities, Incentives and Performance,* Institute of Developing Economies, Japan External Trade Organisation.

Sarkar, S.K. and L. Srivastava. 2001. 'The Regulatory Framework: Experience and Issues' in Sarkar, S.K. and K. Deb (eds), *Regulation in Infrastructure Services: Progress and the Way Forward.* New Delhi: TERI.

Stigler, G. 1971. The Theory of Economic Regulation. *Bell Journal of Economics,* 2.

Vickers, J. and G. Yarrow. 1998. *Privatization: An Economic Analysis.* Cambridge, MA: MIT Press.

World Bank. 1995. *Bureaucrats in Business: The Economics and Politics of Government Ownership.* Oxford University Press.

Agriculture

S.P. Singh

Introduction

Indian agriculture has remained the most neglected sector in the post-reform period in terms of government policy support. The desertion of the sector has been more acute during governance of the National Democratic Alliance (NDA) at the centre over the last six years. The Bharatiya Janata Party (BJP) led NDA made tall promises for agricultural development in its election manifesto and common minimum programme (CMP). However, a perusal of the promises made in the manifesto and the work done by it for agriculture during its tenure reveals a big difference between its promises and its deeds. During its administration, the cost of cultivation increased; and productivity, efficiency, and profitability of agriculture, and employment in it, significantly declined. The deceleration in productivity growth of almost all crops has serious implications not only for the food security but also for the sustainability of agriculture and the livelihood of the rural populace. The lifting of quantitative restrictions (QRs) on import of agricultural products during this period was another setback for the the Indian farmers, as they will not be exposed to price and output volatility in the global agricultural markets. Moreover, this period has seen heightening of distress among farmers and even thousands of suicides in some regions due to crop failures higher input costs, inadequate institutional credit, lower productivity, depressed prices, and heavy debt burdens.

The National Common Minimum Programme (NCMP), of the Congress-led and Left-supported United Progressive Alliance (UPA) government promises to eliminate these distortions and distresses in the farm sector by focusing on: greater public sector investment in research and development (R&D), extension, irrigation, and rural infrastructure; reinvigoration of the rural cooperative credit system; special programmes for dry-land farming; effective enforcement of laws for the protection of farm workers; adequate protection of farmers from imports; remunerative prices to farmers for their products; a greater stake for farmers in the organisations that supply inputs to them; and bringing constitutional amendments to ensure the democratic, autonomous and professional functioning of cooperatives. However, the effectiveness of the NCMP for agriculture will depend on the quantum of resources allocated and efficiency with which the promised schemes are implemented., In the past also, almost all the political parties had 'given' priority to agricultural development in their election manifestos, but the ground reality is that the condition of agriculture and agriculturists, both, have sharply deteriorated during the 1990s.

The deceleration in productivity growth of almost all crops has serious implications not only for the food security but also for the sustainability of agriculture and the livelihood of the rural populace.

Agricultural Growth in Pre- and Post-reform Periods

After achieving a remarkable growth over three per cent per annum during the decade preceding the reforms, Indian agriculture experienced a slowdown in the 1990s. In order to study how the three sectors of the economy performed in the pre and post-reform periods, we have estimated the annual compound growth rates (ACGRs) in the GDP at factor cost for these periods. The growth rates presented in Table 1 demonstrate that the growth rates of both the primary sector (the agricultural and allied products) and the secondary sector (manufacturing) have decelerated in

Table 1
Sector-wise Annual Compound Growth Rates in GDP at Factor Cost

(at 1993–94 prices)

Period	*Primary Sector*	*Secondary Sector*	*Tertiary Sector*	*Total (entire economy)*
1981–82 to 1990–91	3.37*	6.95*	6.99*	5.58*
1991–92 to 2003–04	2.85*	6.35*	8.05*	6.09*

Source: Calculated from the data of *Economic Survey 2003–04*.

the post-reform period. However, the slowdown is more marked in the primary sector. In contrast, there has been a remarkable growth in the tertiary sector (services) in the post-reform period. As the primary secondary sectors have more forward and backward linkages in the economy, the decrease in their growth rates has far reaching implications for employment generation and poverty alleviation in the country.

Comparative growth rates in area, production and yield of main crops in the three periods, i.e. 1981–82 to 1990–91 (pre-reform period), 1991–92 to 2002–03 (post-reform period) and 1997–98 to 2002–03 (the period of reforms under the NDA governance) are shown in Table 2. It is evident from the Table that all the crops had achieved much higher growth rates in both production and productivity in the pre-reform period than has been achieved during the post-reform period and during the NDA years. If we look at the performance of the agricultural sector during the six-years of the NDA governance, we find a very dismal agricultural scenario. The growth rates in area, production, and yield of almost all crops are either positive, but insignificant, or negative and significant. Except for sugarcane, which recorded a significant positive growth in its cultivation area, all other crops show a decline in their cultivation area. The decline in area is more pronounced in case pf oilseeds, which show a negative growth of over 4 per cent per annum. Next to oilseeds are pulses that lost 2.67 per cent of their area. All food grains lost 1.76 per cent of their cultivation area during this period.

In the case of growth in production of various crops, it is observed that almost all crops have negative, but insignificant, growth in production. The only exception is oilseeds, the production of which has declined by 6.57 per cent per annum during the last six years. It is worth mentioning here that the oilseed sector has been severely affected by the lifting of the QRs. In the case of the per hectare yield, cotton and

Table 2
Compound Growth Rate in Area, Production and Yield of Main Crops

Crops	*Pre-reform Period (1981–82 to 1990–91)*			*Post-reform Period (1991–92 to 2001–02)*			*Last Six Years of reform (1997–98 to 2002–03)*		
	A	*P*	*Y*	*A*	*P*	*Y*	*A*	*P*	*Y*
Rice	0.60	4.20*	3.58*	0.25	1.10***	0.84**	–1.10	–1.27	–0.18
Wheat	0.36	3.39*	3.02*	0.71***	2.17*	1.40*	–1.60	–0.17	1.26
Coarse cereals	–1.49*	0.72	2.24***	–1.78*	–0.07	1.73**	–2.01	–1.30	0.72
Pulses	0.09	1.50	1.41**	–0.88**	–0.62	0.27	–2.67***	–3.73	–1.04
Total Food grains	–0.19	2.99*	3.18*	–0.40	1.08***	1.48*	–1.76***	–1.25	0.51
Nine Oilseeds	3.02*	5.80*	2.70*	–1.51*	–1.07**	0.44	–4.25*	–6.57***	–0.25
Sugarcane	1.35	2.97*	1.61*	1.86*	2.09*	0.25	2.41*	0.39	–1.85*
Cotton	–0.97	3.32	4.31**	1.21***	–2.47*	–1.28	–2.26	–3.08	–5.29**

Note: A stands for Area; P for production and Y for yield.
* Significant at 1 per cent level;
** Significant at 5 per cent level; and
*** Significant at 10 per cent level.

Source: Based on the data collected from the official website of Department of Agriculture and Cooperation and *Economic Survey 2003–04*.

As the primary secondary sectors have more forward and backward linkages in the economy, the decrease in their growth rates has far reaching implications for employment generation and poverty alleviation in the country.

sugarcane showed a 5.29 and 1.85 per cent decrease, respectively, over the last six years. Comparing the growth rates in area, production, and yield of these crops during the three periods, it is found that the condition of farming has drastically deteriorated in the post-reform period. The last six years have been particularly bad for the sector.

Decrease in the area under cultivation, production, and yield of food grains has serious implications for the food security of the country. As is evident from the Table 2, the growth rate of total food grains, which was about 3 per cent per annum during the decade preceding reform, has fallen sharply to 1.08 per cent in the post-reform period, a rate even lower than the rate of population growth in the country. Consequently, per capita net availability of food grains has declined steeply, from 510 grams per day in 1991 to 438 grams per day in 2003. (Government of India 2004a) It is generally argued that as the consumption pattern of people is changing due to increase in the per capita income, urbanisation, the convergence of food habits, and greater availability of horticulture and livestock products, food security should not be confined to the mere availability of food grains and it should be extended to the overall availability of edibles including fruits, vegetables, dairy products, eggs, meat, and fish. Based on this argument, the focus of the government policy on agriculture has been gradually shifting to diversification of agriculture, comprising high-value horticulture and livestock products and non-food commercial crops, which cater to requirements of the fast growing middle and upper middle class households. It is beyond doubt that diversification of the farm sector can ensure productive and remunerative employment in the farm sector and in the rural non-farm sector, such as, agro-processing and marketing. However, in the absence of an adequate marketing infrastructure and institutional arrangements, the farmers growing fruits, vegetables and other cash crops of a perishable nature bear the brunt of price and output volatility. Unlike food grains, farmers cannot hold on to stocks of these products when their prices drop. As a result, when there is a glut in the market, they suffer and are not able to repay the crop loans.

...in the absence of an adequate marketing infrastructure and institutional arrangements, the farmers growing fruits, vegetables and other cash crops of a perishable nature bear the brunt of price and output volatility.

Productivity of Major Crops in India vis-a-vis Other Selected Countries

The per hectare productivity of major crops in India is much lower than in the rest of the world. Table 3 shows comparative yields of major crops in selected countries in 2003. It is apparent from the Table that India achieved a much lower per hectare yield of all the considered crops than the world averages for these crops. For instance, in the case of paddy, the average yield in Australia was about 3.5 times that of India; in China and the USA, it was twice and 2.5 times, respectively. The productivity of

Table 3
Comparative Yield of Major Crops in Selected Countries in 2003

(kg/Ha)

Country	*Paddy*	*Wheat*	*Maize*	*Groundnut*	*Sugarcane*
India	3000.3	2617.1	2114.3	937.5	62859.2
China	6074.1	3906.5	4854.4	2623.7	69555.7
Australia	10289.5	1999.0	5266.7	1681.8	85134.8
Canada	–	2250.0	7819.3	–	–
USA	7448.2	2973.8	8923.6	3540.4	77515.1
Indonesia	4537.5	–	3252.2	2016.3	73142.9
Thailand	2454.5	615.4	3913.0	1517.2	66399.7
Pakistan	3054.8	2380.2	1457.1	10,60.0	47933.5
Brazil	3238.1	2371.2	–	2082	72289.5
South Africa	2285.7	1777.8	2899.8	1041	63388.6
Japan	5849.8	4030.2	–	2308.5	60869.6
World Average	3837.4	2665.0	4471.7	1347.5	65292.6

Source: FAO database 'FAOSTAT' (accessed in July 2004).

wheat in China was over 1.5 times that of India. The per hectare yield of maize and groundnut in the USA was 4 times the yield in India. Even in the case of sugarcane, the yield in India was much lower than that obtained by most of the cane producing countries. Considering that the scope for bringing more land under cultivation is almost zero, the future increases in the production of agricultural products can only come from enhancing the productivity of land. However, due to the utter neglect of the farm sector in the recent past, the productivity for the major crops has not only slowed down, but even become negative for several crops (Table 2).

Capital Formation in Agriculture

The dismal performance of Indian agriculture in the post-reform period can largely be attributed to the steep reduction in capital formation in the sector, an outcome directly related to liberalisation and the fiscal crunch. The sector, which contributes a quarter of the gross domestic product (GDP), provides direct employment to about 57 percent of the total workforce, and supports two-thirds of the total population, receives just 1.3 per cent of the total investment in the economy. Table 4 shows the trend in the gross capital formation in the agricultural and allied products sector for the last two decades. The share of the agriculture and allied products sector in the total capital formation has come down from 21 per cent in the 1970s to 10.82 per cent in the 1980s, and further to 7.57 per cent in the 1990s. If the pre-and post-reform positions of the sector is compared in terms of capital formation, an utter neglect of agriculture is apparent in the 1990s. Its share in gross capital formation has declined sharply, from 15.4 per cent in 1980–81 to 8.6 per cent in 2001–02. The most worrying fact is that the public sector investment has come down from 17.7 per cent to 6.1 per cent during the same period. Declining public investment in the sector is a serious issue because it is not only critical for the development of the agricultural infrastructure but also for attracting private sector investment in the sector. Public sector investment has a multiplier effect on investment in any sector. For example, public investment made in building a canal can boost private sector investment in installation of tube-wells in the canal command, as the cost of extracting ground water in the canal command is lower than that of a non-canal area. During the Ninth Plan period, over 400 medium and major irrigation projects were in the pipeline at various stages. However, the the decline in public investment and the thin spread of resources over a large number of projects have delayed the completion of these projects. (Rao 2003)

Sustainability of the groundwater-based minor irrigation systems depends largely on the growth of public investment in major and medium irrigation projects. Nevertheless, in the recent past, the government's policy and attention has shifted from major and medium irrigation projects to minor irrigation projects on various grounds such as efficiency, low cost, less gestation period, quick water yield, and lesser government investment. The Tenth Plan also lays emphasis on minor irrigation projects. It is now a known fact that public investment in major and medium irrigation projects is positively associated with the private sector investment in minor irrigation, albeit with a time lag. This implies that the relatively higher private investment in agriculture during the1990s might have been due to the relatively higher public investment in agriculture during the 1980s.

Declining public investment in the sector is a serious issue because it is not only critical for the development of the agricultural infrastructure but also for attracting private sector investment in the sector. Public sector investment has a multiplier effect on investment in any sector.

We have estimated the average annual capital formation in the public and private sectors for the three periods shown in Table 4. The Table shows that the public sector capital formation has not only gone down in the percentage terms but also in absolute figures. As against an average gross capital formation of Rs. 6,311 crore per annum in the public sector in the decade preceding the reforms, it is estimated that the amount declined to Rs. 4,823 crore in the post-reform period, and it was only Rs. 4,676 crore in the past five years. The percentage share of the public sector

Table 4
Gross Capital Formation in Agriculture & Allied Sector

(at 1993–94 prices)

Year	*GCF in Agriculture & Allied Sector*			*Share of Agriculture & Allied Sector in Total GCF (in %)*		
	Public Sector	*Private Sector*	*Total*	*Public Sector*	*Private Sector*	*Total*
1980–81	7301	6932	14233	17.7	13.6	15.4
1985–86	6213	7919	14132	10.2	9.5	9.8
1990–91	4992	11424	16416	7.1	11.9	9.9
1995–96	5322	12367	17689	7.1	5.9	6.2
1999–2000	4756	15268	20024	5.4	8.5	7.5
2000–01	4417	15161	19578	5.3	8.9	7.7
2001–02*	5260	15880	21140	6.1	9.9	8.6
Average Pre-reform (1980–81 to 1990–91)	6311	8166	14477	11.16	11.32	11.24
Average Post-reform (1991–92 to 2001–02)	4823	12968	17787	6.34	8.50	7.75
Average (1997–98 to 2001–02)	4676	14625	19301	5.74	8.52	7.62

Note: *Quick estimate.
Source: Department of Agriculture and Cooperation, Government of India.

investment in agriculture also declined from 11.16 per cent during the 1980–81 to 1990–91 period to 6.34 per cent during the 1991–92 to 2001–02 period and further to 5.74 per cent during the past five years. Although the average annual private sector capital formation in agriculture has increased in absolute figures, from Rs. 8,166 crore during the 1980–81 to 1990–91 period to Rs. 14,625 crore during the last five years, its share in the total private sector capital formation has actually declined from 11.32 per cent in the 1980s to 8.50 per cent in the 1990s. This implies that in the post-reform period, other sectors have attracted much higher private sector investment than agriculture.

...the public sector gross fixed capital formation (GFCF) in agriculture has sharply declined from Rs.7,368 crore in 1980–81 to Rs. 4,737 crore in 1999–2000, while the GFCF for agriculture has increased from Rs. 9,855 crore to Rs. 9,902 crore during the same period. As a result, the share of the public sector GFCF in agriculture in the total GFCF for agriculture has declined from 74.66 per cent in 1980–81 to 46.83 per cent in 1999–2000.

Another concern about capital formation in agriculture is that the public sector gross fixed capital formation (GFCF) in agriculture has sharply declined from Rs.7,368 crore in 1980–81 to Rs. 4,737 crore in 1999–2000, while the GFCF for agriculture has increased from Rs. 9,855 crore to Rs. 9,902 crore during the same period. As a result, the share of the public sector GFCF in agriculture in the total GFCF for agriculture has declined from 74.66 per cent in 1980–81 to 46.83 per cent in 1999–2000. Although the per cent shares of both the public sector GFCF in agriculture and of agriculture in the country's GDP have declined during the past two decades, the decline is more pronounced in the per cent share of GFCF in agriculture, which has come down from 1.8 per cent in 1980–81 to 0.4 per cent in 1999–2000. (Government of India 2003)

Table 5
GFCF in Agriculture and for Agriculture at 1993–94 Prices

(Rs. crore)

Year	*GFCF*		*Per cent share in GDP of GFCF*	
	in Agriculture	*for Agriculture*	*in Agriculture*	*for Agriculture*
1980–81	13721 (79.41)	17279 (100)	3.4	4.3
1985–86	13061 (73.97)	17656 (100)	2.5	3.4
1990–91	15805 (73.31)	21560 (100)	2.3	3.1
1995–96	16824 (66.54)	25283 (100)	1.9	2.8
2000–01	18364 (65.71)	27946 (100)	1.5	2.3
2001–02	19880 (68.96)	28830 (100)	1.6	2.3

Note: Figures in parentheses are percentages of the total.
Source: Government of India, Department of Agriculture & Cooperation, Ministry of Agriculture, *Report of the Committee on Capital Formation in Agriculture,* March 2003.

The trends in the total GFCF in agriculture and for agriculture are shown in Table 5. The broad trends in both the GFCF in agriculture and agriculture itself are similar during the 1980–81 to 2001–02 period. However, the share of GFCF in agriculture in the total GFCF for agriculture has declined from 79.41 per cent in 1980–81 to 68.96 per cent in 1999–2000, which indicates that the GFCF in agriculture has grown slower than the GFCF in agriculture related activities. As a percentage of the GDP, GFCF in agriculture has declined from 3.4 per cent in 1980–81 to 1.6 per cent in 2001–02. The corresponding share of GFCF for agriculture has also halved during this period.

Table 6 exhibits that the share of agriculture and allied sector in the total Plan outlay has decelerated from 3.40 per cent (revised estimate) in 1997–98 to 2.59 per cent (revised estimate) in 2003–04. Similarly, the budget estimate of the Plan allocation for the sector has declined from 3.23 per cent to 2.61 per cent during the same period. The Union Budget for 2004–05 has allocated only Rs. 4,643 crore for agriculture and allied sector, which is only 2.84 per cent of the total Plan allocation. Thus, what the finance minister stated in his Budget speech, does not reflect in the Plan allocation for the sector.

Reasons for Declining Investment in the Farm Sector

There may be several reasons for the declining share of public sector investment in agriculture. Prominent among them are: (a) diversion of resources from direct investment to subsidies, (b) increase in the cost of maintenance of the existing projects, (c) delays in completion of projects, and (d) inadequate institutional credit support. Above all, the process of macro-economic contraction and declining developmental role of the state in the post-liberalisation period is the main cause of dwindling public sector investment in the farm sector. As curtailing non-Plan expenditure to reduce fiscal deficit was difficult for the government, it cut down capital expenditure, especially on agriculture and the social sector. Although, the government could not succeed in bringing fiscal deficit under control, productive investment in the farm sector has significantly declined because reform policies have eroded the revenues of the government. This has happened due to liberalisation of the tax structure. During the reform period, almost all types of tax rates have been reduced. Consequently, the tax to GDP ratio has gone down from 10.6 per cent in 1989–90 to 8.1 per cent in 2001–02. According to Prof. C.P. Chandrashekher (2003), the adverse impact of reforms on

Table 6
Central Plan Outlay for Agricultural and Allied Sector

(Rs. crore)

Year		*Total Plan Outlay*	*Agriculture and Allied Sector*	*Irrigation and Flood Control*	*Agricultural Research and Education*
1997–98	BE	91839	2969 (3.23)	323 (0.35)	331 (0.36)
	RE	81033	2756 (3.40)	268 (0.33)	331 (0.41)
1998–99	BE	105187	3864 (3.67)	374 (0.36)	531 (0.50)
	RE	88482	2777 (3.14)	345 (0.39)	400 (0.45)
1999–2000	BE	103521	3736 (3.60)	348 (0.34)	574 (0.55)
	RE	96310	3017 (3.13)	347 (0.36)	504 (0.52)
2000–01	BE	117334	3381 (3.47)	452 (0.38)	630 (0.54)
	RE	108587	2982 (2.75)	402 (0.37)	550 (0.51)
2001–02	BE	130181	3380 (2.60)	477 (0.37)	684 (0.53)
	RE	127856	3351 (2.62)	428 (0.33)	684 (0.53)
2002–03	BE	144038	3733 (2.59)	443 (0.31)	775 (0.54)
	RE	136867	2219 (1.62)	381 (0.28)	725 (0.53)
2003–04	BE	147893	3866 (2.61)	443 (0.30)	775 (0.52)
	RE	141766	3671 (2.59)	275 (0.19)	775 (0.55)
2004–05	BE	163720	4643 (2.84)	458 (0.28)	1042 (0.64)

Note: Figures in parentheses are percentages to the total plan outlay.
Source: Compiled from Annual Budget Documents of Government of India

The Union Budget for 2004–05 has allocated only Rs. 4,643 crore for agriculture and allied sector, which is only 2.84 per cent of the total Plan allocation.

revenue generation has occurred through a reduction of a range of tax rates and through curtailing capital and social sector expenditures.

The mid-term review of the Ninth Plan emphasises the fact that the whole approach to agriculture in the past decade has been directed at securing increased agricultural production through input-subsidisation rather than through increased investment in productive fixed assets and infrastructure .The productive base of the sector can be enhanced through direct public sector investment in projects involving irrigation, soil and water conservation, wasteland development programmes, agricultural R&D programmes, and building of a sound marketing and storage infrastructure. However, it is observed that irrigation and flood control, which are important determinants of agricultural productivity, have not been allocated adequate funds by the government in recent years. Its share in the total central plan outlay has decelerated from 0.33 per cent in 1997–98 to 0.19 per cent (revised estimates) in 2003–04 (Table 6). The current budget makes a provision of only Rs. 458 crore for Plan outlay for irrigation and flood control.

Agriculture is a state subject. Most of the states are in severe fiscal crisis due to fiscal mismanagement and the populist measures adopted by them. Moreover, the share of states in the central taxes has declined from 28.32 per cent (budget estimate) in 1996–97 to 25.35 per cent (budget estimate) in 2003–04. The bad fiscal situation of state governments has had an adverse effect on the real investment in agriculture. The cumulative expenditure of the states on agriculture and allied activities as a percentage of the total expenditure has hovered around 4–6 per cent since the mid -1990s, compared to 8 per cent in 1980–81. The maximum decline in the proportion of fund allocation to agriculture and allied activities has been witnessed in the southern states—from 7 per cent in 1996 to almost 5 per cent in 2003 (Ahuja 2004).

Institutional Credit to Agriculture

During the reform period, almost all types of tax rates have been reduced. Consequently, the tax to GDP ratio has gone down from 10.6 per cent in 1989–90 to 8.1 per cent in 2001–02.

Agriculture is a priority sector and 18 per cent of total institutional credit flow is meant for it. However, bank credit to this sector has never reached this percentage. For instance, the relative share of agriculture credit in the net bank credit stood at 12.8 per cent in March 1997 and 11.7 per cent in March 1998 as well as in March 1999. (Government of India 2002) In the present low interest rate regime, big industrialists, businessmen, professionals, and middle and upper middle class consumers are getting easy credit at low cost, while farmers, especially the small and marginal ones, have to depend on the usurious informal sources. The lack of information with farmers, cumbersome lending procedures, and repugnant behaviour of bank officials often restrict farmers from availing the institutional credit. Banks usually avoid giving credit to farmers due to relatively higher transaction and operation costs. Instead of given loans to many small and marginal farmers, they prefer to finance the big customers. Some knowledgeable farmers of Western Uttar Pradesh told the author that the procedure of recovery of bank loans is so cumbersome and complicated that the interest that the farmers have to pay often exceeded the borrowed amount. . When a farmer is unable to repay a loan, the lending bank issues a Recovery Certificate (RC) to the revenue department of the state government. After the issue of an RC, a 10 per cent recovery charge has to be paid by the debtor/ farmer. To avoid such a situation, many farmers prefer getting loans from informal sources, even though the interest rates are much higher than the rates banks charge.

...irrigation and flood control, which are important determinants of agricultural productivity, have not been allocated adequate funds by the government in recent years.

No doubt, the flow of institutional credit to the farm sector has increased significantly during the post-reform period, still about 40 per cent of the farmers' credit requirement is met by the informal sources. Table 7 demonstrates that the total credit flow to the farm sector has increased from Rs. 26,411 crore in 1996–97 to Rs. 80,000 crore in 2003–04, a more than three-fold rise. However, the proportion of the long and medium term credit in the total credit flow is low and has even

Table 7
Flow of Institutional Credit to Agricultural Sector

(Rs. crore)

	1996–97	*1997–98*	*1998–99*	*1999–2000*	*2000–2001*	*2001–02*	*2002–03*	*2003–04 (Estimated)*
Short-term	16998	20640	23903	28965	33314	40509	46281	52000
	(64.36)	(64.71)	(64.85)	(62.60)	(63.06)	(65.29)	(65.36)	(65.0)
Medium/	9413	11316	12957	17303	19513	21536	24529	28000
Long term	(35.64)	(35.41)	(35.15)	(37.40)	(36.94)	(34.71)	(34.64)	(35.0)
Total	26411	31956	36860	46268	52827	62045	70810	80000
	(100)	(100)	(100)	(100)	(100)	(100)	(100)	(100)

Note: Figures in parentheses are percentages to total institutional credit.
Source: Compiled from *Economic Survey 2003–03*, Government of India.

declined slightly, from 35.64 per cent to 35 per cent, during this period. The long and medium term credit is taken for creating physical assets, whereas the short-term credit is taken for procuring inputs like seeds, pesticides and fertilisers. The government policy of providing short-term credit to farmers by issuing Kisan Credit Cards (KCCs) and passbooks has proved effective in catering to the short-term credit needs of farmers. However, this scheme entails an eligibility criteria and access to credit is contingent on the size of the borrowing farmers' operational holdings. This confines the benefits of the scheme to large and medium farmers and small and marginal farmers are mostly by-passed. This will further widen the skewness in credit availability across different farm sizes. The Reserve Bank of India's (RBI) *Report on Currency and Finance 2001–02* finds that the ACGRs in the commercial banks' disbursements of direct finance to small and marginal farmers has declined from 15.1 per cent and 18.1 per cent in the 1980s to 11.0 per cent and 13.0 per cent in the 1990s, respectively. The ACGRs of medium and long term loans disbursed to agriculture and allied activities, which are vital for the private sector capital formation in agriculture, have also declined to 9.7 per cent in the 1990s from 11.5 per cent in the preceding decade. In contrast, growth rate of the short-term credit flows to agriculture has increased from 12.2 per cent to 14.5 per cent during the same period. The shift in the composition of the agricultural credit in favour of short-term advances is a matter of concern, as it is likely to further accentuate the declining private sector capital formation in agriculture.

The UPA government has made a provision for an additional 30 per cent credit flow to the farm sector in the current budget and has targeted doubling of it in the coming three years. The moot point here is: Can credit enhancement to the farm sector alleviate problems in agriculture and reduce indebtedness among farmers? There is a fear that easy availability of credit to farmers may widen their debt burden and as a consequence it may increase distress and despair among them. Agricultural development cannot be ensured only through doubling the credit. What farmers really need are viable and profitable agricultural ventures, which actually depend on policy initiatives ranging from an increase in the public sector investment in agricultural infrastructure, R&D, and extension services, to developing a sound agro-processing, marketing, and insurance system. In the absence of a suitable agricultural marketing and insurance mechanism, farmers may not always get remunerative prices for their produce, and as a result the loans taken by them could turn into bad loans, which may further increase their debt-burden.

No doubt, the flow of institutional credit to the farm sector has increased significantly during the post-reform period, still about 40 per cent of the farmers' credit requirement is met by the informal sources.

Declining Profitability, Rising Indebtedness, and Farmers' Suicides

Agriculture is facing a severe crisis in the post-reform period. The rising input-costs, depressed prices, and declining productivity have made agriculture an unprofitable activity. Recently, the Central Institute of Agricultural Engineering (CIAE) conducted a study to examine the profitability in the sector. The study was based on CACP data on the cost of cultivation, production, and market prices for the period 1990–

91 to 1997–98. The study found that the profitability has declined on account of lower productivity and the market prices failing to keep pace with the rising input costs. The percentage share of profit in paddy has declined from 7.5 per cent in 1995–97 to 3.84 per cent in 1997–98, in wheat from 8.4 per cent to 0.64 per cent, and in gram from 8.08 per cent to –6.42 per cent. The share of profit in coarse cereals and groundnut remained negative. Farmers' incomes have declined sharply during the past five years. The rice farmers in West Bengal earned 28 per cent less in 2002–03 than they had earned in 1996–97. In 2002–03, the sugarcane growers in Uttar Pradesh and Maharastra got 32 per cent and 40 per cent less, respectively, than they had received in 1996–97. (Sharma 2004) Indebtedness among farmers has been on the rise. The Working Group on Agricultural Credit, Cooperation and Crop Insurance (Government of India 2001) has also highlighted the issue of indebtedness among farmers in its report.

The share of profit in coarse cereals and groundnut remained negative. Farmers' incomes have declined sharply during the past five years. The rice farmers in West Bengal earned 28 per cent less in 2002–03 than they had earned in 1996–97. In 2002–03, the sugarcane growers in Uttar Pradesh and Maharastra got 32 per cent and 40 per cent less, respectively, than they had received in 1996–97. Indebtedness among farmers has been on the rise.

Caught in a cycle of debt and crop failure, thousands of farmers have committed suicide in different parts of the country. The spate of suicides shows no signs of ending even after the UPA government at the centre, took several measures to alleviate distress and debt-burden of the affected farmers. Although farmers have been committing suicide in almost all major farm-producing states, the intensity is particularly high among farmers in the arid and semi-arid regions of southern states such as Andhra Pradesh (AP) and Karnataka. In Karnataka, between 1996 and 2000, 10,959 farmers committed suicide, an average of 2,192 suicides per annum. (Deshpande 2002) In AP, over 3,000 farmers have taken their lives since 1997. In Anantapur district of AP alone, 1,826 farmers have killed themselves over the last five years. Recently, suicide deaths among farmers of Kerala and Maharashtra have also been reported. Over 300 farmers in the Vidharbha region of Maharashtra have ended their lives during the past three years. In the Wyanad district of Kerala, about 100 farmers have committed suicide in the recent past. Even in the agriculturally developed state of Punjab, the heavy indebtedness forced more than 200 farmers to take their lives. A probe into the reasons for suicides among farmers reveals that no single factor is accountable for these suicides. Pre-eminence of a reason may vary from region to region. For instance, in the Telengana region of AP, farmers have repeatedly made heavy investments in bore wells and failed to draw adequate water. They had to take loans at relatively higher rates of interest from the informal sources, as institutional credit virtually collapsed in the state. (Sridhar 2004) Apart from chronic illness and family problems, the main reasons for suicides among farmers are:

Although farmers have been committing suicide in almost all major farm-producing states, the intensity is particularly high among farmers in the arid and semi-arid regions of southern states.

(a) drought and failure of rainfall,
(b) loss of crops due to inferior quality of inputs,
(c) sudden attacks of pests and diseases on crops,
(d) crash of market prices,
(e) mounting debt-burden and interlocking of input-credit and product market,
(f) failure of extension services,
(g) changed market conditions,
(h) commercialisation of farming,
(i) technology failure,
(j) spurious seeds, pesticides and other inputs
(k) and an inefficient and inadequate support system.

Above all, the intensity of suicides has been high among the farmers of rain-fed regions, who attempted to innovate and diversify their farming, but due to crop failures and/or market failures, could not repay the loans taken for this purpose and were caught in the debt trap.

The UPA government has abolished the excise duty on tractors and substantially increased the credit flow to the farm sector. These two initiatives of the government should increase the sale of tractors and give a boost to the tractor manufacturing firms. However, there is a fear that instead of alleviating the farming problems, these measures will further aggravate the problems of the already debt-ridden farmers, as these will motivate the small and semi-medium farmers to purchase tractors, which they cannot afford to maintain on their economically unviable holdings. Rising diesel prices and high maintenance costs of tractors may push many such farmers into the debt-trap.

Agriculture Extension and R&D

Agricultural extension has undergone a change over a period of time. The community development, block- based extension system, which served well during the Green Revolution period and thereafter, became defunct after 1980. After commencement of beneficiary-oriented poverty alleviation programmes, village level workers (VLWs) practically engaged in providing loans to the beneficiaries and extension services were totally neglected. The training & visit (T&V) extension system, started in the mid 1970s, also has weak linkages between research-extension and farmers. Due to its uniform top-down approach, the T&V system could not focus on area-specific needs, disadvantaged regions, and target groups. (Sharma 2002) The whole approach of the public extension services has been supply-driven, not demand-driven, and the involvement of farmers in the public extension system has remained minimal. Due to inadequate extension services, most of the farmers did not have access to information about the right doses of inputs such as fertilisers, pesticides, irrigation water, and seeds.

Recently, the private sector has also entered into agriculture extension. Private companies are providing information to farmers as well as arranging supply of inputs. Companies like ITC Ltd. have started using information technology (IT) to provide information to farmers on weather, market prices, and recommended practices for crop production. If the private extension system is found to be effective, the government may consider establishing such extension service centres on a self-sustaining basis. (Government of India 2001) The private sector generally creates extension services for those regions, crops, and farmers where it expects significant returns. The economically backward regions and small and marginal farmers may not attract private investment in extension services. Therefore, the public investment in agricultural extension services is crucial for rain-fed regions, backward areas, and small and marginal farmers.

...the intensity of suicides has been high among the farmers of rain-fed regions, who attempted to innovate and diversify their farming...

With inadequate or no access to information from the government institutions on technology, prices, selection of right inputs, value addition, crop-diversification, credit, and market channels, farmers often depend on local traders and vendors for the choice and use of inputs. These traders quite often provide credit to farmers for the purchase of inputs. Due to interlocking of inputs, credit, and production, farmers are forced to buy substandard inputs from the traders and to sell their produce at relatively lower prices to them.

The whole approach of the public extension services has been supply-driven, not demand-driven, and the involvement of farmers in the public extension system has remained minimal.

A study conducted by Evenson et al. (1999) found that the rates of return to the public sector agricultural research in India are high and increasing public investment in research and extension would lead to even greater gains. The study also estimated that the marginal internal rates of returns to the public agricultural research are greater than that of the private sector. However, agricultural R&D and extension services have not been given much weight in the Plan allocations. Although the central plan outlay for agricultural research and education has increased in absolute figures as well as in percentage, it is still much below what has been recommended by the Indian Council for Agricultural Research (ICAR). Table 6 shows that the

Table 8
R&D Expenditure on Agriculture, Forestry and Fishing

(Rs. crore)

Year	*Central Govt.*		*State Govts.*		*Public Sector*		*Private Sector*		*Total*	
	Amount	*%*	*Amount*	*%*	*Amount*	*%*	*Amount*	*%*	*Amount*	*%*
1996–97	545.50 (27.27)	10.46	768.50 (38.42)	89.88	16.32 (0.82)	3.18	669.73 (33.49)	34.30	2000.05 (100)	23.43
1997–98	681.07 (33.00)	10.73	823.91 (39.91)	88.90	17.78 (0.86)	3.30	541.43 (26.23)	27.09	2064.19 (100)	21.04
1998–99	957.75 (37.73)	11.89	902.35 (35.54)	87.90	20.48 (0.81)	3.15	658.06 (25.92)	29.30	2538.64 (100)	21.18

Note: Figures in parentheses are percentages to the total.
Source: Department of Science and Technology, GOI.

share of agricultural research and education in the total Plan outlay (budget estimate) has gone up from 0.50 per cent in 1997–98 to 0.64 per cent in 2004–05. However, it is just half of that recommended by the ICAR. The R&D expenditure on agriculture, forestry, and fishing is shown in Table 8. Their share in the total central government R&D expenditure has increased from 10.86 per cent in 1996–97 to 11.89 per cent in 1998–99, while the R&D expenditure on them as a percentage of the total R&D expenditure of state governments has declined. The public and private contribution has also gone down. On an average, about 21 per cent of total R&D expenditure has been made on agriculture, forestry, and fishing in 1998–99. Considering the contribution of agriculture in the GDP and workforce absorption, 21 per cent of the total R&D expenditure on this sector seems to be inadequate.

India has achieved tremendous growth in the use of tractors in farm operations.

India has attained the second highest annual growth in the number of tractors used in farm operations.

Trends in Farm Mechanisation

The share of the mechanical power in India has increased from 39.43 per cent in 1971–72 to 83.62 per cent in 2001–02. (Government of India 2004a) India has achieved tremendous growth in the use of tractors in farm operations. Table-9 gives the details of the number of tractors used in agriculture in India vis-à-vis other selected countries. The table shows that India's share in the world tractor market has significantly increased, from 1.87 per cent in 1981 to 5.71 per cent in 2002. India has attained the second highest annual growth in the number of tractors used in farm operations. Thailand tops the lists. However, the growth in the post-reform period was much lower than that achieved in the decade preceding the reforms. Disparity among different states in the use of tractors is also noticeable. In 2002–03, the sale of tractors was highest in Uttar Pradesh (UP), followed by West Bengal. In the agriculturally developed regions such as Punjab, Haryana, and Western UP, aggressive tractor marketing and availability of bank loans have tempted many small

Table 9
Growth in Use of Tractors in Agriculture of Selected Countries

Country	*Number of Tractors (in 1000)*			*Annual compound growth rates*		
	1981	*1991*	*2002*	*1981–2002*	*1981–1990*	*1991–2002*
India	417.77 (1.87)	1063.01 (4.05)	1525.00 (5.71)	6.55	9.14	3.42
China	796.87	795.71	926.03	–0.26	0.57	1.92
Thailand	20.80	65.01	220.00	14.10	12.27	12.05
Brazil	569.00	730.00	806.00	1.61	2.61	0.91
Canada	6865.87	7348.10	6953.53	–0.12	0.90	–0.41
Australia	326.00	316.00	315.00	–0.17	–0.31	–0.01
France	1484.60	1410.00	1264.00	–1.02	–0.32	–1.00
USA	4697.00	4800.00	4800.00	0.14	0.36	0.00
Whole Total	22311.08	26244.97	26704.74	0.68	2.07	0.18

Source: Calculated from FAO database "FAOSTAT' (accessed in July 2004).

farmers to purchase tractors. Since the sizes of their operational holdings are too small to maintain a tractor, many of them get into debt traps. Fragmentation and division of holdings due to breaking-up of families is a vital factor in the growth of tractors, especially in the agriculturally developed regions of the country.

Agricultural Trade

Effective implementation of the Agreement on Agriculture (AoA), prima facie, seems to be the most significant factor for ensuring a transparent trade in agriculture. However, various loopholes in the AoA provide enough space for developed countries to heavily subsidise their agricultural products. During the Uruguay Round of negotiations in the World Trade Organisation (WTO), it was expected that, following the Agreement, distortions in agricultural trade would be reduced and the scope for exports of products from the developing countries will increase. It was also expected that the contemplated fair trade regime will help the efficient producers in realising higher prices for their products. However, even after nine years of existence of the WTO, the production and trade of agricultural products across the world is highly distorted. The Organisation for Economic Cooperation and Development (OECD) countries give a whopping $400 billion subsidy to their farmers every year. Contrary to the claims of the WTO, which maintains that the developed countries have reduced agricultural subsidies, we see that the US Farm Bill for 2002 shows an increase of $83 billion. (Swaminathan 2003) But in these countries also, the farm subsidy is mostly grabbed by the big farmers. In the US, 25 per cent farmers received 89 per cent of the support, an average of $275,000 (Rs. 1.2 crore) per farm; in Europe, 25 per cent of farms received 70 per cent of the support, an average of Rs. 90 lakh per farm. Farm incomes in many OECD countries are higher than the national average income. (Bajaj 2004) How can Indian farmers be efficient producers in such a distorted production and trade environment? These countries plead for better market access for their agricultural products in the developing countries through tariff reduction and increased in-tariff quotas, but they usually avoid negotiating on reduction of domestic support and elimination of export subsidies.

However, even after nine years of existence of the WTO, the production and trade of agricultural products across the world is highly distorted. The Organisation for Economic Cooperation and Development (OECD) countries give a whopping $400 billion subsidy to their farmers every year.

...that the US Farm Bill for 2002 shows an increase of $83 billion...

Farm incomes in many OECD countries are higher than the national average income.

The adverse effectsof the lifting of QRs on international trade and high export and production subsidies given by the developed countries on India's agricultural exports are quite evident. The share of agricultural export in India's total exports has been declining. Table 10 exhibits that the share has shrunk from 20.33 per cent in 1996–97 to 13.10 per cent in 2001–02. In contrast, the share of agricultural imports in the total imports of the country has increased from 4.76 per cent to 5.77 per cent during the same period. This shows that the prospects of India's agricultural exports have become gloomy under the WTO regime. Now, with greater volatility in the global market for agricultural products, any sizeable decline in their prices can be disastrous for Indian farmers. Oilseeds producers in the country have already been facing hardship due to volatility in international prices. Therefore, suitable policy actions have to be taken to protect Indian farmers from the onslaughts of foreign producers. Due to low crop-productivity and high cost of production, prices of agricultural products in India are less competitive. For example, in 2001, as against $107.7 per tonne in USA, the price of wheat in India was $131 per tonne.

Table 10
Import and Export of Agricultural Commodities during the Post-reform Period
(per cent of India's Total Import and Export)

	1996–97	*1997–98*	*1998–99*	*1999–00*	*2000–01*	*2001–02*	*2002–03*
Import	4.76	5.7	8.17	7.45	5.29	6.63	5.77
Export	20.33	19.1	18.25	15.91	14.23	14.22	13.10

Source: Official website of Department of Agriculture and Cooperation, Government of India (accessed in July 2004).

Table 11
Cost of Production and Export Price of Selected Crops of the USA in 2001

Item	*Cost of Production (in $ per bushel)*	*Export Price (in $ per bushel)*	*Export price as percentage of the production cost*
1. Wheat	6.24	3.50	56.09
2. Soya Bean	6.96	4.93	70.83
3. Maize	3.47	2.28	65.71
4. Cotton	0.93	0.39	41.94
5. Rice	18.66	14.55	77.97

Source: http://www.cpiml.org/liberation/year%202003/May2003/WTO.htm

Assessing the situation on the basis of the three components of the AoA, viz., market access, domestic support, and export subsidies, it is observed that India will stand to gain in the global market for agricultural products provided domestic support and export subsidies were substantially reduced by the developed countries and market access enhanced through reducing above-quota tariffs. After the removal of QRs, the main problem for India is from the heavily subsidised agricultural exports of industrialised countries. Table 11 shows the cost of production and the export price per bushel of some selected agricultural products in the USA in 2001. That year, the export price of cotton in the USA was about 42 per cent of the cost of production, the export price of wheat was 56 per cent of the cost, and the price of maize was about 66 per cent of the cost. This clearly indicates the extent of support given by the US to its farmers.

...with greater volatility in the global market for agricultural products, any sizeable decline in their prices can be disastrous for Indian farmers. Oilseeds producers in the country have already been facing hardship due to volatility in international prices.

Economics of Agricultural Subsidy

The constant rise in the agricultural subsidy including food subsidy has become a major concern for the government. While the public investment in agriculture is declining, the subsidy bill accruing toward agriculture is increasing. The share of fertiliser subsidy in the total explicit subsidies has gone up from 35 per cent in the 1980s to 49.8 per cent in the second half of the 1990s. Fertiliser subsidy, which was just Rs. 4,389 crore in 1990–91, increased to Rs. 12,567 crore in 2003–04. Another big chunk of subsidy is the food subsidy, which has increased tremendously, from Rs. 6,066 crore in 1996–97 to Rs. 25,160 crore in 2003–04. Besides food and fertiliser subsidies, other input-subsidies such as irrigation and power have also been on the rise.

The steep rise in the agriculture subsidy is crowding out the real investment in the farm sector, as the resource-striven central government finds it difficult to raise public investment in the sector. Moreover, due to inequitable distribution of these subsidies across regions and farmers, their benefits are availed mainly by the big farmers, especially in the agriculturally developed regions. For instance, a sizeable portion of fertiliser subsidy is cornered by the farmers of irrigated regions, as fertiliser consumption in rainfed regions is very low. Heavy subsidies on irrigation and power not only deplete the water table, but also distort the cropping pattern and adversely affect the sustainability of agriculture. Further, inefficiency and leakages in the delivery system of these subsidies restrict their accessibility by the targeted beneficiaries. For example, fertiliser subsidy is not given directly to farmers; it is given to the fertiliser industry. Besides possible manipulations in cost estimation to keep the price of fertilisers artificially high, a significant part of the fertiliser subsidy is absorbed by production inefficiency.

Food subsidy has three components—consumers' subsidy, implicit subsidy for producers, and subsidy pertaining to the maintenance of buffer stocks. The amount of consumers' subsidy depends on the quantity of food grains distributed through the Public Distribution System (PDS), while the carrying costs for maintaining the stocks at the buffer norm level is the price for food security. The cost of carrying stocks in excess of designated levels may be considered as an implicit subsidy for fertiliser producers. The share of producers' subsidy in the total food subsidy has increased drastically, from 12.8 per cent in 1993–94 to 48.9 per cent in 2001–02, whereas the share of consumers' subsidy has declined tremendously, from 56.5 per cent to 29.2 per cent during the same period, and the subsidy pertaining to maintaining the buffer stock has declined from 30.7 per cent to 21.9 per cent during the period (RBI, 2002). This implies that only a small fraction of the total food subsidy has actually been received by the poor consumers. In the Union Budget 2004–05, a provision of Rs. 27,746 crore has been made for food subsidy (Government of India, 2004b). Considering the official estimate of people below poverty line, the average food subsidy per household in India works out to be over Rs. 5,000, sufficient to purchase about seven quintals of food grains from the open market. Thus, if the amount of subsidy is given directly to the poor in the form of food stamps, a poor person could get 850 grams of food grains per day, which is much higher than the national average of 438.2 grams per capita per day. Even if half of this food subsidy is provided directly to the poor, the food security of the poor could be ensured. But only a very small part of these subsidies go to the consumers.

The economic cost (EC) of food grains to the Food Corporation of India (FCI) has been increasing continuously. Table 12 shows that the EC of wheat has increased from Rs. 838.26 per quintal in 2001–02 to Rs. 952.51 in 2003–04, a net increase of Rs.114 per quintal. The ratio of the EC to minimum support price (MSP) has increased from 1.38 to 1.51, highlighting the inefficiency in food management. Therefore, if food stocks were to be stored as per food security norms and the subsidy was to be better targeted to save public money, it will be possible to create real investment in the farm sector.

The MSP policy was initiated with the objective to provide remunerative prices to farmers,to procure food grains for maintaining food security, and provide incentives for diversification of agriculture. The policy has grossly failed in achieving crop-diversification and in providing remunerative prices to farmers. Farmers have been facing uncertainties not only in weather but also in the prices of farm produce. In the absence of effective price protection, sometimes bumper crops become a curse for farmers. Every year the government announces MSP for different crops, as per the recommendations of CACP. In the case of a few crops, such as paddy and wheat, the MSPs have been higher than the cost of production, while in the case of coarse cereals, it has been lower than the actual cost of production. For instance, in 1997–98, as against a cost of production of Rs. 499 per quintal for coarse cereals, their MSP was only Rs. 360 per quintal. In contrast, the MSP for wheat was Rs. 510, much higher than the actual cost of production (Rs. 418 per quintal). (RBI 2002) The MSP policy has made cultivation of the superior cereals relatively more profitable than the coarse cereals, pulses, and oilseeds and thus distorted the cropping pattern. It has prevented the much needed diversification of the cropping pattern.

...only a small fraction of the total food subsidy has actually been received by the poor consumers.

Considering the official estimate of people below poverty line, the average food subsidy per household in India works out to be over Rs. 5,000, sufficient to purchase about seven quintals of food grains from the open market.

Table 12
Minimum Support Price, Economic Cost and Issue Price of Wheat

(Rs. per quintal)

Year	*MSP*	*Issue price(BPL)*	*Economic Cost*	*Ratio of economic cost to MSP*
2001–02	620	415	838.26	1.38
2002–03	620	415	914.71	1.48
2003–04	630	415	952.51	1.51

Source: Compiled from *Economic Survey 2003–04*.

Marginalisation of the Workforce and Size of Operational Holdings

Although the percentage of the workforce dependent on agriculture has declined in 2001, the absolute number has increased from 185 million in 1991 to 235 million in 2001. Simultaneously, the share of agriculture in the GDP declined sharply, from 34.93 per cent in 1990–91 to about 22 per cent in 2003–04. The widening gap between per worker GDP in agriculture and non-agricultural sectors provides a clear indication of the marginalisation of the agricultural workforce. The Vision-2020 document prepared by the Planning Commission visualises that the share of agriculture in the GDP will decline to 6 per cent in 2020, while dependence of the workforce on agriculture may fall to less than 45 per cent. If this happens, imagine what would be the economic condition of farm workers vis-a-vis workers of other sectors.

The number of agricultural labourers has increased from 27 million in 1951 to 107 million in 2001, a nearly four-fold rise. Consequently, their share in the total workforce has also increased from 19.5 per cent to 26.7 per cent during the same period.

The number of agricultural labourers has increased from 27 million in 1951 to 107 million in 2001, a nearly four-fold rise. Consequently, their share in the total workforce has also increased from 19.5 per cent to 26.7 per cent during the same period. A startling fact about the composition of the workforce in the 2001 census is that the share of main workers as well as non-workers has come down, while the share of marginal workers has substantially increased. Rural Labour Enquiry Report on General Characteristics of Rural Labour Households (55th Round of NSS 1999–2000), shows that the average daily earnings of both the agricultural labourers and rural labourers have remained much lower in agricultural operations than in non-agricultural activities. For instance, in 1999–2000, an agricultural labourer earned Rs. 40.14 per day as against Rs. 54.09 in non-agricultural activities. Between 1993–94 and 1999–00, anagricultural labourer's daily earnings (at current prices) increased by 88 per cent in agricultural operations and 100 per cent in non-agricultural operation. A similar change is also observed in the case of the daily earnings of a rural labourer. This reveals that the average earnings grew faster in non-farm activities than in farm activities.

In India, the number of landless and nearly landless households in rural areas has shown a steady rise. ...Among the agricultural labourers, about 12 per cent were landless and 69 per cent owned less than 0.40 hectare land. Overall, 10 per cent of the rural households were landless and about 49 per cent were nearly landless.

In an agro-based rural economy, access to land is a good indicator of the socio-economic status of a household. A rising trend in the number of marginal and small holdings in any economy points towards marginalisation of the agricultural workforce. In India, the number of landless and nearly landless households in rural areas has shown a steady rise. As per the 1999–2000 NSSO Survey, 77.90 per cent farm households possessed land holdings below 2 hectares. Nearly half the total farm households owned less than one hectare land. Among the agricultural labourers, about 12 per cent were landless and 69 per cent owned less than 0.40 hectare land. Overall, 10 per cent of the rural households were landless and about 49 per cent were nearly landless. The highly skewed distribution of land among rural households also indicates the marginalisation of workers. The declining share of agriculture in the GDP with a marginal reduction in its share in the workforce, the growing proportion of agricultural labourers, the declining regular employment elsewhere, the increasing cost of production and reducing farm profitability, the rising indebtedness among farmers, and the corporatisation of the agricultural sector, all indicate that the farm workers in the post-liberalisation period have been marginalised.

According to the Agricultural Census 1995–96, over 80 per cent of agricultural holdings in the country are less than 2 hectares. Table 13 demonstrates that between 1990–91 and 1995–96, marginal holdings (less than 1 hectare) have increased both in terms of number as well as area. Comparing the data of the Agricultural Census 1990–91 to that of 1995–96, we find that the total number of agricultural holdings has increased from 106,637 thousand to 115,580 thousand. However, the total operated area has declined from 165,506 thousand hectares to 163,357 thousand

Table 13
Distribution of Operational Holdings-All India

Category of Holdings	*No. of Operational Holdings (in %)*		*Area Operated (in %)*		*Average Size of Operational Holdings (ha)*	
	1990–91	1995–96	1990–91	1995–96	1990–91	1995–96
Marginal (less than 1ha)	59.4	61.6	15.0	17.2	0.39	0.40
Small (1.0–2.0 ha)	18.8	18.7	17.4	18.4	1.43	1.42
Semi-medium (2.0–4.0 ha)	13.1	12.3	23.2	23.8	2.76	2.73
Medium (4.0–10.0 ha)	7.1	6.1	27.1	25.3	5.90	5.84
Large (10.0 ha & above)	1.6	1.2	17.3	14.8	17.33	17.21
All holdings*	106637 (100)	115580 (100)	165507 (100)	163357 (1000)	1.57 (100)	1.41 (100)

Note: *Number in 1000 and area in 1000 hectares.
Source: Official website of Department of Agriculture and Cooperation, GOI (accessed in July 2004).

hectares during the same period. Looking at the categories of holdings, it is observed that except for the marginal category, the numbers of all sizes of holdings have declined. The area operated by marginal farmers as a percentage of the total operated area has also increased from 15 per cent in 1990–91 to 17.2 in 1995–96. Consequently, the average size of operational holding under the marginal category has increased slightly, from 0.39 hectare to 0.40 hectare, during this period, while the average sizes of operational holdings under all other categories have declined. Hence, the changing structure of operational holdings highlights the marginalisation of agricultural workers.

...over 80 per cent of agricultural holdings in the country are less than 2 hectares.

The area operated by marginal farmers as a percentage of the total operated area has also increased from 15 per cent in 1990–91 to 17.2 in 1995–96.

Consequently, the average size of operational holding under the marginal category has increased slightly, from 0.39 hectare to 0.40 hectare, during this period, while the average sizes of operational holdings under all other categories have declined.

Contract Farming

Commercialisation of agriculture through contract farming is a new policy initiative in the country. Contract farming is being considered a win-win situation for both the farmers and the contracting companies. The Tenth Plan document also focuses on its promotion. In the present era of trade liberalisation and expanding agri-business, the small and marginal farmers in India may find themselves incapable of participating in the market economy due to constraints such as lack of essential inputs, scarcity of reasonable credit, technical guidance, and marketing support. It is argued that contract farming can provide a viable option for making agriculture a profitable venture for farmers. In India, several big companies, such as Pepsi Foods, Kellogg, Cadbury India, ITC, and Cargill have already entered into contract farming. Theoretically, it appears that contract farming is a viable option for raising the farm income and adding value to agricultural products. However, the experience of farmers with contract farming has not always been sweet. As contract farming is an agreement between unequal partners, there is always the possibility of exploitation of farmers by the big companies.

Therefore, in order to make the small and marginal holdings economically viable and to provide productive employment to farmers, we have to evolve a farming system, which is better than corporate and contract farming. Effective participation of cooperative institutions in various facets of agriculture may be a better option. Another alternative could be the promotion of collective farming among small and marginal farmers through self-help groups (SHGs) that can be formed with the intervention of the local non-governmental organization (NGOs), agricultural extension staff, and the Panchayati Raj system of village management. Instead of providing credit to individual farmers, banks can provide credit to a group of small and marginal farmers for procuring capital assets, such as tractors and irrigation pump sets. To encourage the farmers to form such groups, the government can provide subsidies for procuring these assets. Indian agriculture can be competitive in the global market only if the cost of production is reduced and productivity per unit of land is enhanced. Collective farming by groups of small and marginal farmers may eliminate the disadvantages of small-scale farming, which comprises 80 per cent of the total operational holdings and about 36 per cent of the total operated area.

Conclusion

During the post-reform period, Indian agriculture has been facing both internal and external challenges. On the domestic front, we have the problem of declining productivity, efficiency, profitability, and employment in the agricultural sector, which are largely due to drastic decline in real investment in irrigation, water management, R&D, extension services, and infrastructure. Low productivity and high input cost have increased the indebtedness among farmers, forcing many of them to end their lives. External challenges are also being faced due to heavy production and export subsidies by industrialised countries, which have distorted the world trade in agricultural products. Removal of quantitative restrictions in the presence of these subsidies has already shown its adverse consequences for our agriculture. Hence, suitable policy interventions must be made to protect Indian farmers from the onslaughts of foreign producers.

Indian agriculture needs appropriate policy action to augment farm income and employment. The rates of subsidy and MSPneed to be used in a manner that removes distortions in the cropping pattern, encourages crop-diversification, and improves crop-productivity. In order to enhance the real investment in the sector, non-merit subsidies are to be downsized and the resources so generated should be ploughed back into agriculture as investments in irrigation and other infrastructure. As farmers face uncertainty and risk in production and prices due to crop and market failures, implementation of insurance schemes like the Farm Income Insurance Scheme (FIIS) could be effective in protecting farmers' incomes. Generally, farmers do not get the right market signals and, as a result, lose income from their products.

The UPA government needs to set up an Agricultural Production and Marketing Information System (APAMIS) with the purpose of collecting, analysing, and disseminating information on global production, demand, prices, subsidies, quality standards, and export trends in various agricultural products. The system should be well connected to District Information Centres (DICs). The DICs should supply information on these issues fortnightly to the local newspapers so that they can publish the information in the vernacular languages for the benefit of the farmers. Enhancing profitability in agriculture is not only vital for the development of the sector itself, but also for the growth of the secondary and tertiary sectors. As about three-fifths of Indian workers depend directly on agriculture, an increase in their disposable income can raise demand for the secondary and tertiary sectors' products, which is crucial for achieving the targeted 8 per cent GDP growth rate.

As about three-fifths of Indian workers depend directly on agriculture, an increase in their disposable income can raise demand for the secondary and tertiary sectors' products...

References

Ahuja, Shobha. 2004. 'States' Spending on Agriculture Dismal', *The Financial Express*, 5 July.

Bajaj, Rahul. 2004. 'Trade by Terror: Calling the WTO Deadline Bluff', *The Times of India*, 27 July.

Chandrashekar, C.P. 2003. 'Budget 2003: Straitjacketed by Reform', *Frontline*, 20(6), 15–28 March.

Despande, R.S. 2002. 'Suicide by Farmers in Karnataka: Agrarian Distress and Possible Alleviatory Steps', *Economic and Political Weekly*, 29 June.

Evenson R. E. and R.W. Rosegrant. 1999. *Agricultural Research and Productivity Growth in India*, Research Report 109, Washington D.C., USA: IFPRI.

Food and Agriculture Organization. 2004. FAOSTAT Database on Agriculture, http://faostat.fao.org/faostat/collections?subset=agriculture (Accessed in July 2004).

Government of India. 2001. *Report of the Working Group on Agricultural Credit, Cooperation and Insurance for the Tenth Five Year Plan (2002–07)*, New Delhi: Planning Commission.

Government of India. 2002. *Report of the Steering Group on Agriculture and Allied Sector for the Tenth Five Year Plan 2002–07.* New Delhi: Planning Commission.

Government of India. 2003. *Report of the Committee on Capital Formation in Agriculture*, Directorate of Economics & Statistics, Department of Agriculture & Cooperation, Ministry of Agriculture, New Delhi.

Government of India. 2004a. *Economic Survey 2003–04*, Ministry of Finance, New Delhi.

Government of India. 2004b. *Union Budget 2004–05*, Ministry of Finance, New Delhi.

Reserve Bank of India. 2002. *Report on Currency and Finance 2001–02 http://www.rbi.org.in.*

Rao, C.H. Hanumantha. 2003. 'Reform Agenda for Agriculture', *Economic and Political Weekly*, 15 February.

Sharma, Devender. 2004. 'Have Farmers Become a Burden on India?' http://ww1.mid-day.com/news/nation/2004/july/87552.htm.

Sharma, Rita. 2002. 'Reforms in Agricultural Extension: New Policy Framework', *Economic and Political Weekly*, Review of Agriculture, 27 July.

Sridhar, V. 2004. 'An Agrarian Tragedy', *Frontline*, 21(13), 19 June–2 July.

Swaminathan, S. 2003. 'WTO: Agreement on Agriculture', http://www.cpiml.org/liberation/year%202003/May2003/WTO.htm.

Industry

T. Ravi Kumar

Industrial performance improved in the year 2003–04 with the Index of Industrial Production (IIP) growing by 6.9 per cent compared with 5.7 per cent the previous year. Terming of this accomplishment as 'healthy' by the official *Economic Survey 2003–04* tantamounts to ignoring the fact that this growth rate fell well short of the Tenth Plan target of 10 per cent despite a good monsoon and other favourable factors. The performance over the first two years of the Plan, therefore, does not bode well for the achievement of either the average growth target for the industrial sector or the overall Gross Domestic Product (GDP) growth of 8 per cent. However, in assessing the outlook for industry, the *Survey* acknowledges this facet of industrial performance and states that 'one of the most important challenges in Indian economic policy consists of devising strategies for obtaining industrial growth in excess of 10 per cent'.

Sectoral Performance

Two of the three major sectors contributed to the improved performance in 2003–04. The Manufacturing and Electricity sectors grew faster than in the previous year, at rates of 7.2 and 5.0 per cent respectively compared with the rates of 6.0 and 3.2 per cent in 2002–03 (Table 1). The Mining and Quarrying sector witnessed a marginal slow down with a growth at 5.1 per cent compared with 5.8 per cent the previous year.

An examining of industrial performance in terms of use-based classification reveals that three of the four sectors showed improved performance in 2003–04—Basic Goods, Capital Goods, and Intermediate Goods grew at 5.4, 12.7, and 6.2 per cent respectively compared with 4.9, 10.5, and 3.9 per cent the previous year (Table 2). However, the Basic Goods and Intermediate Goods sectors, despite their better performance, grew more slowly than the industry average. Though Consumer Durables sector grew at the same rate as the previous year, 7.1 per cent, there was a complete reversal within the sector in terms of the performance of the sub-sectors compared with 2002–03. Consumer Durables, which exhibited negative growth in 2002–03, grew strongly at 11.6 per cent, while Consumer Non-Durables experienced a severe deceleration in growth—from 12 per cent to 5.7 per cent in 2003–04.

The performance over the first two years of the Plan, therefore, does not bode well for the achievement of either the average growth target for the industrial sector or the overall Gross Domestic Product (GDP) growth of eight per cent.

There was a vast variation in the growth experienced by the different groups of industries (two-digit) within the Manufacturing sector—the major sector exhibiting

Table 1
Annual Growth Rates of Industrial Production

(per cent)

Sectors	*Weight*	*1997–98*	*1998–99*	*1999–00*	*2000–01*	*2001–02*	*2002–03*	*2003–04*
Mining	10.47	6.9	–0.8	1.0	2.8	1.2	5.8	5.1
Manufacturing	79.36	6.7	4.4	7.1	5.3	2.9	6.0	7.2
Electricity	10.17	6.6	6.5	7.3	4.0	3.1	3.2	5.0
General	100.00	6.7	4.1	6.7	5.0	2.7	5.7	6.9

Source: Derived from Index of Industrial Production (Base: 1993–94 =100) data reported in the *Economic Survey 2003–2004*.

Table 2
Growth Rates of Industrial Production by Use-Based Classification

(per cent)

Sectors	*Weight*	*1997–98*	*1998–99*	*1999–00*	*2000–01*	*2001–02*	*2002–03*	*2003–04*
1. Basic	35.5	6.9	1.6	5.5	3.7	2.6	4.9	5.4
2. Capital	9.3	5.8	12.6	6.9	1.8	–3.4	10.5	12.7
3. Intermediate	26.5	8.0	6.1	8.8	4.7	1.5	3.9	6.2
4. Consumer	28.7	5.5	2.2	5.7	8.0	6.0	7.1	7.1
4a Durables	5.4	7.8	5.6	14.1	14.5	11.5	–6.3	11.6
4b Non-Durables	23.3	4.8	1.2	3.2	5.8	4.1	12.0	5.7
General	100.0	6.7	4.1	6.7	5.0	2.7	5.7	6.9

Source: Derived from Index of Industrial Production (Base: 1993–94=100) data reported in the *Economic Survey 2003–2004*.

the strongest growth and accounting for nearly four-fifths of the industrial output. Many agro-based industries such as Food Products, Cotton and Jute and other vegetable fibre textiles, Textile Products, and Leather and Leather Products witnessed negative growth. On the other hand, Machinery and Equipment, including Transport Equipment, as well as Paper and Paper Products exhibited growth in excess of 15 per cent. The other groups that grew at rates above the average growth rate for the Manufacturing sector as a whole included Beverages, Tobacco and Products, Basic Chemicals (excluding Petroleum and Coal) and Basic Metals and Alloys.

The Public Sector Enterprises: Enhanced Performance

Though the public sector enterprises (PSEs) form an important segment of industry, contributing significantly to industrial development in the country, the *Economic Survey 2003–04* continues with the policy introduced in the last *Survey*. It too does not have a separate section in the Industry chapter assessing the performance of the PSEs. Despite their growing productivity and profitability, the only aspect of PSEs considered relevant seems to be that of privatisation and the actual mechanism of disinvestment. This is indeed surprising, as the PSEs have performed extremely well over the past several years. The most recent data on the PSEs is from the *Public Enterprises Survey 2002–03* which reports that in 2002–03, of the 100 PSEs that had signed performance related Memoranda of Understanding (MoU) with the government, *45* were rated *excellent* and *26* as *very good.*

Despite their growing productivity and profitability, the only aspect of PSEs considered relevant seems to be that of privatisation and the actual mechanism of disinvestment.

Figure 1
Rising Public Sector Profitability

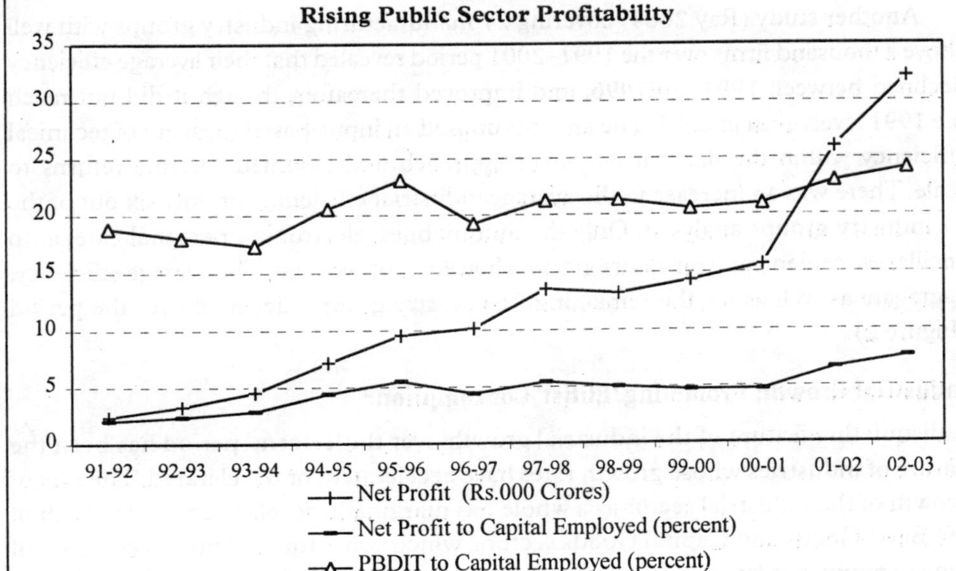

Besides fulfilling a number of objectives assigned to them, some of which impinge directly on their profitability, the PSEs as a whole earned a return on investment (RoI) of 17.4 per cent during the fiscal year 2002–03 and their turnover/operating income increased by 13.7 per cent over the previous year. They also reported an increase of 29.6 per cent in net profit before tax (PBT) and a growth of 12.7 per cent in profit before depreciation, interest, and taxes (PBDIT). The enhanced performance of the PSEs over the past decade may be seen from Figure 1 in terms of three financial indicators—Net Profit, Net Profit to Capital Employed ratio, and PBDIT to Capital Employed ratio.

Reforms and Efficiency in Indian Industry

The 'reformist' agenda for industry has neither succeeded in achieving the targeted growth rates for industry in the Eighth and the Ninth Five-Year Plans—the two Plans that were conceived and implemented within the first decade of the 'reform' period—nor in accelerating growth rates to levels above those prevailing in the immediate 'pre-reform' period. One of the key objectives of the Statement on Industrial Policy tabled in the Parliament on 24 July, 1991 was to maintain a sustained growth in productivity. The *Economic Survey 2002–03* states, 'the essence of the reform process has been the quest for efficiency, or the establishment of a framework of incentives whereby the highest possible value added is obtained using a given stock of labour and capital'. However, even in terms of this fundamental parameter, the 'reform' process does not seem to have achieved any major success.

A study (Das 2004) covering a wide range of industries that have been the beneficiaries of the trade and industrial policy changes of the 1980s and the 1990s concluded that there was no indication of any significant change in total factor productivity (TFP) growth following the liberalisation regime initiated in the early 1990s. The industries covered by the study included cotton textiles, textile products, leather and leather products, basic chemicals, rubber, plastics and petroleum products, basic metals, metal products, non-electrical machinery, electrical machinery, transport and equipment.

...'the essence of the reform process has been the quest for efficiency, or the establishment of a framework of incentives whereby the highest possible value added is obtained using a given stock of labour and capital'. However, even in terms of this fundamental parameter, the 'reform' process does not seem to have achieved any major success.

As in case of 1980s, much of the output growth in 1990s was due to factor accumulation rather than an increase in productivity levels. (Das 2004) The study, utilising the *Annual Survey of Industries* (ASI) data relating to 75 three-digit manufacturing industries, further concluded that the TFP growth in the 1990s was lower than in the 1980s and that 'productivity performance seemed to worsen as the pace of the trade reforms gathered momentum'.

Another study (Ray 2004) covering 27 manufacturing industry groups with well above a thousand firms over the 1991–2001 period revealed that their average efficiency declined between 1991 and1996, and improved thereafter, though it did not reach the 1991 levels even in 2001. The analysis utilised an input-based measure of technical efficiency within the data envelopment approach and assumed variable returns to scale. There was an increase in the average industrial efficiency for only six out of the 27 industry groups analysed. Only the automobiles, electronics, personal care, auto ancillaries, cement, and fertilisers groups showed improvement. The average efficiency, aggregate as well as for the remaining 21 industry groups, declined over the period (Figure 2).

Industrial Growth: Promoting 'Elitist' Consumption?

A disquieting feature of the industrial growth over the 'reform' period has been the nature of industries whose growth rates have accelerated, or decelerated. The rate of growth of the industrial sector as a whole has marginally decelerated. The growth of the Basic Goods and Capital Goods sectors, which constitute the productive base of the economy, has been relatively lower.

Figure 2
Average Industrial Efficiency Levels—1991 and 2001

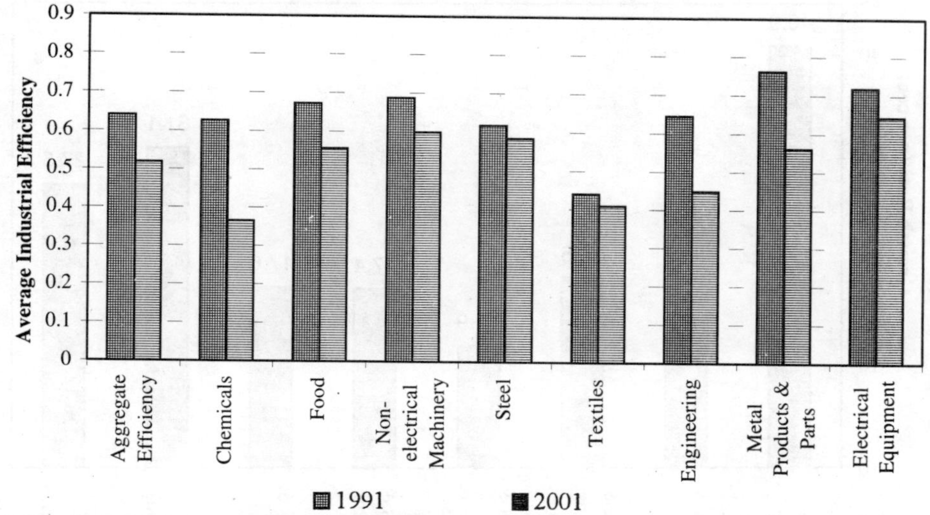

Source: From results in Ray (2004).

Only in the Intermediate Goods segment has there been a significant acceleration. The rate of growth in the Consumer Durables segment has also increased marginally.

The results of a more disaggregated analysis, utilising data from the *Handbook of Industrial Policy and Statistics* (Ministry of Commerce and Industry) and *Trends in Industrial Production* (Centre for Monitoring the Indian Economy), suggests that many industries producing goods for consumption by the higher economic strata of society have experienced rates of growth much higher than the average for the industrial sector as a whole. Production of cars—a conventional and established indicator of elitist consumption in a poor country—grew by an average of 14.6 per cent annually during the 'reform' period, which was two-and-a-half times the average growth rate of 5.76 per cent for industry as a whole (Figure 3).

Production of motorcycles, scooters etc., increased by nearly twice the industry average (11 per cent) while that of the colour televisions grew by nearly three times (17 per cent). Manufacture of refrigerators increased at 12.2 per cent, while that of telephones grew at 19.7 per cent.

Figure 3
Annual Average Growth Rates for Selected Industries 1991-92 to 2003-04

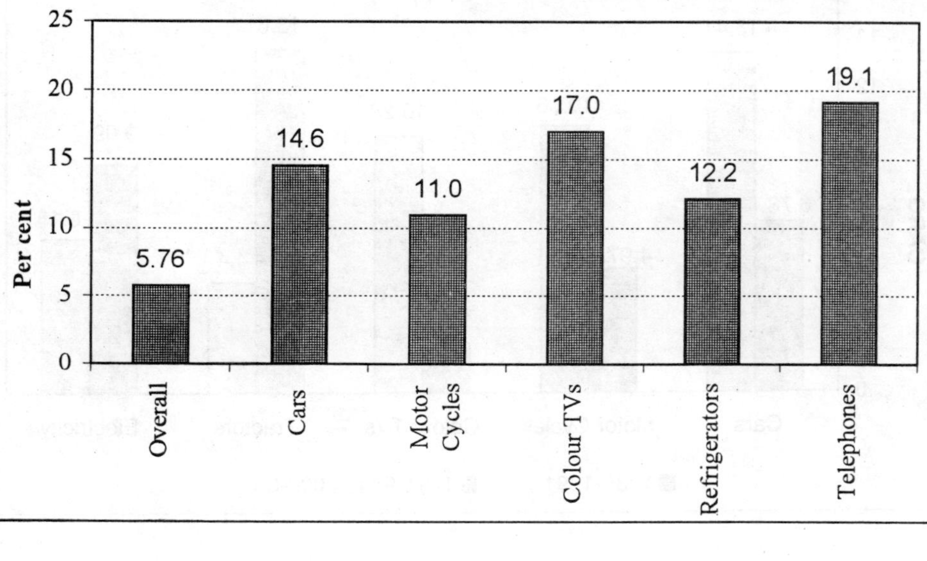

Another study covering 27 manufacturing industry groups with well above a thousand firms over the 1991–2001 period revealed that their average efficiency declined between 1991 and1996, and improved thereafter, though it did not reach the 1991 levels even in 2001.

The rate of growth of the industrial sector as a whole has marginally decelerated. The growth of the Basic Goods and Capital Goods sectors, which constitute the productive base of the economy, has been relatively lower.

Figure 4
Growth in Gross Value Added in Selected Consumer Durable Industries 1989–90 to 1997–98

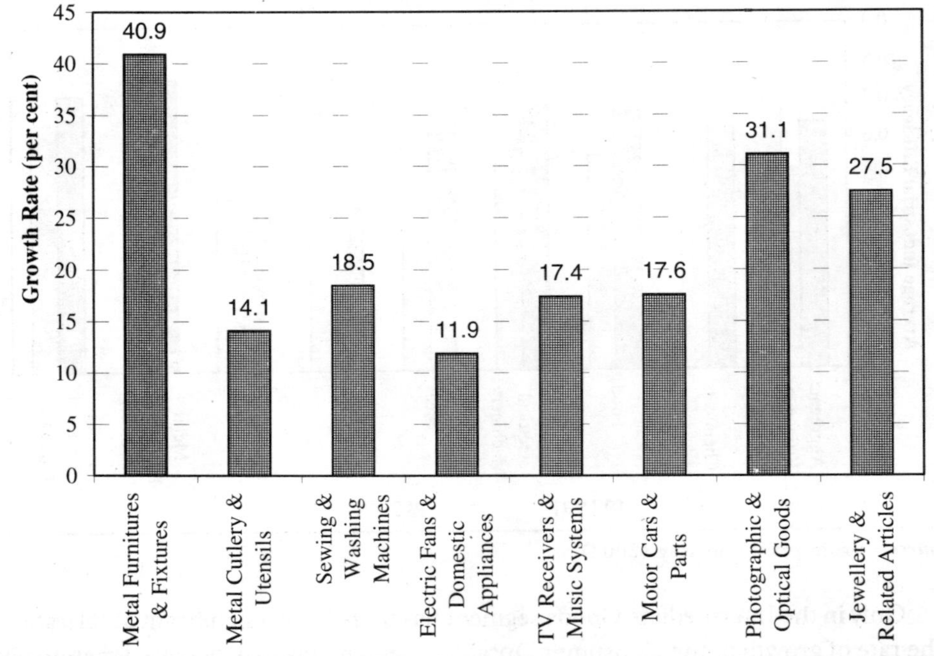

Source: From results in Ramaswamy 2002.

The high growth consumer durable industries have been those whose products are consumed by the richer sections of society.

The results of a study of 21 three-digit consumer durable industry groups based on ASI data (Ramaswamy 2002) are equally revealing (Figure 4). The growth rates in the figure have been determined from values of Gross Value Added (GVA) of the three-digit sectors deflated by using industry specific Wholesale Price Index (WPI) with 1981–82 as the base year. The high growth consumer durable industries have been those whose products are consumed by the richer sections of society.

Comparing compound annual rates of growth (CARG) of selected industries over the period 1986–1991 with the period 1991–2003 on the basis of the produced units in terminal years being the three-year averages reveals that the growth rate of production of cars nearly doubled compared with the preceding period while that of motorcycles, scooters etc. more than doubled (Figure 5). The rate of growth of the

The variations in the rates of growth among specific products and industries are significant and lend credence to the views expressed by many analysts that the 'reformist' agenda for industry has promoted a pattern of elitist consumption in the country.

Figure 5
Comparison of Growth rates for Selected Industries

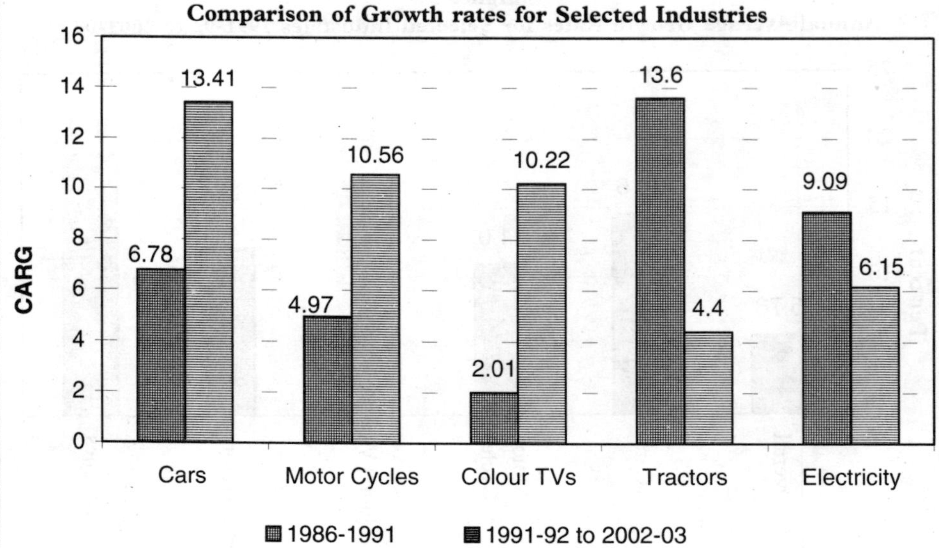

colour televisions increased by more than four times. Conversely, the growth rate of production of tractors declined in the 'reform' period to less than one-third of the preceding period while that of electricity generation dropped by nearly 30 per cent. Machine tools production, which had experienced low rates of growth for much of the 1990s, declined 1997 onwards with negative growth rates for the next four years (Indian Machine Tool Manufacturer's Association, as quoted in Nagraj 2003). The variations in the rates of growth among specific products and industries are significant and lend credence to the views expressed by many analysts that the 'reformist' agenda for industry has promoted a pattern of elitist consumption in the country.

Factor Shares

Besides the varied pace of growth experienced by different industries, the income distribution generated by this kind of industrial growth is as important a factor as the growth itself. The ASI provides data on factor shares as components of Net Value Added, which are Wages, Total Emoluments, Rents, Interest and Profits. The latest available ASI data relate to the year 2001–02. The movements in factor shares over the last twenty years may be seen from Figure 6. The share of workers' Emoluments in Net Value Added (shown as Wages in Figure 6) experienced a sharp decline, from 46.7 per cent in 1981–82, when it was roughly equal to the share accruing to Rents, Interest and Profits, to 29 per cent in 1996–97 and then stabilised at about 31 per cent over the next three years. The decline in the share of Emoluments was principally the result of a steep decline in the Wages component in Emoluments from 30.3 per cent of Net Value Added to 16.9 per cent in 1996–97.

Conversely, the share of Rents, Interest and Profits increased sharply from 47.1 per cent at the beginning of the period to 65 per cent in 1996–97, from where it declined to 61.8 per cent in 1999–2000. The share of Profits alone increased from a low of 11.6 per cent in 1987–88 to 36.5 per cent in 1996–97, from where it declined to 30.5 per cent in 1999–2000. The notable feature of the declining share of Wages and the increasing share of Rents, Interest and Profits is that it occurred primarily in the 'reform' decade of the 1990s, which strengthens the proposition that the 'reform' process redistributed income towards the high-income groups. In comparison, for most of the 1980s, the share of Emoluments in Net Value Added was actually higher than that accruing to Rents, Interest and Profits. The increase in the share of Emoluments to about 35 per cent, to which Wages contributed a rise of approximately 2 per cent in the first two years of the new millennium, is a development that needs to be actively encouraged by appropriate policies if industrial growth is to generate higher living standards for the mass of the population.

The decline in the share of Emoluments was principally the result of a steep decline in the Wages component in Emoluments from 30.3 per cent of Net Value Added to 16.9 per cent in 1996–97.

The increase in the share of Emoluments to about 35 per cent ...in the first two years of the new millennium, is a development that needs to be actively encouraged by appropriate policies if industrial growth is to generate higher living standards for the mass of the population.

Figure 6
Factor Shares in Net Value Added: 1981-82 to 2001-02

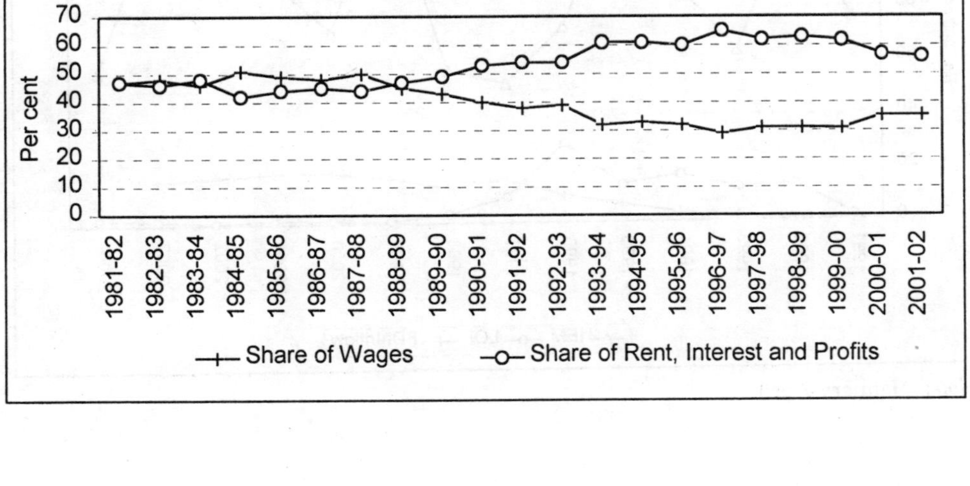

Prospects for Growth

The proposed investment in industry in terms of Industrial Entrepreneur Memorandum (IEM) at Rs. 118,612 crore for 2003 was well above that for the previous year at Rs. 91,291 crore but still below the peak of Rs. 128,892 crore in 1999 (Figure 7). IEMs between January and April, 2004 at Rs. 1,516 crore were above that for the corresponding period in 2003 (Rs. 1,141 crores), which may be indicative of an improving industrial investment climate. Industrial investment intentions filed through Letters of Intent (LOI) in 2003 at Rs. 1,395 crore, were more than double those for the previous year (Rs. 649 crore), but well below the high of Rs. 29,932 crore reached in 1996. Howeverforeign direct investment (FDI) inflows in 2003–04 at Rs. 16,409 crore were below those in 2002–03 by about Rs. 1,359 crore. (In Figure 7, the data for FDI inflows for the years 2002 and 2003 relate to the financial years 2002–03 and 2003–04 respectively). India's share in the global FDI inflows in the year 2002 was 0.5 per cent as compared with China's 8.1 per cent. It should be noted that the Reserve Bank of India (RBI) has adopted a new and broader definition of FDI and consequently it has revised the FDI data for the period beginning 2000–01. The amended definition includes three categories of capital flows: equity capital, reinvested earnings, and other direct capital. The earlier definition included only the equity capital. The adoption of a broader coverage system has resulted in revised estimates that are, on average, 70 per cent larger.

The *Economic Survey 2003–04* identifies five major constraints to industrial growth while suggesting that 'the outlook for Indian industry appears bright if these impediments are removed'. These constraints are:

(a) reservation for the small scale sector,

(b) high customs tariffs,

(c) rigidities in the labour laws acting as an impediment to building large firms and reaping the economies of scale and scope,

(d) frictions faced in the creation and closure of firms in response to normal competitive market dynamics, and

(e) distortions in the structure of indirect taxes, which affect resource allocation.

It should be noted that the *Survey* identifies the same five constraints as the primary causes inhibiting efficiency and productivity in Indian manufacturing.

India's share in the global FDI inflows in the year 2002 was 0.5 per cent as compared with China's 8.1 per cent.

Figure 7
IEMs, LOIs, and FDI Inflows

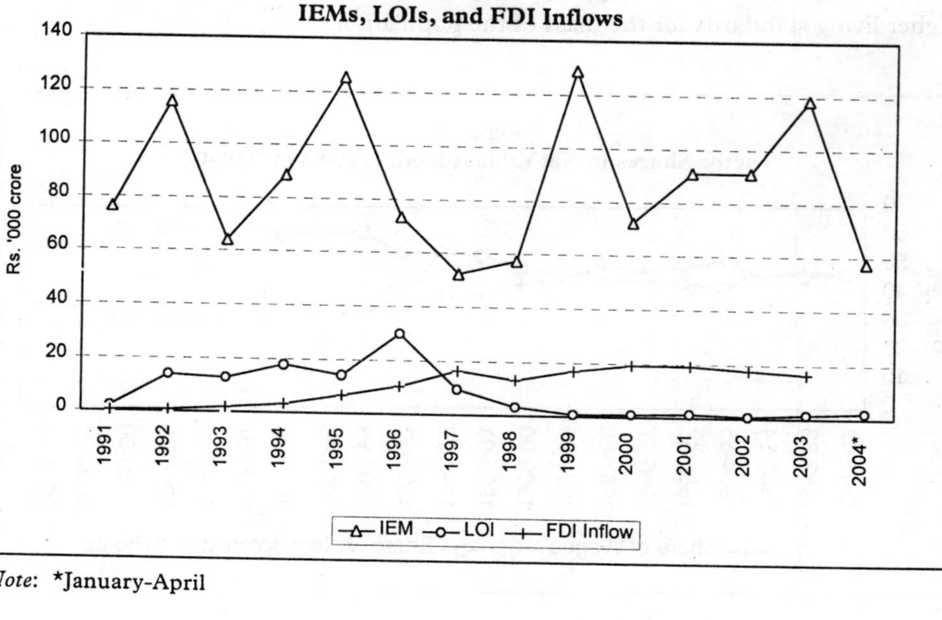

Note: *January-April

Incidentally, these factors also underlie the core of the policy changes recommended under the 'second-generation' reforms. It does indeed seem strange that the very failures of the 'first-generation' reforms are frequently utilised to justify strident demands for the 'second-generation' reforms.

A number of short and medium-term factors that stem from the macroeconomic stabilisation programme have been advanced as the direct trigger for the recessionary trend in Indian manufacturing. These factors are: import compression, fiscal contraction, and inflationary pressures. It has also been suggested that the tight monetary policy in 1995–96 might have had an adverse impact on industrial growth. More fundamental is the fact that the investment boom in fixed investment in the 1990s was not accompanied by a corresponding increase in production, which resulted in excess capacities and higher incremental capital-output ratios in many industries. This would seem to suggest that industrial performance is constrained by a lack of demand and not by policy-inhibited supply. Two features that have emerged within the economy in 1990s are:

(a) a weakening of the performance of the agriculture sector, and

(b) a declining public investment.

Both aspects are in fact interlinked, as there has been a lowering of the growth of public investment in agriculture, which has been only partially compensated by an increase in private investment. Given the considerable linkages between the agricultural and industrial sectors, indifferent performance by the former impacts adversely on the demand originating from the rural sector not only for consumer goods but also for capital, basic and intermediate goods. In addition, a large proportion of the reduction in the public expenditure is accounted for by a decline in the public investment, especially in infrastructure. This may be expected to affect investment demand unfavourably—both domestic and foreign—and also create bottlenecks for supply of several basic inputs such as power and transport. Besides these factors, the declining share of wages in the industrial value added and the 'elitist' nature of industries that have experienced high growth also contribute to restricting domestic demand. To enhance industrial performance on a sustained basis, these fundamental issues have to be addressed.

...the declining share of wages in the industrial value added and the 'elitist' nature of industries that have experienced high growth also contribute to restricting domestic demand. To enhance industrial performance on a sustained basis, these fundamental issues have to be addressed.

References

Das, Deb Kusum. 2004. 'Manufacturing Productivity under Varying Trade Regimes, 1980–2000,' *Economic and Political Weekly*, 31 January.

Government of India (GOI). 2003. *Economic Survey 2002–03*. New Delhi: Ministry of Finance.

Indian Machine Tool Manufacturer's Association. 2003. As quoted in R. Nagraj, 'Growth and Distribution in Indian Industry in the Nineties', *Economic and Political Weekly*, 30 August.

Ramaswamy, K.V. 2002. 'Economic Reforms, Industrial Structure and Performance: The Case of Consumer Durable Goods Industry in India', in Shuji Uchikawa (ed.), *Economic Reforms and Industrial Structure in India*. Delhi: Manohar.

Ray, Saon. 2004. 'MNEs Strategic Alliance and Efficiency of Firms: Emerging Trends', *Economic and Political Weekly*, 31 January.

Public Enterprises

R.K. Mishra

The performance of the Public Enterprises (PEs) was severely criticised by the National Democratic Alliance (NDA) government. It is high time that the performance of the PEs is evaluated to find the truth. This chapter presents the policy of the NDA government relating to the PEs and discusses the various aspects of their performance. It finally suggests a policy framework which could enable the PEs to further enhance their efficiency and be a superior fit with the Indian economy.

PE Policy of the NDA Government

The NDA government's policy on the PEs had a clear influence of the economic reforms that did not have the element of human face. The policy advocated winding up of the continuously loss making PEs, withdrawal of the state from non-strategic areas of economic activity and an embargo on setting up of new PEs. The policy showed a clear tilt towards the private sector and its progressive expansion. The key elements of this PE policy are reproduced below:

(i) Portfolio of public sector investments will be reviewed with a view to focus the public sector on strategic, high-tech and essential infrastructure. Whereas some reservation for the public sector is being retained, there would be no bar for area of exclusivity to be opened up to the private sector selectively. Similarly, the public sector will also be allowed entry in areas not reserved for it.

(ii) Public enterprises which are chronically sick and unlikely to be turned around will, for the formulation of revival/rehabilitation schemes, be referred to the Board for Industrial and Financial Reconstruction (BIFR), or other similar high-level institutions created for the purpose. A social security mechanism will be created to protect the interests of workers likely to be affected by such rehabilitation packages.

(iii) In order to raise resources and encourage wider public participation, a part of the government's shareholding in the public sector would be offered to mutual funds, financial institutions, general public and workers.

(iv) Boards of public sector companies would be made more professional and given greater powers.

(v) There will be a greater thrust on performance improvement through the Memoranda of Understanding (MOU) system through which management would be granted greater autonomy and will be held accountable. Technical expertise on the part of the government would be upgraded to make the MOU negotiations and implementation more effective.

(vi) To facilitate a fuller discussion on performance, the MOU signed between government and the public enterprises would be placed in Parliament. While focusing on major management issues, this would also help place matters on day-to-day operations of public enterprises in their correct perspective.

The NDA government's policy on the PEs had a clear influence of the economic reforms that did not have the element of human face.

The main objectives of the policy followed between July 1991 and April 2004 were stated to be:

- Bring down government equity in all non-strategic PEs to 26 per cent or lower, if necessary;
- Restructure and review potentially viable PEs;
- Close down that PEs which can not be revived; and
- Fully protect the interest of workers.

Have the PEs performed very inefficiently? Have they been a heavy burden on the national exchequer? Have they been a drain on Plan finances? Have they approached capital market to fund their expansion and operations, and deepened and widened the capital market? Have they carried out reforms with human face? The next section revolves around answering these questions and several other issues which could provide a holistic assessment of the performance of the PEs.

The capital employed in the PEs increased by about 300 per cent between 1992–93 and 2002–03.

Financial Performance of PEs

Table 1 provides the various financial aggregates of the central PEs (CPEs).

(i) The capital employed in the PEs increased by about 300 per cent between 1992–93 and 2002–03.

(ii) PEs obtained an increase of 400 per cent in cash profit between 1992–93 and 2002–03.

(iii) Their Profit before Interest and Tax (PBIT) to Capital Employed ratio was 14 per cent in 1992–93, which increased to 17.4 per cent in 2002–03.

(iv) Their quality of profit earning improved during this period. The profit of the profit making enterprises increased by 5.83 times, whereas the loss of the loss making enterprise increased by only 2.66 times.

Table 1

Trend Analysis of Performance Indicators of Central Public Enterprises

(Rs. in crore)

S.No	Particulars	92–93	93–94	94–95	95–96	96–97	97–98	98–99	99–00	00–01	01–02	02–03
1.	No. of operating Enterprises	239	240	241	239	236	236	235	232	234	230	227
2.	Capital employed (CE)	140110	159836	162451	173948	231178	249855	265093	302367	331401	390261	418758
3.	Profit before dep. Int. & tax (PBDIT)	25227	27707	33384	40161	44457	53062	56495	62212	69287	89619	100918
4.	Depreciation	9270	9151	10754	12574	13542	15856	16768	19942	20520	26362	27841
5.	Profit before int. & tax (PBIT)	15957	18556	22630	27587	30915	37206	39727	42270	48767	63257	73077
6.	Interest	10881	11901	12862	13966	15537	17990	20025	20233	23800	24958	23506
7.	Profit before tax	5076	6655	9768	13621	15378	19216	19702	22037	24967	38299	49571
8.	Tax provisions	1805	2110	2581	4047	5192	5634	6499	7706	9314	12254	17430
9.	Net profit	3271	4545	7187	9574	10186	13582	13203	14331	15653	26045	32141
10.	Profit of profit-making PEs	7384	9768	12070	14763	16125	20279	22508	24633	28494	36432	43085
11.	Loss of loss incurring PEs	4113	5223	4883	5188	5939	6697	9305	10302	12841	10387	10944
12.	PEs in profits	131	121	130	132	129	134	126	126	123	119	118
13.	PEs in losses	106	116	109	102	104	100	107	105	110	109	107
14.	PEs in no profit/loss	2	3	2	5	3	2	2	1	1	2	2
15.	Dividend	792	1028	1436	2205	2836	3609	4932	5455	8260	8067	13735
16.	Dividend tax					261	464	537	790	842	9	1712
17.	Retained profit	2479	3517	5751	7369	7089	9509	7734	8086	6551	17969	16694
	Financial Ratio (%)											
A	PBDIT to CE	18.0	17.3	20.6	23.1	19.2	21.2	21.3	20.5	20.9	23.0	24.10
B.	PBIT to CE	11.4	11.6	13.9	15.9	13.4	14.9	15.0	14.0	14.7	16.2	17.45
C	Dividend payout	24.2	22.6	20.0	23.0	27.8	26.6	37.4	38.1	52.8	31.0	42.73
	Turnover											

Source: Public Sector Survey 2002–03, Volume 1, Department of Public Enterprises, New Delhi, p. 24.

(v) Their Capital Employed to Turnover/Operating Income ratio was 105 per cent in 1992–93, which increased to 130 per cent in 2002–03.

(vi) Their Dividend Pay-out ratio increased from 24.2 per cent in 1992–93 to 42.7 per cent in 2002–03. The dividends repatriated registered a speculator increase of 17 times.

The dividend performance of the CPEs was very heartening, which can be seen from Table 2, which shows that not only the number of dividend declaring CPEs increased but the quantum of dividends declared also attained a new high in 2002–03.

The financial performance of the PEs is derided for their accumulated losses, which amounted to Rs. 4,735 crore in 2000–01, Rs. 6,002 crore in 2001–02, and Rs. 7,197 crore in 2002–03. While it is true that the PEs are carrying the burden of the past, it should be noted that their contribution to the exchequer during the same period not only wipes out this loss but also earns kudos for them for their financial contribution to the national economy. Table 3 depicts the dividends declared on the investment by the government, interest paid on debentures, and taxes paid by way of excise duty, custom duty, corporate tax, dividend tax, sales tax, and other duties and taxes.

The Value Added to Capital Employed ratio, as indicated in Table 4, reveals the efficiency of the manufacturing PEs. The manufacturing CPEs manifest an improvement in this ratio during the period 2001–02 to 2002–03. This ratio increased from 51.87 per cent in 2001–02 to 59.62 per cent in 2002–03. This increase very clearly reflects the enhancement in the conversion efficiency of the CPEs and also a promising trend for the future.

Their Profit before Interest and Tax (PBIT) to Capital Employed ratio was 14 per cent in 1992–93, which increased to 17.4 per cent in 2002–03.

Their Dividend Pay-out ratio increased from 24.2 per cent in 1992–93 to 42.7 per cent in 2002–03.

The dividend performance of the CPEs was very heartening...

Table 2
Dividend Declared by CPEs

S.No.	*Particulars*	*2002–03*	*2001–02*	*2000–01*
1.	Number of enterprises	81	82	84
2.	Dividend declared* (Rs. in crore)	13735	8068	8260

Note: *Includes the dividend declared on the share capital contribution of the government to the CPEs.

Source: Public Sector Survey 2002–03, Volume 1, Department of Public Enterprises, New Delhi.

Table 3
Contribution to Central Exchequer on Actual Basis

(Rs. in crore)

S.No.	*Particulars*	*2002–03*	*2001–02*	*2000–01*
1.	On investment by Central Govt. in PSUs			
	A Dividend	9507.48	5768.68	3492.38
	B Interest	1367.92	1950.01	1985.31
	Total (1)	10875.40	7718.69	5477.69
2.	Taxes & Duties			
	A Excise Duty	40000.10	30656.07	31411.04
	B Custom Duty	7344.81	8049.98	8645.88
	C Corporate Tax	18018.12	11620.89	10894.71
	D Dividend Tax	320.10	352.74	670.81
	E Sales Tax	4164.04	3410.43	3072.44
	Other duties and taxes	1203.91	1056.73	864.91
	Total (2)	71051.08	55146.84	55559.79
3.	Total contribution (1+2)	81926.48	62865.53	61037.48

Source: Public Sector Survey 2002–03, Volume 1, Department of Public Enterprises, New Delhi.

Table 4
Value Added to Capital Employed in CPEs

(Rs. in crore)

Year	*Value Added*	*Capital Employed*	*% of Value added to Capital Employed*
2001–02	106387.17	205100.35	51.87
2002–03	129706.85	217552.64	59.62

Source: Public Sector Survey 2002–03, Volume 1, Department of Public Enterprises, New Delhi.

The external sector has become an important component of the Indian economy. The export performance determines the role of this sector to a great extent. The CPEs registered increasing gains on the exports front. Table 5 shows the export earnings of the CPEs during the period 2000–01 to 2002–03.

PEs' Contribution to Plan Finance and Capital Market Development

The internal resources generated by the PEs contribute to financing of the five-year Plans. These resources also provide the wherewithal to the PEs for financing their working capital and expansion projects. The trend in the generation of internal resources, as shown by Table 6, indicates a sharp rise in the internal resource generated by the CPEs. The seventh and eighth Plans saw a quantum jump in the PEs' generation of internal resources. A superior profit earning was largely responsible for this quantum jump. Also, the government's insistence on finding more resources internally drove the CPEs to perform better on this count.

The composition of the PEs' internal resources underwent an appreciable change. In the pecking order, retained profits and depreciation occupied the place of prime importance and the deferred revenue expenditure and write-offs receded to the last position. This clearly shows a constant improvement in the quality of resource contribution by the CPEs to the Plan finances of India.

While it is true that the PEs are carrying the burden of the past, it should be noted that their contribution to the exchequer during the same period not only wipes out this loss but also earns kudos for them for their financial contribution to the national economy.

The manufacturing CPEs manifest an improvement in this ratio during the period 2001–02 to 2002–03.

The trend in the generation of internal resources indicates a sharp rise in the internal resource generated by the CPEs.

Table 5
Export Earnings

(Rs. in crore)

S.No.	*Particulars*	*2002–03*	*2001–02*	*2000–01*
1.	Export of goods on FOB basis	25499	17039	20606
2.	Royalty, know-how, professional and consultancy fee	147	132	117
3.	Interest and dividend	61	134	381
4.	Other income	1273	3582	3668
	Total	26980	20887	24772

Source: Public Sector Survey 2002–03, Volume 1, Department of Public Enterprises, New Delhi.

Table 6
Generation of Gross Internal Resources Between Third and Ninth Plans

(Rs. in crore)

Sl.No.	*Plan*	*Amount*
1.	III	287
2.	IV	1260
3.	V	3439
4.	VI	13768
5.	VII	37678
6.	VIII	101212
7.	IX	188782
8.	X (2002–03)	54160

Source: Public Sector Survey 2002–03, Volume 1, Department of Public Enterprises, New Delhi.

Table 7
Composition of Internal Resources Generated by CPEs

(Rs. in crore)

Year	*No. of enterprises Generating Gross Internal Resources*	*Details of Internal Resources*			
		Depreciation	*DRE Written off*	*Retained Profits*	*Total*
VIII Plan					
1992–93	146	7184.34	1198.71	6409.34	14792.39
1993–94	135	8013.27	287.18	8375.63	16676.08
1994–95	140	9717.72	488.79	9825.54	19992.05
1995–96	143	11777.35	461.53	11958.71	24197.59
1996–97	144	12826.77	298.99	12427.93	25553.69
Total VIII Plan		49519.45	2695.20	48997.15	101211.80
IX Plan					
1997–98	144	15279.67	288.61	15623.19	31191.47
1998–99	136	14410.76	285.38	16606.49	31302.63
1999–00	135	17520.62	246.69	18165.12	35932.43
2000–01	134	19363.85	343.79	18103.36	37811.00
2001–02	130	34360.90	255.24	27927.67	52543.81
Total IX Plan	128	90935.80	1419.71	96425.83	188781.34
X Plan					
2002–03	128	26475.48	620.53	27064.35	54160.36

Source: Public Sector Survey 2002–03, Volume 1, Department of Public Enterprises, New Delhi, p. 97.

The budget receipts from the PEs obtained by the government show that the PEs make a significant contribution to the annual budgets. In 2003–04, these receipts were revised upwards from Rs. 24,815 crore to Rs. 32,655 crore.

The budget receipts from the PEs obtained by the government show that the PEs make a significant contribution to the annual budgets. In 2003–04, these receipts were revised upwards from Rs. 24,815 crore to Rs. 32,655 crore. The budget estimate for receipts from the PEs during 2004–05 has been put at Rs. 20161 crore. The total Plan expenditure target for the year 2004–05 has been estimated at Rs. 145,590 crore. The Plan investments in the PEs have been estimated at Rs. 92,161 crore of which they themselves will have to organise Rs. 75,834 crore. The budgetary support to the CPEs has been restricted to Rs. 16,326 crore. Tables 8a and 8b show the budget receipts from the CPEs and the Plan investments there in.

...the Plan outlay is supported more by the extra-budgetary resources, which saw a phenomenal rise from 68,766 crore in the Eighth Plan (1992–93 to 1996–97) to Rs. 87,614 core in the Ninth Plan.

The PEs have contributed significantly to the Plan investments by constantly reducing their dependence on the budgetary support and increasing their reliance on the extra-budgetary resources. Table 9 shows that the Plan outlay is supported more by the extra-budgetary resources, which saw a phenomenal rise from 68,766 crore in the Eighth Plan (1992–93 to 1996–97) to Rs. 87,614 core in the Ninth Plan (1997–98 to 2001–2002). The performance of the CPEs continued to remain encouraging in 2002–03 and they increased their extra-budgetary resources to Rs. 21,017 crore. The extra-budgetary resources were raised from the capital market on the same conditions that apply to the private sector. A greater penetration of the CPEs in the capital market shows their greater acceptance among the investing public and institutions.

The diversification of the sources of finance by the CPEs has strengthened the capital market in India in terms of introduction of a variety of new financing instruments, larger trading and enhanced liquidity. The capital market has achieved a greater deepening and widening with the CPEs tapping it more and more. The investors' confidence has gone up and its erosion due to the malpractices indulged by private enterprises has been checked.

Table 8a
Budget Receipts from PEs*

(Rs. in crore)

Head	*Budget 2003–04*	*Revised 2003–04*	*Budget 2004–05*
Dividend from PEs	7,136.43	10,841.18	12,978.57
Other Investments			
Disinvestment of equity holding in PEs	1,3200.00	14,500.00	4000.00
Recovery of loans and advances from PEs, Statutory Bodies etc	4,478.45	7,314.03	3,183.00
Total	24,814.88	32,655.21	20,161.57

Note: *Does not include taxes paid by PEs, royalties from oil companies and licence fees paid by telecom PEs like BSNL & MTNL.

Source: Kaleidoscope 'Be it Left or Right: PSUs Continue to be Corner Stone of Plan Development', New Delhi, Vol.24: 3 August, 2004, p. 7.

Table 8b
Plan Investment and Resources in PEs

(Rs. in crore)

Head	*Budget 2003–04*	*Revised 2003–04*	*Budget 2004–05*
Total Plan Outlay	90878.18	84901.16	9216.00
(a) Equity	12661.26	13048.70	14194.40
(b) Loans	2475.91	2933.41	2038.20
Total Budget support	15137.17	15982.11	16326.98
(a) Internal Resources of PEs	–	36254.69	41930.44
(b) Bonds/Debentures	–	18022.24	21499.27
(c) ECB/SuppliesCredit	–	3655.83	4469.16
(d) Others	–	10986.29	7945.18
Total Resources of PEs	–	68919.05	75834.04

Source: Kaleidoscope, 'Be it Left or Right: PSUs Continue to be Corner Stone of Plan Development', New Delhi, Vol.24: 3 August, 2004, p. 8.

Table 9
Resource Mobilisation and Plan Investment by Central Public Sector Enterprises

(Rs. in crore)

Year	*Net Internal Resources*	*Extra Budgetary Resources*	*Budgetary Support*	*Plan Outlay*
VIII Plan				
1992–93	10081.30	11001.43	3443.66	24526.89
1993–94	9862.03	14743.93	4067.65	28673.61
1994–95	14932.00	13445.53	4379.59	32757.12
1995–96	16726.90	12674.02	3919.46	33320.38
1996–97	13157.81	16901.23	3644.37	33703.41
Total VIII Plan	64760.54	68766.14	19454.73	152981.41
IX Plan				
1997–98	15111.81	14912.25	3840.56	33864.62
1998–99	19294.95	12280.46	4250.32	35825.73
1999–00	13245.95	17700.37	4528.66	354745.98
2000–01	25046.96	18007.71	4472.09	47526.76
2001–02	25744.98	24713.19	4909.70	55367.87
Total IX Plan	98444.65	87613.98	22001.33	208059.96
X Plan				
2002–03	32858.83	21017.05	5313.91	59189.79

Source: Public Sector Survey 2002–03, Volume 1, Department of Public Enterprises, New Delhi, p. 98.

The diversification of the sources of finance by the CPEs has strengthened the capital market in India in terms of introduction of a variety of new financing instruments, larger trading and enhanced liquidity.

Table 10
Public Sector's Contribution in Total Industrial Production

Item	National Production (PSP)		Public Sector's Production (PSP)		PSP to NP(%)	
	1968–69	2002–03	1968–69	2002–03	1968–69	2002–03
Fuel (Million Tonnes) Coal	71.40	341.25	12.61	325.40	17.66	95.36
Lignite	3.98	26.02	3.98	26.02	100.00	100.00
Petroleum (Million Tonnes)						
Crude Oil	6.06	33.04	3.08	28.95	50.83	87.62
Natural Gas	NA	31.40	NA	25.99	NA	83.73
Refinery crude	16.55	112.56	8.09	74.76	48.88	66.42
Basic Metal Industries (MT)						
Finished Steel	4.58	33.63	2.55	10.97	55.68	32.62
Non Ferrous Metals (000 Tonnes)						
Alumiunium	125.3	689.19	Nil	244.71	Nil	35.51
Primary Lead	1.9	39.1	1.9	Nil	100.00	Nil
Zinc	17.0	235.5	13.7	Nil	80.59	Nil
Fertilisers (000 Tonnes)						
Nitrogenous	563	10562	401	2854	71.23	27.02
Phosphatic	213	3904	53.0	307	24.88	7.87

Source: Public Sector Survey 2002–03, Volume 1, Department of Public Enterprises, New Delhi.

Despite the industrial liberalisation manifested in the expansion of the private sector, public sectors' contribution in total industrial production continues to remain phenomenal.

PEs' Contribution to Development Efforts

Despite the industrial liberalisation manifested in the expansion of the private sector, public sectors' contribution in total industrial production continues to remain phenomenal. Table 10 shows the contribution of the public sector in the various sectors of industrial production.

While the CPEs have gone a long way in removing the spatial imbalance, the private sector has to do a lot more to catch up with the public sector.

The regional imbalances in economic development have always remained a complex problem for the policy makers. Unless the regional imbalances are minimised, the socio-economic and political integration of the country will remain just a pious wish. While the CPEs have gone a long way in removing the spatial imbalance, the private sector has to do a lot more to catch up with the public sector. Table 10 shows the state-wise distribution of gross block and employment created by the CPEs in India. Table 11 shows that even smaller states have benefited from the presence of the CPEs.

...the CPEs made an important contribution to the economic development of India.

The cost of production and the labour content in the value of production could be taken as important indicators from the point of view of the economic development. Viewed from this point, the gross block per employee could further throw some light in this regard. Table 12 shows that the CPEs made an important contribution to the economic development of India.

PEs' Social Contribution

...CPEs, their contribution to employment was quite impressive in sectors such as financial services and travel and tourism.

The PEs have been contributing significantly to the 'social side' of the economic development. Table 13 shows the percentage of women employed in the CPEs. Though women formed only 7 per cent of the total work force of the CPEs, their contribution to employment was quite impressive in sectors such as financial services and travel and tourism.

The share of the weaker sections of the society in employment is considered an important indicator of social development. The CPEs have done their bit very well in this regard. The present controversy about reservation of jobs for the weaker sections in the private sector, including the multinational corporations (MNCs), explains the position of the private sector and its apex associations in this regard. Table 14 shows that the representation of the weaker sections in the form of employment to the scheduled castes and scheduled tribes under the various categories of employment rose from 11.91 per cent as on 1 January 1971 to 27.42 per cent as on 1 January 2003.

The PEs are considered model employers. They recognise their responsibility towards the welfare of their employees. Housing has been considered one of the major contributing factors of employee's satisfaction, which in turn promotes better industrial climate resulting in high productivity. The CPEs have also taken lead in providing other essential community facilities such as health care, education, shopping, and recreation centers. Table 15 indicates the capital expenditure incurred on townships by the CPEs in relation to their gross fixed assets and gap between the gross expenditure and the receipts on township maintenance and social overheads between 2001 and 2003.

The average annual per capita emoluments in the CPEs show a constant increase at current prices.

The average annual per capita emoluments in the CPEs show a constant increase at current prices. The average annual per capita emolument increased from Rs. 56,508

Table 11
State-Wise Distribution of Gross Block and Employments

(Gross Block—Rs. in crore)/(Employment—Nos. in lakhs)

Sn	State/Union Territory	*As on 31.3.2003* Gross Block	*As on 31.3.2003* Employ-ment	*As on 31.3.2002* Gross Block	*As on 31.3.2002* Employ-ment	*% share as on 31.3.2003* Gross Block	*% share as on 31.3.2003* Employ-ment	*Ranking as on 31.3.2003* Gross Block	*Ranking as on 31.3.2003* Employ-ment
1.	Andhra Pradesh	40197.64	1.05	38172.40	1.11	7.65	5.61	2	7
2.	Arunachal Pradesh	1869.88	0.01	1759.98	0.01	0.36	0.08	24	29
3.	Assam	22677.71	0.60	21191.92	0.60	4.32	3.19	11	12
4.	Bihar	9858.49	0.19	8823.37	0.24	1.88	1.02	19	19
5.	Chhattisgarh	13402.97	1.06	11057.83	1.12	2.55	5.65	15	6
6.	Delhi	25755.17	0.85	24988.84	0.88	4.90	4.55	9	10
7.	Goa	366.41	0.03	315.49	0.03	0.07	0.17	29	26
8.	Gujarat	29284.45	0.47	34417.60	0.63	5.57	2.51	6	14
9.	Haryana	11028.62	0.22	9618.10	0.21	2.10	1.17	17	18
10.	Himachal Pradesh	14680.30	0.09	12326.18	0.10	2.79	0.48	13	21
11.	Jammu& Kashmir	10439.14	0.09	9705.10	0.09	1.99	0.50	18	20
12.	Jharkhand	19233.24	2.55	21415.19	2.77	3.66	13.66	12	2
13.	Karnataka	27040.17	0.91	18111.50	0.97	5.15	4.85	8	9
14.	Kerala	14547.84	0.48	13504.05	0.49	2.77	2.56	14	13
15.	Madhya Pradesh	23541.55	1.18	21870.83	1.24	4.48	6.33	10	4
16.	Maharashtra	91245.68	2.36	81322.39	2.43	17.37	12.60	1	3
17.	Manipur	940.25	0.01	877.15	0.06	0.18	0.08	27	30
18.	Mizoram	202.07	0.00	139.65	0.00	0.04	0.02	30	33
19.	Meghalaya	730.26	0.04	623.62	0.05	0.14	0.24	28	24
20.	Nagaland	1038.52	0.05	911.71	0.01	0.20	0.28	26	23
21.	Orissa	29936.36	0.71	27131.11	0.75	5.70	3.82	5	11
22.	Punjab	8254.42	0.29	7353.59	0.28	1.57	1.53	20	16
23.	Rajasthan	12807.88	0.32	13167.11	0.40	2.44	1.71	16	15
24.	Sikkim	1286.48	0.01	940.82	0.01	0.24	0.05	25	32
25.	Tamilnadu	37641.47	1.10	33956.63	1.10	7.17	5.89	3	5
26.	Tripura	2283.06	0.03	1316.58	0.02	0.43	0.17	22	25
27.	Uttar Pradesh	37160.64	0.94	33851.58	1.07	7.07	5.03	4	8
28.	Uttaranchal	7368.09	0.22	8074.36	0.24	1.40	1.18	21	17
29.	West Bengal	27834.04	2.70	26711.54	2.88	5.30	14.43	7	1
30.	Andaman & Nicobar Islands	180.75	0.02	161.81	0.02	0.03	0.11	31	28
31.	Chandigarh	85.87	0.01	89.32	0.01	0.02	0.06	32	31
32.	Pondicherry	70.34	0.02	73.63	0.03	0.01	0.13	33	27
33.	Others and Unallocated	2313.17	0.07	6416.26	0.04	0.44	0.37	23	22
	Total	525302.93	18.71	490397.24	19.92	100.00	100.00		

Source: Public Sector Survey 2002–03, Volume 1, Department of Public Enterprises, New Delhi.

in 1991–92 to Rs. 2,24,099 in 2002–03, an increase of about 400 per cent. The percentage increase in average annual emoluments was very high except for the year 2001–02 when it was negative. This increase was far higher than the growth in the general price level. Table 16 shows the employment and average annual emoluments in the CPEs.

Although, economic reforms have adversely affected the employment scenario in the CPEs, the social safety net extended by these enterprises has provided a great support to their employees. About 4.24 lakh employees availed of the Voluntary Retirement Scheme (VRS) till 31 March 2003. The government set up a National Renewal Fund in 1992, broadly to cover the expenses on the VRS and to provide counselling, retraining, and redeployment. Table 17 depicts the number of employees availing these facilities and the expenditure incurred on their extension.

the representation of the weaker sections in the form of employment to the scheduled castes and scheduled tribes under the various categories of employment rose from 11.91 per cent as on 1 January 1971 to 27.42 per cent as on 1 January 2003.

Public vs Private Sector Performance

Although the PEs are considered to be the engine of development in India, often their performance is compared with the private sector and adverse conclusions are drawn about them. However, many studies do not agree with such conclusion. A study of India's 100 best performing non-financial and non-banking companies shows that of the top 10 ranked companies, as many as 6 were from the public sector and only 4 were from the private enterprises. Importantly, the former were picked from a total of only 240 PEs whereas the latter were picked from a crowd of thousands, which included companies from the best-known private business houses, management groups, and MNCs. Even in terms of market capitalisation, which is highly depleted for the PEs because of the uncertainties created by losses and the talk of disinvestments and privatisation, 3of the top 10 companies and 8 of the top

Table 12
Total Employment, Gross Block, Cost of Production and Labour Content in Commodity Groups during 2002–03

S. No.	*Commodity Group*	*No. of Employees*	*Gross Block*	*Gross Block per employee in thousands*	*Cost of Production (Rs. in crore)*	*Labour content (Rs. in crore)*	*Labour content as % of cost of production*
1.	Enterprise Under construction	3280	14156.79	43160.95	0	0	0
2.	Steel	177593	37849.7	2131.26	22842.78	4587.49	20.08
3.	Minerals and Metals	38717	12852.48	3319.6	4866.13	864.5	17.77
4.	Coal and Lignite	516311	36636.83	70.59	21516.05	8574.03	39.85
5.	Power	51746	78254.09	15122.73	21150.17	1238.81	5.86
6.	Petroleum	117274	154699.3	13191.27	263792.6	4867.35	1.85
7.	Fertilisers	21172	9935.35	4692.68	10682.13	980.73	9.18
8.	Chemicals and Pharmaceuticals	15192	1345.95	885.96	1417.84	289.73	9.18
9.	Heavy Engineering	60314	4164.17	690.42	7913.58	1723	21.77
10.	Medium & Light Engineering	80297	4492.37	559.47	8359.86	1557.16	18.63
11.	Transportation Equipment	70336	3118.78	443.41	6792.05	1608.27	23.68
12.	Consumer Goods	11916	2939.1	2466.52	1900.06	260.74	13.72
13.	Agro based Industries	5711	122.03	213.68	160.97	65.64	40.78
14.	Textiles	89256	786.01	88.06	3580.11	1187.22	33.16
15.	Trading and Marketing Services	78034	2067.64	264.97	55263.75	1498.33	2.71
16.	Transportation Services	60668	26162.63	4312.43	16215.63	3348.35	20.65
17.	Contract and Construction Services	17987	4116.49	2288.59	2920.8	374	12.8
18.	Industrial Development and Tech Consul. Services	21296	22187.59	10418.67	4481.32	878.15	19.6
19.	Tourist Services	7705	257.26	33.89	436.62	126.64	28.98
20.	Financial Services	3294	710.35	2156.5	7004.54	143.7	2.05
21.	Telecommunication and IT services	420437	108342.7	2576.91	28033.56	7700.39	27.47
22.	Section 25 Co.	2149	105.36	490.27	158.91	54.87	34.53
	Grand Total	1870685	525302.9	2808.08	41928.62		

Source: Public Sector Survey 2002–03, Volume 1, Department of Public Enterprises, New Delhi.

Table 13
Cognate Group-Wise Women Employment during 2002–03

Sl. No	Cognate Group	Managerial & Supervisory	Non-Executive	Total	No. of Employees	Share of Women Employment in Total Employment
1.	Enterprises Under Construction	0	2	2	3280	0.06
2.	Steel	1028	8279	9307	177593	5.24
3.	Minerals & Metals	482	1997	2479	38717	6.40
4.	Coal and Lignite	2101	30172	32273	516311	6.25
5.	Power	1172	2263	3435	51746	6.63
6.	Petroleum	3475	3766	7241	117274	6.17
7.	Fertilisers	428	861	1289	21172	6.08
8.	Chemicals & Pharmaceuticals	137	480	617	15192	4.06
9.	Heavy Engineering	1143	1853	2996	60314	4.96
10.	Medium & Light Engineering	1926	10805	12731	80297	15.85
11.	Transportation Equipment	712	1910	2622	70336	3.72
12.	Consumer Goods	176	727	903	11916	7.57
13.	Agro Based Industries	13	210	223	5711	3.90
14.	Textiles	379	6271	6650	89256	7.45
15.	Trading and Marketing Services	459	3070	3529	78034	4.52
16.	Transportation Services	5084	4984	10068	60668	16.59
17.	Contract & Construction Services	248	450	698	17987	3.88
18.	Industrial Dev & Tech.Consul.Services	706	693	1399	21296	6.56
19.	Tourist Services	377	611	988	7705	12.82
20.	Financial Service	337	484	821	3294	24.92
21.	Telecommunications and Information Technology Services	3485	27282	30767	420437	7.31
22.	Section 25 Companies	95	219	314	2149	14.61
	Grand Total	23963	107389	131352	1870685	7.02

Source: Public Sector Survey 2002–03, Volume 1, Department of Public Enterprises, New Delhi.

20 were CPEs. The comparative shares of non-dividend declared companies in the two sectors were: CPEs 24 per cent, private sector 60 per cent. In terms of the position of top 50 corporates, the position of the CPEs was as follows:

A survey of 2,436 companies conducted by the Centre for Industrial and Economic Research shows that over 41 per cent of the CPEs had an earning per share (EPS) exceeding Rs. 10, against only about 16.5 per cent of the private sector comapnies. Nearly 32.7 per cent of private sector companies had registered none or negative EPS against only about 17 per cent in the case of the CPEs[5] Even in respect of Price to Earning (P/E) ratio, the CPEs faired better—while about 50 per cent of the private sector companies showed P/E ratios of less than one, only 19 per cent of the CPEs qualified for inclusion in this category. Similarly, while 88 per cent of the PEs recorded prices at or above par, the comparable proportion of private sector companies was only about 62 per cent.

About 4.24 lakh employees availed of the Voluntary Retirement Scheme (VRS) till 31 March 2003.

New Framework for PE Functioning

The government realises that the CPEs have a potential to perform much better. In terms of unlocking the value in their assets, the government will have to think innovatively. Liabilities management offers as much scope for economy as income

Table 14
Share of Weaker Sections in Total Employment in 2002–03

Group	*Total no. of employees*	*Representation of SCs/STs* SCs No.	% age	STs No.	% age
As On 1.1.1971 (Based on information furnished by about 85 enterprises)					
Group 'A'	31,311	163	0.52	53	0.17
Group 'B'	35,751	549	1.54	57	0.16
Group 'C'	3,51,347	19,302	5.59	4,519	1.29
Group 'D' (Safai Karamcharis)	5,551	4,547	81.75	77	1.39
Grand Total	5,53,180	45,187	8.17	12,386	2.24
As on 1.1.2003 (Based on information furnished by about 218 enterprises)					
Group 'A'	1,88,846	22,196	11.75	6577	3.48
Group 'B'	1,81,088	22,527	12.44	9335	5.15
Group 'C'	9,32,261	1,80,635	19.38	86,105	9.24
Group 'D'	3,30,803	71,030	21.47	36,487	11.03
Group 'D' (Safai Karamcharis)	18,880	17,529	92.84	583	3.09
Grand Total	16,51,878	3,13,917	19.00	1,39,087	8.42

Source: Public Sector Survey 2002–03, Volume 1, Department of Public Enterprises, New Delhi pp.174,176.

Table 15
Capital and Revenue Expenditure on Townships and Their Maintenance by CPEs

(Rs in crore)

As on	*Gross Block including Capital Work in Progress*	*Total Capital Expenditure on Townships*	*Percentage of col. 3 to col. 2*	*Gap between Gross Expenditure & Receipts*	
1	2	3	4	5	6 (3+6)
31.3.2001	411865	6572	1.60	3573.15	10145.15
31.3.2002	490397	6681	1.36	2933.15	9614.15
31.3.2003	525303	5771	1.10	2932.40	8703.4

Source: Public Sector Survey 2002–03, Volume 1, Department of Public Enterprises, New Delhi pp.193,195.

Table 16
Employment and Average Annual Emoluments

Year	*No. of employees (in lakhs)*	*Average annual per capital emoluments (Rs.)*	*% increase in average annual emoluments*
1991–92	21.79	56508	14.90
1992–93	21.53	64983	15.00
1993–94	20.70	72043	10.86
1994–95	20.62	82517	14.54
1995–96	20.52	106876	29.52
1996–97	20.08	110662	3.54
1997–98	19.59	129582	17.10
1998–99	19.00	138179	6.63
1999–00	18.06	168339	21.83
2000–01	17.40	219672	30.49
2001–02	19.92*	193554	(–)11.89
2002–03	18.71	224099	15.78

Note: *During the year 2001–02, BSNL has been included in the Survey.
Source: Public Sector Survey 2002–03, Volume 1, Department of Public Enterprises, New Delhi, p. 31.

A study of India's 100 best performing non-financial and non-banking companies shows that of the top 10 ranked companies, as many as 6 were from the public sector and only 4 were from the private enterprises.

Table 17
Employees Availing VRS Covered by NRF and Expenditure on VRS and NRF: 1992–93 to 1998–99

Year	*Budgetary allocation*	*Amount transferred to public account*	*Expenditure incurred on NRF*	*VRS*	*No. of VRS availees covered by NRF*
1992–93	*8.297	8.297	5.967	5.667	39.751
1993–94	#10.200	7.000	4.782	4.781	34.232
1994–95	2.000	1.000	2.519	2.508	16.206
1995–96	1.400	1.400	2.170	2.096	12.583
1996–97	1.500	1.500	1.956	1.880	6.980
1997–98	3.069	3.069	3.304	3.267	14.815
1998–99	4.013	4.013	3.773	3.721	4.482
Total	30.478	26.278	24.172	23.920	129.049

Note: *Includes Rs. 5 billion received from IBRD/IDA and # Includes Rs. 5 billion received from IDA.

Source: Government of India, Ministry of Industry.

Table 18
Top Fifty Corporates 2000–01

Parameter	*Number (%)*		*Share (%)*	
	Public Sector	*Private Sector*	*Public Sector*	*Private Sector*
Turnover	40	60	68	32
Assets	42	58	63	37
Market cap	24	76	18	82
Net profit	36	64	56	44
Taxes paid	38	62	64	36

Source: Mohnot, S.R., *Reinventing the Public Sector,* Centre for Industrial and Economic Research and Rajiv Gandhi Institute for Contemporary Studies, Sanskriti, New Delhi., 2003, p. 37.

and expense management. The government will have to formulate a new accountability relationship with these enterprises, limiting its role to discussions on profitability and corporate mission and goals. The Parliament will have to exercise the right of self-denial curtailing its freedom to discuss their performance through starred and unstarred questions, reports of the Committee on Public Undertakings, and debates. The Parliament will have to also amend 'Article 12' of the Indian Constitution. The Comptroller and Auditor General of India (CAGI) would be required to exclude these enterprises from the scope of its audit. These enterprises should become board-led ventures, which should create conditions for their alignment with the markets.

Conclusion

The PEs are an essential mechanism to spur economic growth and enhance it to the targeted rate of 8 per cent per annum. By any financial, economic, and social parameter, they could not be denied a place of pride in the country's development. On no performance parameter have the PEs given an unsatisfactory performance. As compared with the private sector enterprises, they have done better. However, in the new economic setting, these enterprises have to redefine their role, tasks, and strategies. The debate about the choice between the public or the private sector is meaningless. What the country needs today is an efficient public sector. The PEs could achieve this by internal and external reforms. Internally, systemic changes must be effected to bring about the vision-mission-goal clarity, strategise decision making, and tone up day-to-day operations. Externally, the government will have to formulate a policy regime which could enable these enterprises to align with the markets, provide level-playing field, and turn them into global players.

What the country needs today is an efficient public sector. The PEs could achieve this by internal and external reforms.

References

Economic Times. 2004. 'Privatisation Still Alive, but it ain't Kicking Now', Friday, 9 July.

Government of India (GOI). 2002. *Public Enterprises Survey 2001–02*. Vol. 1: 3–4. Department of Public Enterprises, New Delhi.

Government of India (GOI). 2003a. *Economic Survey 2002–03*. Ministry of Finance, New Delhi.

Government of India (GOI). 2003b. *Public Sector Survey 2002–03*, Vol. 1. Department of Public Enterprises, New Delhi.

Kaleidoscope. 2004. 'Be it Left or Right: PSUs Continue to be Corner Stone of Plan Development', Vol. 24, 3 August.

Mohnot, S.R. 2003. 'Reinventing the Public Sector', Centre for Industrial and Economic Research and Rajiv Gandhi Institute for Contemporary Studies, New Delhi: Sanskriti.

External Sector

Man Mohan Krishana and Pushpa Kumari

From the North-South summit at Cancun in 1974 to the WTO's Ministerial Conference, again at Cancun, in 2003, a lot of water has flown down the Ganges. In 1974, India was a leading spokesman and champion of the South. Many groupings such as the Non-aligned Movement (NAM) or the Group of 77, with a proactive lead role of India, were negotiating and bargaining with the developed countries at different international fora for the right of the poor countries. When the North-South dialogue in Cancun was proposed, India was the automatic choice for representing the South. Since the Uruguay Round of General Agreement on Tariffs and Trade (GATT), in which India chose to deliberately keep a low profile, India's leadership has been questioned by many developing countries. This has been particularly true for the post-1991 period, when Indian policy makers adopted the policies of liberalisation, privatisation, and globalisation (LPG), formulated on the basis of Washington Consensus.[1]

India chose the path of economic reforms without adequate discussion and analysis at home. The reasons they forwarded included:

- Growth rate of Indian economy was quite low.
- India was facing huge deficits in balance of trade, current account, and capital account.
- Controls and licensing policies of the government were hindering private investment and economic growth.
- Lack of competition from inside and outside had created monopolies and the consumer had become a hostage in the hands of corrupt and inefficient producers.
- The country's foreign exchange reserves were very low and exchange crises were imminent.
- PSUs were running in huge loses and straining India's public expenditure.

Many official reviews and documents have sought to tailor the facts regarding the performance of the economy to retrospectively justify the LPG. However, even on the external front, the cat is out of the bag and India's unjustified dependent status in the global economy remains intractable at least, as of now. In a similar vein, the *Economic Survey 2003–04* seeks to suggest that India has achieved external account viability with positive 'current account balance for the 3rd successive year. The capital account balance also continued to strengthen. The size of the capital account surplus during April-December 2003–04 was more than that for the full year of 2002–03'. The survey further points out that the foreign exchange (forex) reserves have been increasing throughout the period of economic reforms. In 1990-91, the reserves were rather low and could pay for imports of only five weeks and now they are sufficient enough to pay for imports of 21 months. In fact, they touched an all times high of US$ 118 billion in the year under review. The survey further claims that the

...India's unjustified dependent status in the global economy remains intractable at least, as of now.

1. Washington Consensus is the policy mix developed by economists of World Bank for economic revival of debt-ridden developing countries.

growth of Indian exports has been praiseworthy throughout the period of reforms, especially so in the later years of economic reforms. It projects that in the year 2003–04 the growth of exports will be 12.5 per cent. The reasons cited for such a high growth rate include:

- The US economy is poised to bounce back onto a high growth path in 2003–04 after three or four years of depression.
- Global economic activity is gaining momentum, although it still remains vulnerable to a relapse.
- Japanese economy will achieve its highest growth since 1996.

Thus India is expected to reap the benefits of integration with the global economy. Clearly, only external factors have been credited for the potential surge in exports. There is no mention of the role of domestic economy in boosting India's exports; or, for that matter, any policies that might build its intrinsic competitive strengths to support a high rate of growth of exports.

Continuing with external focus, the *Economic Survey 2003–04* cautions, 'The optimism about global trade growth can translate into reality only if the roadblocks encountered by the failed talks is Cancun are negotiated successfully through meaningful efforts by the international community'. Further, the Survey heaps praise on the performance of exports: 'Export growth in 2002–03 was broad based with both commodity groups and manufacturing groups… Major traditional exports like textiles, gems and jewellery, non-ferrous metal, chemicals and related products and handicrafts contributed bulk of such increase in manufacturing goods of exports'. A close scrutiny must be made in order to obtain a complete and non-distorted picture (Table1).

It can be seen from the above data that India's trade balance has remained negative throughout the period of economic reforms, and the provisional statistics shows that the deficit for 2003–04 would be around $ 19,000 million, nearly double the trade deficit India had at the start of the reforms. This indicates that even a 12.5 per cent growth in exports is not enough to reduce the size of trade deficit. This also suggests that during the period of reforms the growth in imports has been faster than the growth in exports. It shows how the G-7 countries have been able to increase the penetration of the Indian economy. Our narrow home market is not able to support full utilisation of domestic capacities and capacity utilisation is getting further reduced owing to liberalisation-led import spree. Easy and cheap imports are also hindering the industrial sector's opportunity to upgrade to value-added products, as often many industries are reduced to merely assembling imported components and inputs. India,

...India's trade balance has remained negative throughout the period of economic reforms, and the provisional statistics shows that the deficit for 2003–04 would be around $ 19,000 million, nearly double the trade deficit India had at the start of the reforms.

Table 1
Balance of Payment—Summary

(Figures in $ US Million)

Major heads/years	*1990–91*	*1995–96*	*2000–01*	*2001–02*	*2002–03*	*2003–04 (Apr-Dec)**
Exports	18477	34133	44894	44915	52512	43237
Imports	27915	48948	59264	57618	65422	58233
Balance of Trade	–9438	–14815	–14370	–12703	–12910	–14996
Invisibles	–243	10196	10780	13485	17047	18222
(of which) Private Transfer	2069	12387	12798	12125	14807	14494
Foreign Investment (Net)	103	5963	5862	6693	4555	10135
(of which) FDI	97	2651	3272	4741	3611	2513
FII	0	1926	1677	1436	342	7219
N R Deposits	1537	3350	2317	2754	2979	3502

Note: *Provisional
Source: *Economic Survey 2003-04*: 101.

described suggestively as an emerging market, has become a large and attractive market for the major trading countries.

As far as the balance of current account is concerned, it was negative throughout the 1990s though it has become marginally positive during the last three years. The government claims that this is due to the success of economic reforms. But, the fact of the matter is that in the net invisible income, the role of private transfers, mostly money sent home by the Indians working abroad, has been the single largest factor. In 1991, private transfers were nearly $ 2,069 million, which have increased to nearly $ 17,750 million in 2003–04—an increase of more than eight times! So the private transfers have more than offset the negative trade balance. Private transfers from expatriate Indians may increase further in the short run, as the global demand for trained Indian workers is currently on the rise. This trend may, however, not sustain for a variety of reasons. More importantly, this factor has nothing, yes, nothing to do with the opening up of the Indian economy; this trend began way back in the mid-1970s.

The most important reason is that migration rules are becoming tough in Europe and North America, the destinations for the Indian techie brigade and the local residents of these countries facing massive job cuts and downsizing are complaining against the inflow of manpower from the Asian countries. Another important reason is the coming back of the Middle East based semi-skilled and less skilled Indians due to unfriendly working conditions and the uncertain political climate of the region.

Liberalisation of markets, low tax rates, availability of officially sanctioned routes for tax evasion and free play to speculators in the form of derivatives trading have enticed foreign investment investors (FIIs), which are now calling the shots on the Indian bourses. (For details, see the chapter on stock markets.) The inflow of foreign direct investment (FDI) during this period amounted to about $ 4 billion. The FII inflows dollars and the expatriates' repatriations add up to about $ 17 billion. Thus, it is clear that the deficit in trade balance is considerably offset by repatriated dollars and the net capital account surplus is generated mainly with the help of non-earned, liability-creating FDI and FII inflows. These foreign flows have significant impact on Indian interest rates. Also, a great part of FDI has come for mergers and acquisitions of the existing Indian companies, which helps foreign companies to gain control of not only the Indian market but also the Indian exports. It means over a long period there will be considerable repatriation of India's export profits by the foreign companies that are investing in India.

Further, the investment from FIIs is not only short-term and volatile but also very risky. Less than ten years have passed since the world witnessed the infamous currency crisis in South East Asia, as a result of which five countries with booming economies suddenly found themselves facing a meltdown of their currencies because of an abrupt, large-scale withdrawal of FII dollars from their financial markets. Malaysia's prime minister, Mahatir Mohammad had then remarked, 'Alberto Moron should be treated as a criminal'. Alberto Moron was a big portfolio investor in Malaysian companies when the weather was fair and when some problems arose he withdrew his investment in a hurry. He was not alone in such opportunistic retreat. Generally, FIIs are fair weather friends and invest where they can earn huge amount of capital gains quickly. Their investment is not rooted to the ground in physical and human assets, but mostly in freely tradable securities; hence it is very easy for them to pull out their investment and walk away from any country. Theirs is hot money, which is very risky to boot. There is no way to know when and to what extent would an FII withdraw from a market. Of course, it is true that India has still not opted for full convertibility of its currency and e there are luckily certain restrictions on movement of foreign currency, which precludes any immediate likelihood of huge transfers of currency form India to elsewhere, yet the dangers posed by FIIs are

Liberalisation of markets, low tax rates, availability of officially sanctioned routes for tax evasion and free play to speculators in the form of derivatives trading have enticed foreign investment investors (FIIs), which are now calling the shots on the Indian bourses.

Table 2
Terms of Trade

Year	Export growth		Import growth		Terms of Trade	
	Volume	Unit Value	Volume	Unit value	Net	Income
1998-99	3.4	3.8	14.6	0.9	2.9	6.4
1999-00	15.5	-1.2	9.4	10.5	-10.5	3.3
00-01	23.9	3.3	-1.0	8.2	-4.5	18.3
01-02	3.7	-1.0	5.0	1.1	-2.1	1.5
02-03	21.7	0.3	9.5	10.7	-9.4	10.3

Source: DGCIS.

serious. There is nothing to be happy about in amassing foreign currency reserves in such non-sustainable ways. They are essentially a means for enabling India to facilitate imports, open up Indian market to MNCs, and provide a safe and lucrative market to international finance. A very important area of concern in external sector is that of the deterioration of the net barter terms of trade. The official *Economic Survey* does not even care to explain the full impact of this phenomenon.

Table 2 presents the growth rates of exports and imports and the terms of trade for the last five years. India's net barter terms of trade have been negative for the last four years. Net barter term of trade represent the price comparisons of exports per unit vis-a-vis imports per unit. If the net barter terms of trade are negative, it means the prices of commodities exported by India are falling in comparison to the prices of commodities that India imports. The explanation given by the official *Economic Survey* for this phenomenon is the continuous increase in prices of petroleum products. The prices of petroleum products are likely to remain high in the near future as crude oil prices have been very high of late, at the level of $ 45–50 per barrel, thanks mainly to the US occupation of Iraq. Therefore, the negative barter terms of trade are likely to continue if the explanation provided in the official *Economic Survey* is true. The impact of these negative terms of trade is likely to justify the theory of inmiserising growth, according to which a country ends up in a greater misery while trying to promote exports because of negative barter terms of trade. The fact of the matter is that the policies adopted by developed countries are such that in order to promote exports to the rich industrialised countries, the poor countries would compete with each other and end up exporting more commodities for less return. There are many ploys used by the developed countries to restrict export of value-added products from the developing countries and also to push their prices down; these include sanitary and phytosanitary measures, income support subsidies, the child labour prevention clause, and the environmental protection clause. Recently many American states have moved to restrict outsourcing. This has been done basically to create pressure on Indian IT companies to further lower their prices. The result would be that Indian companies would have to do much more for fewer dollars. Raul Prebisch and E.W. Singer in their well-known theory had clearly illustrated the impact of adverse net barter terms of trade on growth of less developed countries. This theory is now being put into practice by the rich countries.

...the negative barter terms of trade are likely to continue if the explanation provided in the official *Economic Survey* is true. ...a country ends up in a greater misery while trying to promote exports because of negative barter terms of trade.

The official *Economic Survey* claims that Indian exports in the income terms of trade have been positive throughout the last decade. Income terms of trade explain the importing capacity of a country. They are deduced by multiplying prices of exports per unit with total quantity of exports. Income terms of trade are positive in case of India because the growth in quantum of exports has exceeded the deterioration in terms of trade. But, in future export promotion measures are likely to bring negative results if net barter terms of trade remain negative. Moreover, the reasons the government has put forward for future export growth suggest a dependence on the American economy bouncing back from depression and the Japanese economy doing

Table 3
Commodity Structure of Exports of India, 1980–2000

(Percentage of Total Non-oil Exports)

Commodity group	*1980*	*1990*	*2000*
Group I: Primary Commodities Manufactures	40.9	26.6	18.9
Group II: Mainly based on labour and natural resources	38.5	51.1	52.6
Textiles	15.3	12.8	14.2
Clothing	7.9	14.9	14.5
Footwear, leather, and travel products	6.3	6.8	3.6
Wood and paper products	0.3	0.1	0.2
Paper, print and publishing	0.2	0.2	0.5
Non-metallic products	8.5	16.4	19.7
Group III: Low-technology intensive	5.7	4.8	6.6
Iron and steel	1.1	1.7	3.2
Fabricated metal products	2.9	2.0	2.5
Simple transport equipment	1.6	0.9	0.6
Ships and boats	0.0	0.2	0.2
Group IV: Medium-technology intensive	7.0	6.6	6.6
Rubber and plastic products	0.6	1.1	1.3
Non-electrical machinery	3.4	3.2	2.6
Electrical machinery (excluding semiconductors)	1.5	1.2	1.5
Road motor vehicles	1.6	1.1	1.2
Group V: High-technology intensive	5.1	9.3	11.7
Industrial chemicals	2.8	5.1	7.2
Pharmaceuticals	1.5	2.7	3.0
Computers and office equipment	0.0	0.6	0.4
Communication equipment and semicond.	0.2	0.4	0.4
Aircraft	0.0	0.0	0.1
Scientific instruments	0.6	0.4	0.6
Other manufactures	2.7	1.6	3.6

Source: UNCTAD, *Trade and Development Report,* 2003.

well this year. This means that the growth of Indian exports will last only as long as the conditions in the developed world continue to be favourable to India and all the developing nations abide by the World Trade Organisation (WTO) charter and remain solid followers of the agreement. This implies that India has to act according to the wishes of the developed countries, or suffer.

It is quite true that when a country opens up to trade with the major economic powers of the world, it also opens up to foreign economic pressures due to the asymmetric economic relationship. But the threats like the one mentioned above has a different connotation. Only sometimes back the European Union (EU) criticised the 'one country one vote' principle of WTO. It said that because of this principle the developing countries are able to stall the progress of WTO negotiations. The fact of the matter is that the developing countries are using this principle to stop their economic exploitation. Prior to WTO, all global economic and political institutions were based on the principle of power aristocracy where some countries could dictate terms. India, the one time leader of the developing nations, should take a lesson from such countries resisting the US and its allies in order to keep their interests, identity, and existence intact rather than surrendering their sovereignty.

...when a country opens up to trade with the major economic powers of the world, it also opens up to foreign economic pressures due to the asymmetric economic relationship.

Composition and Direction of Foreign Trade

The official claim of a wonderful export performance on the basis of exports' growth rate of 13.8 per cent during 2002 should be seen against the low growth rate of 2.3 per cent during 2001; or it should be compared with the 19.1 per cent growth rate of developing countries during 2002. If India's place in the world's exports is to be

Table 4
Direction of Exports

(Percentage shares)

Country Group	*1990-91*	*2000-01*	*2002-03*
OECD	53.7	52.7	50.0
of which EU	27.5	22.7	21.2
US	14.7	20.9	20.7
OPEC	5.6	10.9	13.1
Eastern Europe	17.9	2.4	1.8
Other LDCs	16.8	26.7	30.8
Others	6.2	7.3	4.2
Total	100.0	100.0	100.0

Source: Economic Survey 2003-04.

seen, then her share in world exports is a better index, which has been a lowly 0.8 per cent during 2002 and 2003 though it used to be 2 per cent at the time of Independence. China's share in global trade in 2003 was 5.9 per cent (*Economic Survey 2003–04* and *RBI Annual Report 2002–03*). The official claim that 'various policy initiatives taken by the government in the recent years for exporting products and market diversification have helped in improving export competitiveness' can also be analysed by using the United Nations Conference on Trade and Development (UNCTAD) data on commodity structure of exports (as per cent of total non-oil exports) for the years 1980, 1990, and 2000 and data on direction of exports for the years 1990–91, 2000–01, and 2002–03.

Table 3 shows that between 1980 and 2000 the share of primary commodities in total non-oil exports declined from 41 per cent to 19 per cent, and naturally the share of manufactures has gone up. The share of group II has increased from 39 per cent in 1980 to 53 per cent in 2000, whereas that of Group III saw a small increase, Group IV has actually declined and Group V has seen a good increase over the years. Disproportionate rise in exports based on labour and natural resources on one side and high technology on the other implies an unequal spread of technology across industries. Moreover, increased exports seemed to be highly concentrated in clothing, non-metallic mineral products, fabricated metal products, industrial chemicals and pharmaceuticals. The share of most of the other categories has either stagnated or fallen. Diversification of markets is generally considered an important element for sustaining export growth. Continued high dependence of Indian exports on the Organisation for Economic Cooperation and Development (OECD) markets is visible in Table 4. Though exports have started going to other markets, even greater efforts are required to bring about a change in direction, especially towards the South, which can make our trade really symmetrical and mutually beneficial.

If India's place in the world's exports is to be seen, then her share in world exports is a better index, which has been a lowly 0.8 per cent during 2002 and 2003 though it used to be 2 per cent at the time of Independence.

Continued high dependence of Indian exports on the Organisation for Economic Cooperation and Development (OECD) markets is visible.

Composition of imports[2] too needs due attention. During 2002–03, petroleum and oil (POL) imports now make about 29 per cent of the total import bill. During the 1987–90 period this percentage was 17.1 and during the 1992–97 period it was 23.9. This is a sure indication of our reduced energy security and dependence-fostering transport policy and industrial growth. Remarkably, during 1992–97, the share of imports of gold and silver in total imports was 7 per cent (8.7 per cent during April-Feb 2003–04) and the value of these imports at $ 4.3 billion ($ 6 million in 1991–92) was slightly less than the net FDI inflows of $ 4.6 billion. The expenditure on foreign travel by Indians was Rs. 16,761 crore during 2002–03 in comparison with merely Rs. 703 crore during 1990–91. If you consider the fact that nearly 5 million Indians travelled abroad in the period under review while only

2. Data used in the relevant description is taken from *Economic Survey 2003–04, and RBI, Report on Currency and Finance 2001–02.*

70,000 people declared annual taxable income in excess of Rs. 10 lakh, you can see who is benefiting from the prevalent external trade management.

India's exports financed about 86 per cent of the total imports during 2002–03; the deficit was covered by the surplus from invisibles, especially private transfers (15.8 per cent of total current receipts). Most of our imports are used for producing luxury and high-income goods that feed the growing inequality of income. Freer trade has become a means for supporting conspicuous consumption of high-income groups. Even most of the POL imports go for non-public automobiles costing between Rs. 2 lakh and Rs. 50 lakh.

Without an analysis of the earnings from and spending on the invisibles, our discussion of the country's external current account will remains incomplete. With the policy shift with regard to foreign capitalinflows—now weighed in favour of non-debt-creating inflows—the balance of payments appears to have been relieved of the debt repayment burden. But, the ratio of profits and dividend-exports (PD-X) happens to be very high. If an interest-exports (Int-X) ratio of between 12 and 20 per cent can make an economy a moderate debtor, India's PD-X ratio in the 13–15 per cent range in recent years (Table 5) is in no way low so far as the claim on the current receipts is concerned. Non-debt-creating inflows are preferred over debt-creating inflows because of former's risk-sharing and therefore viable nature. But

Table 5
Income Payment-Exports Ratio, 1990–2003, Select Years

(In Per cent)

Item	*1990–91*	*1997–98*	*1998–99*	*1999–00*	*2000–01*	*2001–02*	*2002–03*
Int/X	12.1	3.3	3.2	2.8	2.2	2.0	1.4
PD/X	10.6	11.3	13.3	12.1	14.9	14.7	13.3

Notes: Int/X stands for interest/exports, PD/X for profit-dividend/exports.
Source: Calculations are based on the data from *Economic survey 2003–04*.

Table 6
Export Intensity in Percentage of Foreign Investment Companies in India, 1990–2002

(In Per cent)

Items	*Average* 1990–91 to 2001–02	*Average* 1990–91 to 1996–97	*Average* 1997–98 to 2001–02	*2001–02*
Engineering	7.5	7.5	7.8	NA
Chemicals/Chemical Products	8.7	7.6	10.4	11.4
Tea Plantations	19.1	19.5	18.4	21.6
Trading/Whole Sale and Retail Trade	11.4	12.8	9.4	13.1
All TextilesRubber/ Plastic Products	35.1	33.8	44.4	NA
Food Products and Beverages	8.7	8.4	9.1	10.7
Machinery and Machine Tools	12.4	NA	12.4	11.6
Electrical Machinery and Apparatus	11.5	NA	11.5	13.7
Motor Vehicles and Other Transport	6.8	NA	6.8	10.3
Equipments	7.7	NA	7.7	7.6
Computer and Related Activities	14.3	NA	14.3	12.2
Total	8.9	8.2	10	11.2

Note: Exports referred to in this table pertain to foreign currency earnings through exports only.
NA : Not Available.
Source: RBI, *Report on Currency and Finance 2002-03*.

Most of our imports are used for producing luxury and high-income goods that feed the growing inequality of income. Freer trade has become a means for supporting conspicuous consumption of high-income groups.

the possibility of private viability co-existing with balance of payments non-viability cannot be ignored for a country like India, which has a high level of volatile FIIs inflows. This can also be seen from the low level of export-intensity of foreign companies over the years (Table 6). Except for few businesses like textiles and tea plantation, export intensity is less than 15 per cent.

India has been experiencing increasing current account surplus for the last two years (the current year is the third one in the row). Whereas, a policy of maintaining the current account deficit (CAD) of about 2 per cent has been considered by RBI quite sustainable for Indian economy. (RBI 2002: VII–18) The CAD-GDP ratio averaging just over 1 per cent in the 1990s and even showing a surplus during recent years could reflect the limited absorptive capacity of Indian economy and infrastructural and other bottlenecks in it, which hamper higher levels of investment and, hence, current and future rates of economic growth. (RBI 2002: VII–20)

References

Government of India (GOI). 2004. *Economic Survery 2003–04*. Ministry of Finance, New Delhi.
Reserve Bank of India (RBI). 2002. *Report on Currency and Finance, 2001–02*.
Reserve Bank of India (RBI). 2003. *Annual Report, 2002–03*.

But the possibility of private viability co-existing with balance of payments non-viability cannot be ignored for a country like India, which has a high level of volatile FIIs inflows.

Power Sector

Surinder Kumar

Power sector 'reforms' were initiated in India in 1991. After a series of 'reforms' for a decade, a very comprehensive Electricity Bill was introduced in the Parliament in 2001. It generated a lot of debate and discussion on various platforms and thereafter it was passed by the Parliament in May 2003. The Electricity Act 2003 came into force on 10 June 2003. The new Act has been characterised as 'distilled wisdom' of a series of commissioned international and national consultancy studies, seminars, and conferences held at the all India level during the last three years. It is further claimed to be the roadmap for the electricity industry, which will help hasten the pace of economic reforms in the country (Godbole 2003). The other set of opinions is that 'the entire legislation has been jetsamed, and inspired by external agencies—the World Bank, the Governments of the UK, the USA (through the DFID and the USAID), Multinational Corporations and Multinational accountancy and consultancy firms—new and untried laws and institutions have been 'imposed' on the nation. The various organs of the Indian State and the media have been reduced to mere hands that execute, not the heads that originate ideas and programmes'. (Rao 2003)

In this context, we propose to examine the status of the power sector, the new laws and subsequent institutional arrangements and their likely impact on various stakeholders.

...Multinational Corporations and Multinational accountancy and consultancy firms, and new and untried laws and institutions have been 'imposed' on the nation.

Performance of the Power Sector

The total installed power generating capacity in the utility sector as on 31 March 2004 was 1,12,058 MW. Of that, thermal power generation capacity was 77,968 MW or 69.6 per cent of the total capacity, hydroelectric (hydel) power 29,500.23 MW (26.3 per cent), nuclear 2,720 MW (2.4 per cent), and wind 1869.66 (1.7 per cent). Though the installed capacity of hydel power has increased by more than 6000 MW over the last three years, its share in the total electricity generation has remained about the same. In 2003–04, there was an increase in electricity generation by 4.5 per cent as compared to the previous year, but the major share of the increase was contributed by thermal power due to increase in its plant load factor (PLF) from 69.9 per cent to 72.7 per cent. The total installed capacity in non-utility sector was about 18,000 MW. The total energy generated during the year was 558.134 billion units (BUs) whereas the demand, according to the16th Annual Electric Power Survey, was for 597.95 Bus, which meant a shortage of more than nine per cent. Consumers continued to experience serious problems in terms of reliable access to electricity. (GOI 2004)

Transmission and distribution (T&D) losses (commercial losses) are reported to have increased from 21.8per cent in 1992–93 to 33.98 per cent in 2001–02. The increase in T&D losses was not necessarily due to deterioration in the T&D system; rather it was due to improvement in data collection as a result of strengthening of the metering system. However, the estimates of T&D losses remain an 'intelligent' guess because a significant part of supply continues to be unmetered. While T&D systems in some states have been strengthened, whereby losses are expected to have reduced, yet T&D losses in India remain at an unacceptable level by international standards.

...the estimates of T&D losses remain an 'intelligent' guess because a significant part of supply continues to be unmetered.

Financial performance of the state power sector, including the state electricity boards (SEBs), continues to be unsatisfactory. The rate of return (ROR) of the states on average capital base during 2003–04 was (–) 31 per cent as compared with the statutory provision to earn 3 per cent ROR. Gross subsidy for 2003–04 was Rs. 31,941 crore, which is expected to increase to Rs. 33,797 crore in 2004–05. During 2003–04, state governments paid a subvention of Rs. 11,427 crore to the state electricity undertakings *in lieu* of subsidised supply of electricity to various categories of consumers as per directions of the state governments. The net subsidy (deficit) left was Rs. 20,514 crore, which the SEBs were forced to bear. As a result, the SEBs have had to borrow heavily from various financial institutions.

In the last decade and a half, the government has been reluctant to invest more in the power sector and is leaving it to private sector initiative. In the Seventh Five Year Plan (1985–90), the share of Plan expenditure on power sector was 17.33 per cent, which was reduced in the Eighth Plan (1992–97) to 15.79 per cent. For the Ninth Plan (1997–2002), it is estimated to be about 13 per cent of the total Plan expenditure. Moreover, the actual investments were quite off the planned targets. In the Ninth Plan, the actual addition to generating capacity was 19,015 MW against the target of 40,245 MW, that is only 47.2 per cent of the target. In the central sector, the addition to power generation capacity was 4504 MW against the target of 11,909 MW, achievement of mere 37.8 per cent of the target, and in the state sector, the addition was 9,450 MW against the target of 10,748 MW, a much better 87.9 per cent achievement. The addition through independent power producers (IPPs) is woefully short of expectations. During the Eighth Plan, against the target of 2,810 MW the actual achievement was only about half of that at 1,430 MW. In the Ninth Plan, against the targeted capacity addition of 17,588 MW through private sector projects, the achievement was only 5,061 MW. (Planning Commission 2003) It is obvious from this analysis that the first phase of the reforms process, which relied on IPPs to add to the generating capacity, failed. The Enron episode clearly brought out that the IPP route was not viable.

One of the major initiatives in 2003–04 was the agreement signed by 26 state governments for one time settlement of the dues of the SEBs to the Central Public Sector Undertakings (CPSUs). After securitising the dues, 27 states issued bonds amounting to Rs. 28,993.95 crore. This mechanism has bailed the CPSUs out of their financial crises, but it has increased the debt servicing burden of the SEBs. Therefore, unless the efficiency of state power systems improves, leading to significant cost reductions, this mechanism appears to have only postponed the dooms day.

The net subsidy (deficit) left was Rs. 20,514 crore, which the SEBs were forced to bear. As a result, the SEBs have had to borrow heavily from various financial institutions.

unless the efficiency of state power systems improves, leading to significant cost reductions, this mechanism appears to have only postponed the dooms day.

Electricity Act 2003

The Electricity Act 2003 came into force with effect from June 10, 2003, though the section 121, related to the appellate tribunal, was kept in abeyance. The government has claimed that the objective of the new law is to provide a 'liberal' and 'progressive' framework for growth of the power sector by introducing competition in the areas of generation, transmission, and distribution of electricity. The government has also claiming that the interests of consumers will be protected and the goal of electricity supply to all regions will be achieved through this Act.

It is proposed to restructure SEBs completely. During the transitional period, the SEBs would be treated as transmission utilities that will be unbundled subsequently. Generation of power has been completely delicensed, except for large hydel projects, and captive power generation is now freely allowed. It allows open access to the transmission network (by paying wheeling charges) under regulatory supervision. Any generation company is now free to seek distribution license. The present blind system of cross-subsidisation will be slowly phased out and replaced by transparent and explicit subsidies to meet the social objectives prioritised by state governments. For rural and inaccessible areas stand alone systems involving generation and distribution are allowed without the requirement of license, and decentralised systems of local distribution is be allowed through Panchayats, user associations, co-operatives, or franchises.

As a follow-up of the Electricity Act 2003, the Central Electricity Regulatory Commission (CERC) has issued regulations for open access to inter-state transmission. The CERC has introduced availability-based tariff in all the five regions in the country. A commercial pricing mechanism known as the unscheduled energy interchange rate (UI rates) has been introduced. This is expected to help improve frequency. The UI mechanism is an alternative to formal trading. These steps are expected to take the market for electricity like other markets in the economy. The Act provides that the State Electricity Regulatory Commissions (SERCs) shall be guided by the principles and methodologies prescribed by the CERC. Future investment projects are to be structured through a tariff-based transparent competitive bidding process.

During the period of transition to a competitive bidding regime, tariff regulation, as far as practical, are to move away from the cost plus approach to regulated normative parameters. These tariff and investment norms are expected to provide incentives for improvements in the efficiency of the power sector and streamline its tariffs. Steps to improve efficiency have been laid down and the provisions to deal with pilferage of power have been made quite stringent. The Electricity Act, 2003 overrides all the existing laws governing the power sector.

The Ministry of Power has prepared an ambitious plan of adding 100,000 MW to the generating capacity during the period 2002–2012. During the Tenth Plan, the planned capacity addition is 45,000 MW. In that the shares of centre, states and the private Sector are to be 51 per cent, 16 per cent and 25 per cent, respectively, and about 7 per cent addition may be from renewable sources. Under the Mission 2012, the government has set a goal of 'Power to All by 2012'. It includes electrification of all villages by 2007 and all households by 2012. If our past experience is any guide, this is a very ambitious goal and may not be tenable. Despite many schemes, and attempts, made by the central and state governments, in the last 57 years of Independence, only 44 per cent of rural households could be electrified. The central government has introduced the Accelerated Power Development Reforms Programme (APDRP) to hurry up the expansion of electricity network in the country. The budgetary allocation for 2003–04 for APDRP was Rs. 3,500 crore. This programme provides fiscal support to state governments that undertake reforms programmes, and it is expected to bring down the aggregate technical and commercial (AT&C) losses of the SEBs from 50 per cent to 15 per cent.

These steps are expected to take the market for electricity like other markets in the economy.

Despite many schemes, and attempts, made by the central and state governments, in the last 57 years of Independence, only 44 per cent of rural households could be electrified.

Implications of the Electricity Act 2003

Though it may be premature to evaluate the impact of the Electricity Act 2003 on the power sector, we can speculate on the possibilities it will spawn. There will now be more players in the power generation, transmission, and distribution businesses, and captive generation will increase. Major bulk consumers, such as Railways, and generators like NTPC or IPPs would enter into direct contracts. The state owned utilities might be left with only the low-tariff and high-cost consumer market. This would adversely affect their financial health, requiring increased tariff rates or subsidisation.

Operationalisation of the Act is expected to segment power consumers into four broad categories with varying terms for buying electricity:

1. *Large consumers*: These consumers would be allowed to access power from new generating capacities at low cost or put up their own captive plants.

These consumers would be allowed to write off or reduce the burden of historical or stranded costs.

2. *Small urban consumers*: These consumers may remain under regulated monopolies for some more time. The private companies may see these urban consumers as captive consumers not just for distribution but also for their proposed generation plants, unless regulatory commissions force competitive bidding for new power plants whereby they may again become vertically integrated monopolies.
3. *Small rural consumers*: These consumers would also be under regulated monopolies. These consumers are the largest in number and would be bearing the largest brunt of tariff increase.
4. *Prospective rural consumers*: The still unconnected rural population will form this category of power consumers. Action plans for these prospective consumers are still in the making. There is urgency to clearly spell out what will be done for these consumers and what is expected through the rural electrification policies of the Ministry of Power.

Small rural consumers ...would also be under regulated monopolies. These consumers are the largest in number and would be bearing the largest brunt of tariff increase.

Conclusion

It is well known that free play of market forces always increases disparities between the rich and the poor. Polarisation of consumers on the basis of their purchasing power will marginalise the poor consumers who live predominantly in villages. The state will have to protect their interests, or areas of darkness in rural India will increase.

Polarisation of consumers on the basis of their purchasing power will marginalise the poor consumers who live predominantly in villages.

The 'reforms' imposed by external agencies like the World Bank, are bound to fail unless accompanied by the required political will and preparedness of the people. The experience of restructuring of the SEBs, into separate generation, transmission, and distribution companies in Haryana shows that unbundling by itself does not improve things; rather, it adds to the overhead costs, which lead to an increase in the tariff.

The 'reforms' imposed by external agencies like the World Bank, are bound to fail unless accompanied by the required political will and preparedness of the people.

The opposition to privatisation or deregulation of power distribution is rooted in the people' distrust of the private sector's priorities and the competence of local self-government bodies and non-government organisations (NGOs). It is a worrying possibility that the Electricity Act 2003 may provide the state a pretext to abdicate its social responsibilities when the results of decentralisation of power distribution are already there to see.

Though the central and state regulatory commissions have been able to identify some of the major areas of weaknesses, ad-hocism, and arbitrariness in the functioning of SEBs and other government-owned power companies and the Electricity Act 2003 provides very broad and flexible alternatives implementation of the corrective measures will have to be based on proper assessment of the ground realities.

There may be a need to review the Act to ensure that the role of central planning is not diluted too much. The critical significance of central planning was demonstrated in the case of the Enron project, which was allowed to be established without financial clearance from the Central Electricity Authority (CEA). Then, there is a danger that public monopolies may now be replaced by private monopolies, which may prove even more harmful. Also, there may be further encouragement for setting up small, inefficient captive power plants. Without central planning, country-wide optimisation of generation and transmission of power may be adversely affected.

References

Rao, K. Ashok. 2003. Transform India Group, October. Mimeo.

Government of India (GOI). 2004. *Economic Survey 2003–04*, New Delhi: Ministry of Finance.

Godbole. 2003. *Economic and Political Weekly*. 27 September.

Stock Market

K.S. Chalapati Rao

The Indian stock market experienced a major change in fortunes during 2003–04. From 3081 points on 1 April 2003, the 30-share Bombay Stock Exchange (BSE) Sensitive Index (Sensex), the bell-weather of the Indian stock market, recorded strong and almost sustained increase until it reached an all-time high of 6,250 points in 9 January 2004. Indeed, in about five weeks during December 2003 and 9 January 2004, the Sensex jumped by more than 20 per cent. The index ended the financial year on 5,591 points.

This boom contributed to the 'feel good' factor and launching of the 'India Shining' campaign by the ruling NDA coalition as a precursor to its election preparations. Thanks to the boom, the market value (market capitalisation) of the companies listed on the BSE more than doubled, from Rs. 5,72,000 crore in March 2003 to 12,01,000 crore at the end of March 2004. Many reasons have been advanced to explain this bull run. Apart from the reported healthy growth of the economy in general and improved performance of the large Indian companies in particular, a decisive factor has been the heavy inflow of funds from foreign institutional investors (FIIs) into the Indian stock market. Net FII inflows, comprising both debt and equity, rose dramatically from Rs. 2,822 crore in 2002–03 to Rs. 48,968 crore in 2003–04.

The stock market is a mechanism of disintermediation to build a direct channel between entrepreneurs and savers (individual investors). Seen in this context, the share of Indian public in the listed companies' equity works out to only 13 per cent. Even the share of mutual funds (MFs), which are supposed to act as vehicles for investment by individual investors, was very little in the increased wealth. The two put together claimed a share smaller than that of FIIs.

Role of FIIs and the Place of Indian Public

To gain some insights into the changes the FII inflows brought about in the shareholding of individual Indian investors and sharing of the market gains, we have examined the data of 2,550 stock exchange listed companies for which we could obtain broad ownership details and other related information at the end of March in 2003 and 2004. While the share of promote:s in this newly created 'wealth' was a staggering 41 per cent, that of FIIs was almost half of that at 19 per cent (Table 1). Together, the two gained to the extent of three-fifths of the total appreciation in stock prices. Since the category 'Others' includes, apart from others, holders of the Global Depository Shares (GDS)/American Depository Receipts (ADRs), non-resident Indians (NRIs), and foreign companies; and promoters' shareholding is

Table 1
Share of Different Categories of Investors in Increased Market Capitalisation between 31 March, 2003 and 31 March, 2004 in Top Companies

Type of Investor	*Share in Increased Market Capitalisation (%)*	*Including Govt. Companies*
Promoters$	41.05	54.40
FIIs	19.57	15.71
Indian Public	13.20	10.12
GDR/ADR, NRIs, etc.#	10.84	9.20
Banks & FIs	8.16	4.86
Private Corporate Bodies	3.85	2.99
Mutual Funds	3.33	2.72
Total	100.00	100.00

Notes: $ Including persons acting in concert.
Includes ADR/GDS, NRIs/OCBs, shares in transit, shares held by non-promoter directors, etc.

generally under-reported by companies, this could be their minimum share. The stock market is a mechanism of disintermediation to build a direct channel between entrepreneurs and savers (individual investors). Seen in this context, the share of Indian public in the listed companies' equity works out to only 13 per cent. Even the share of mutual funds (MFs), which are supposed to act as vehicles for investment by individual investors, was very little in the increased wealth. The two put together claimed a share smaller than that of FIIs.

Not only that, the number of shares held by the Indian public came down drastically in quite a few companies. This happened with MFs also. Of particular significance is the fact that the number of shares held by individual investors declined in companies whose market capitalisation gained the maximum. At the same time, their holdings increased in the companies that were losing market capitalisation (See Table 2). The experience of FIIs was exactly the opposite. It is difficult to say at what stage did the changes take place and to what extent did individual investors, who had to suffer a long bear phase till then, make their exit taking advantage of a spurt in prices to minimise losses or net some gains. They could also have been trapped in some worthless stocks hoping for a bonanza similar to that of the year 2000 would get repeated. They could also have made their exit during share buybacks by companies. Or, is it that they were focusing on fewer and better stocks? They probably did not have an exit route in the losing companies, as their stocks continued to be illiquid. Foreign investors, having created the boom, must now be sitting pretty on huge capital gains.

Whatever be the causes or stages of their exit from a number of large companies, the Indian public held fewer shares in such companies at the end of the financial year 2003–04 (Table 3). In contrast, in most of these companies, the FIIs increased their holdings. Moreover, at the end of the year, Indian public held fewer shares in a good number of large companies compared with FIIs. If the entire foreign holding, comprising shares of foreign parents/partners, NRIs, ADRs/GDS, etc. is taken together, the percentage holding of Indian public would turn out to be even lower. For instance, while about half of Infosys' shares are held abroad, more than three-fourths of the shares of Housing Development Finance Corporation (HDFC) are owned by foreign entities. Similar is the case with ICICI Bank. The share of the foreign investors is even higher in the multinationals' Indian subsidiaries such as Nestle India and Hindustan Lever (HLL). In Oil & Natural Gas Corporation (ONGC) and GAIL Ltd (formerly Gas Authority of India Ltd.), two government companies, which issued shares to the public early this year, foreign shareholding far exceeds the local individual investors. Indeed, the lower share of Indian public

...the number of shares held by the Indian public came down drastically in quite a few companies.

If the entire foreign holding, comprising shares of foreign parents/partners, NRIs, ADRs/GDS, etc. is taken together, the percentage holding of Indian public would turn out to be even lower.

Table 2

Change in the Number of Shares held by Indian Public and FIIs according to the extent of change in Market Capitalisation between 31 March 2003 and 31 March 2004 in Top Companies

Change in Market Capitalisation	*No. of Companies*	*Increase (%) in the No. of Shares held by**	
		Indian Public	*FIIs*
Decline	405	17.95	–58.22
No Change	447	1.25	26.84
up to 25 per cent	240	1.48	35.03
25–50 per cent	248	5.06	31.22
50–100 per cent	411	–1.40	36.89
100–200 per cent	429	2.57	69.02
200–300 per cent	179	1.82	79.31
more than 300 per cent	191	– 0.82	189.81
All Companies	2550	2.95	58.21

Note: * Taking into consideration share splits and consolidations but not bonus issues.

Table 3

Change in the Number of Equity Shares held by FIIs and Indian Public between 31 March 2003 and 31 March 2004 in Top Companies[#]

	Company Name	*Increase (%) in the No. of Shares held by**		*Share (%) in Total Equity as on March 31, 2004*		
		Indian Public	*FIIs' Share*	*Indian Public*	*FIIs' Share*	*Total Foreign Holding@*
	Government Cos./ PS Banks					
1.	Container Corpn. of India Ltd.	–51.94	33.47	1.90	26.00	26.08
2.	*Mahanagar Telephone Nigam Ltd.*	–14.41	9.32	1.84	15.75	23.45
3.	*Bharat Heavy Electricals Ltd.*	–25.63	21.57	0.96	21.00	21.03
4.	*Hindustan Petroleum Corpn. Ltd.*	–17.73	93.59	6.57	19.70	20.03
5.	*State Bank of India*	–11.24	0.23	6.90	11.46	19.39
6.	Bank of Baroda	–34.00	189.13	7.73	16.98	17.99
7.	GAIL (India) Ltd.	476.14	451.00	6.31	10.86	17.82
8.	Bharat Petroleum Corpn. Ltd.	–29.88	49.85	3.15	15.30	15.37
9.	Oriental Bank of Commerce	–46.84	693.52	7.97	15.04	15.10
10.	Punjab National Bank	–46.16	23.48	4.64	5.51	12.88
11.	Canara Bank	–27.17	616.17	9.56	11.76	11.83
12.	*Oil & Natural Gas Corpn. Ltd.*	195.94	1235.08	3.54	6.09	6.18
13.	National Aluminium Co. Ltd.	–17.03	175.70	1.39	2.45	2.52
14.	Steel Authority of India Ltd.	20.89	56.90	4.43	1.58	1.69
15.	Indian Oil Corpn. Ltd.	41.81	841.62	3.50	1.04	1.05
16.	Mangalore Refinery & Petrochem Ltd.	0.66	1011.55	9.62	0.02	0.77
17.	Neyveli Lignite Corpn. Ltd.	57.47	88.28	1.70	0.33	0.36
	Non-Government Cos./Pvt. Banks					
1.	*Housing Development Finance Corp. Ltd. (HDFC)*	–10.21	20.60	13.81	61.55	76.94
2.	*ICICI Bank Ltd.*	–18.27	22.30	7.39	46.71	72.79
3.	Nestle India Ltd.	–5.88	–16.31	19.28	6.72	68.94
4.	Hindustan Lever Ltd.	–4.59	5.84	20.27	13.09	64.95
5.	Motor Industries Co. Ltd.	–2.81	$	10.65	2.37	63.46
6.	*Satyam Computer Services Ltd.*	–28.08	19.80	6.06	51.27	63.28
7.	*Zee Telefilms Ltd.*	–37.57	31.15	6.13	34.93	59.71
8.	Glaxosmithkline Pharmaceuticals Ltd.	–13.41	269.02	19.79	9.76	58.80
9.	*ITC Ltd.*	–11.31	53.21	12.41	14.73	51.75
10.	*Infosys Technologies Ltd.*	–14.31	7.40	9.02	41.82	50.45
11.	*Hero Honda Motors Ltd.*	–22.02	6.85	11.57	24.07	50.33
12.	*Dr. Reddy'S Laboratories Ltd.*	–10.90	–13.59	12.18	20.86	50.17
13.	*Bharti Tele-Ventures Ltd.*	–25.00	72.07	1.03	9.24	47.70
14.	*HDFC Bank Ltd.*	–10.59	16.92	15.27	26.93	46.15
15.	*Cipla Ltd.*	–8.18	91.40	26.89	15.82	41.47
16.	*Hindalco Industries Ltd.*	–27.87	63.39	10.70	19.03	41.13
17.	*Tata Motors Ltd.*	–11.24	81.11	12.69	23.36	39.09
18.	*Gujarat Ambuja Cements Ltd.*	–2.48	55.39	13.14	21.70	37.19
19.	Mahindra & Mahindra Ltd.	–29.90	198.78	11.02	21.99	36.17
20.	*Grasim Industries Ltd.*	–19.85	40.44	16.25	19.82	34.78
21.	*Ranbaxy Laboratories Ltd.*	–9.60	0.46	18.72	22.69	32.98
22.	HCL Technologies Ltd.	–24.13	173.75	3.57	9.53	31.14
23.	*Reliance Industries Ltd.*	–21.38	54.48	13.60	22.63	29.62
24.	Associated Cement Cos. Ltd.	–33.90	25.74	22.63	22.83	26.70
25.	*Bajaj Auto Ltd.*	–7.67	38.04	28.42	17.15	22.32
26.	*Reliance Energy Ltd.*	–23.10	1624.31	6.62	12.98	21.39
27.	Larsen & Toubro Ltd.	–28.37	339.08	22.27	14.86	20.91
28.	Indian Petrochemicals Corpn. Ltd.	66.23	1649.18	14.79	18.98	19.48
29.	Sun Pharmaceutical Inds. Ltd.	–9.92	7.74	7.32	14.34	14.40
30.	Videsh Sanchar Nigam Ltd.	–41.96	–47.82	3.47	1.01	13.97
31.	*Tata Power Co. Ltd.*	–9.81	135.56	25.79	11.52	13.85
32.	*Tata Iron & Steel Co. Ltd.*	–12.12	180.46	28.11	13.31	13.68
33.	*Wipro Ltd.*	–5.91	47.92	6.63	3.91	3.74

Note: Names of companies comprising Sensex have been italicised.

\# Based on the market capitalisation as on 31 March 2004. Excludes Maruti Udyog Ltd which was not listed earlier and which is now part of the Sensex.

* Taking into consideration share splits and consolidations but not bonus issues.

@ Includes apart from FIIs, foreign parent/collaborator, foreign companies, ADR/GDS, NRIs/OCBs, etc.

$ There was no FII shareholding in March 2003.

Table 4

FII Category-wise Net Investment

FII Category	Net Investment (Rs in Cr.)	Share in Total (%)
Mutual Funds	20,449	28
Investment Companies	10,918	15
Private Companies	8,990	12
Investment Adviser	4,137	6
Pension Fund	3,116	4
Investment Trust	2,981	4
Government and Multilateral Agencies	2,975	4
Public Companies	2,768	4
Banks	1,116	2
Investment Fund & Investment Management Cos.	1,157	2
Unit Trust	993	2
Insurance Companies & Endowment Funds	527	1
Others	12,838	16
Total	72,965	100

Source: SEBI Press Release dated October 30, 2003. PR No. 264/2003.

...it is obvious that the market has become a domain of the promoters and foreign investors, with the local individual investors playing only a supporting cast. Back of the envelope calculations show that the dividend outgo on account of all types of foreign investors could be anywhere between 25 and 30 per cent of the dividends declared by the listed private sector companies.

The unsavoury experience of the stockmarket scam of 2000, when some resident Indians including company promoters used the FII route to manipulate share prices and made huge gains, has nagged many.

was built into the issue mechanism itself. Only 25 per cent of the public offer was reserved for retail investors with a limit of Rs. 50,000 on investment by an individual investor. The largest portion was reserved for allotment to the Qualifies Institutional Buyers (QIBs) on a discretionary basis. The QIBs, unlike the retail bidders, are not required to make payment at the time of subscription for a public issue. They have to pay only to the extent of shares allotted to them. Overall, in the market capitalisation of the Sensex 30 companies, as on 31 March 2004, the share of Indian public was as low as 10 per cent while that of FIIs was about 19 per cent. Together with ADRs, NRIs, etc. the total foreign portfolio investment works out to about 24 per cent.

Companies may prefer large shareholders as with them interested there is a better chance of their issues getting subscribed and the cost of servicing fewer shareholders being lower. On its part, the government welcomes FIIs as they would facilitate its huge disinvestment programme. This is in spite of the fact that a widely distributed shareholding in the hands of individual investors works to the advantage of promoters. It is quite possible that the promoters have now become confident of FIIs not meddling with their control as long as they deliver decent returns. The upper limit placed on holding of individual FIIs further acts as a protective shield for them. At worst, FIIs will sell-off their shares, which could adversely affect their share prices. Even otherwise, they are known to 'vote with their wallets' than fight it out at annual general meetings (AGMs) of companies. So far, they have not displayed any proactive approach to corporate governance. Indeed, it is known that managements cosy up to large funds. One needs to look into the implications of such relationship between promoters/managements and large funds, as they would have a bearing on the corporate governance issues on the one hand and on the avenues for investment by domestic small investors. In any case, it is obvious that the market has become a domain of the promoters and foreign investors, with the local individual investors playing only a supporting cast. Back of the envelope calculations show that the dividend outgo on account of all types of foreign investors could be anywhere between 25 and 30 per cent of the dividends declared by the listed private sector companies.

One Face of the FII Inflows

The unsavoury experience of the stockmarket scam of 2000, when some resident Indians including company promoters used the FII route to manipulate share prices and made huge gains, has nagged many. Refuting a press report on 30 October

2003, which suggested that about 40 per cent of the FII investment during the year was contributed by NRIs through sub-accounts and participatory notes (PNs), SEBI informed *the same day* that as on 30 September 2003, out of the total net investment of Rs. 72,965 crore, 84 per cent was held by 'Mutual Funds, Asset Management Companies, Investment Companies, Banks, Pension Funds, etc.' (Table 4) Interestingly, SEBI also informed that 12 registered FIIs had issued participatory notes outstanding as on September 30, 2003 and the total value of the underlying investment in equity represented by the PNs was Rs. 19,125 crore. SEBI dismissed the news as conjectural on the basis of its own data on FII investments and the assurances of the FIIs issuing PNs that they/their associates/clients did not issue the PNs directly or indirectly to Overseas Corporate Bodies (OCBs).

It is difficult to take the assertion of SEBI at its face value. While 28 per cent of the inflows are on account of the FIIs that are mutual funds, there is a large unexplained portion of 'Others', which account for 16 per cent of the total net FII investment in Indian stocks. Not only that, the identity of those behind the foreign investment companies that have a 15 per cent share in the total FII investment, the private companies with 12 per cent of the FII holdings, and the public companies with 4 per cent piece of the pie is anybody's guess. According to SEBI, the 'private companies are generally broad-based, but not listed on any exchange'. The assertion that private companies can be broad-based is difficult to comprehend. Strangely enough, SEBI did not expect any problem with the investments of the private companies 'as they are routed through FIIs, which are regulated entities duly registered here'. The real point is: was the data and the type of analysis done by SEBIrelevant for the point under question? Couldn't these three categories include the OCBs that were debarred in November 2001 from participating in the Indian stock market for their role in the scam of 2000? Also, one would have liked to know, how much of this entered India during 2003? OCBs are entities that are owned 60 per cent or more by the NRIs. The nature of OCBs is that often they are difficult to trace. On top of that, the term NRI has become so amorphous that many Indian businessmen, who are actively involved in managing large Indian companies, have turned NRIs. According to press reports, out of the letters sent to some 500 OCBs in more than 300 cases, the letters came back as the addresses were fake! In the early 1980s, investigative reports published in the *Indian Express* revealed the springing up of NRI investment companies with similar sounding names, purported to be related to the promoters in a large Indian company, at two different places.

In spite of SEBI's clean chit, however, the attention continued to rivet on PNs and OCBs. PNs are used by entities that are either not permitted to trade directly on the Indian stock market, such as hedge funds, or by them who wish to keep their identity a secret. Consequently, PNs played a major role in the scam of 2000. In

PNs are used by entities that are either not permitted to trade directly on the Indian stock market, such as hedge funds, or by them who wish to keep their identity a secret. Consequently, PNs played a major role in the scam of 2000.

Figure 1
Fall in Sensex Forllowing Rumours of Ban on PNs and Subsequent Recovery after SEBI's Clarification on 23 January 2004

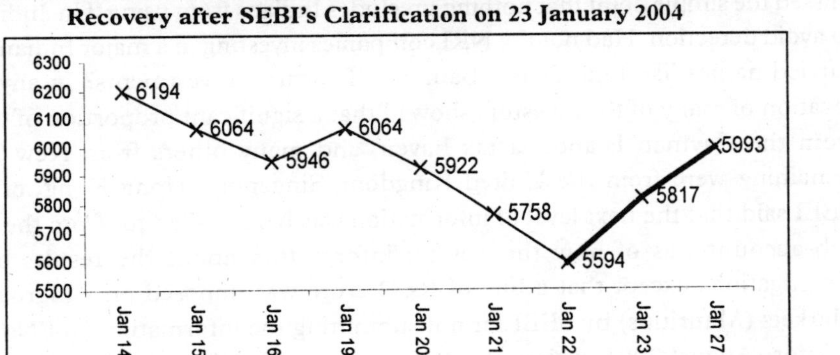

October 2001, as a follow up of investigation into the scam, SEBI ordered the FIIs/ sub-accounts to submit details of issue of PNs. Strangely enough, SEBI did not bother to follow up its own circular until the boom had settled in well. In August 2003, SEBI had to amend its FII regulations to make it mandatory for all FIIs to disclose information about offshore derivative instruments such as PNs where the underlying securities were Indianstocks or indices. In addition to the prevalent disclosure norms, SEBI had asked the FIIs for historical information on these instruments. For FIIs, however, there is no such thing as voluntary compliance.

On 30 December 2003, SE*BI reported that the underlying value of equity investments represented by PNs at the end of November 2003 was Rs. 21,179 crore, representing about 25 per cent of the total investments in equities of Rs. 84,762 crore. And the top ten FII purchases constituted about 86 per cent of total FII investments during September 2003 and about 66 per cent in October 2003. Out of these FIIs, only 12 entities had issued Participatory Notes (PNs) outstanding at the end of November 2003. These included Goldman Sachs Investment Mauritius, Morgan Stanley Dean Witter Mauritius, Merrill Lynch, Copthall Mauritius Investment, Citigroup Global Markets (Mauritius), and Swiss Finance Corporation. It was revealed that Citigroup and Goldman Sachs had even traded with Credit Suisse First Boston (CSFB) whose own FII registration has not been renewed after its dubious dealings with Ketan Parekh, the central figure of the scam of 2000. The information provided by FIIs did not enable SEBI to form a clear opinion of the nature of investments and the involvement of OCBs. SEBI indeed had to go by the names of the beneficiaries, and the list of suspects contained about thrity-one entities whose names sounded 'Indian'. Notwithstanding the declarations given by FIIs and their sub-accounts that they had not issued these derivative instruments, directly or indirectly, to the resident or non-resident Indians, persons of Indian origin and OCBs, SEBI's report indicated that:

- Copthall Mauritius issued PNs to nine OCBs, including OCBs with names like Indus Holdings (Cayman) and Indus Asia Pacific Fund.
- Morgan Stanley issued PNs to eight OCBs, including Ram Trading.
- Merrill Lynch issued PNs to Wadhwani Asset Mgt.
- CGM Mauritius issued PNs to eight OCBs.
- Swiss Finance Corporation issued PNs to three entities including Indea Capital and Everest.
- Goldman Sachs Investment issued PNs to three OCBs based in New York and the Cayman Islands.

...the location of many of the investors showed that a significant proportion of them were from the Cayman Islands, a tax haven, and many others from New York. The remaining were from the United Kingdom, Singapore, Hong Kong, et al.

SEBI noticed that there were several layers, with a minimum of three, of investors in the PNs deals and this information was generally given by the FIIs only up to the next layer and '(W)hat lies beyond this level is not known'. Obviously, the investigation missed the simple point that nothing precludes Indians from using 'Un-Indian' names to avoid detection. Had not the NRI companies investing in a major Indian company carried names like Iota, Victor, Bamford, Thornton Investments? In any case, the location of many of the investors showed that a significant proportion of them were from the Cayman Islands, a tax haven, and many others from New York. The remaining were from the United Kingdom, Singapore, Hong Kong, et al. While SEBI said that the next level of information was being called for from the other FII/ sub-accounts, as of now there is no information about the results of further investigations except that a fine of Rs. 2 crore was imposed on Citigroup Global Markets (Mauritius) by SEBI for not submitting the information on PNs issued by it before August 2003 in time.

Following the rumours that FII inflows could slow down due to imminent strict norms for the FIIs issuing PNs, the Sensex fell by 250 point in two days. After a day's recovery, it fell by further 350 points. In all, it fell by 9.7 per cent. Following SEBI's clarification that PNs issued to unregulated entities were not required to be sold in the market immediately and that they were being offered a five-year grace period and that henceforth such notes can be issued to regulated entities only, the Sensex jumped by 400 points or 7.2 per cent within two days (See Figure 1). Interestingly, the 'regulated entities' cover wide-ranging bodies and include companies, banks, brokers, individuals, and entities such as funds, trusts, collective investment schemes, investment companies, and limited partnerships, subject to the 'know your client' principles. Ultimately, even hedge funds are on their way to invest directly in the Indian stock market.

Have we taken the issue of foreign exchange reserves too far? Now Indian mutual funds can invest in foreign securities, individual Indians can do the same up to $25,000 per year, Indian companies can invest abroad more freely through the automatic approval route. While this can be a part of the process of moving to full convertibility, a question arises as to the purpose of the FII investments.

Summing Up

The last year's experience has shown beyond any reasonable doubt that the Indian stock market has become heavily dependent on foreign portfolio capital flows and hence it has become vulnerable to the swings and strategies of the foreign investors. Even assuming that the foreign investors are now wiser and would be moderate in their 'irrational exuberance' and 'panics', given the importance gained by portfolio capital and the direct entry of hedge funds, the Damocles sword will continue to hang over the Indian stock market. It does appear that the current boom has been fuelled, to a significant extent, by entities that were not eligible to trade in the Indian stock market. Ultimately, these had to be recognised and regularised. Otherwise, one would not know to what depths the share prices would have sunk.

...even hedge funds are on their way to invest directly in the Indian stock market.

In terms of compliance with the official guidelines, FIIs did not seem too eager to oblige. It is said that FIIs prefer to invest in companies adopting good corporate governance practices. But with their own responsibility to the law of the land so doubtful, as was evident even in the US, home to many of the FIIs, could one expect them to be more responsible in India? After all, when they saw the potential for good returns, they did not hesitate to invest even in the companies with poor corporate governance records. After all, it is not the colour of the cat that is important; what matters is whether one can make money or not by banking on it.

In terms of compliance with the official guidelines, FIIs did not seem too eager to oblige. It is said that FIIs prefer to invest in companies adopting good corporate governance practices. But with their own responsibility to the law of the land so doubtful, as was evident even in the US, home to many of the FIIs, could one expect them to be more responsible in India?

While company managements may be happy with foreign portfolio investments, as they can raise large amount of funds and probably at low cost, the real problem is for the individual Indian investors. Just as a sudden fall of the market prices catches them off-guard, they may not be able to take full advantage of the sudden jumps engineered by large international investors. The small ones have no way of finding out when the inflows would slow down or even reverse. The Indian case clearly illustrates how the involvement of FIIs could push out individual investors. While it could be said that but for the large FII inflows during the year, the individual investor would have continued to suffer the bear phase, the point is that he got stuck there because of the earlier unregulated heavy inflows.

From a position of suspicion and possible disqualification not so long ago, we have moved to a position of acceptance of hedge funds that reportedly command about $ 750 million of assets and are feared for their high volume trading and the resultant volatility. With the stock market thrown further open to such big players, it is difficult to imagine the future role of the Indian small investors. They too might benefit, but only as marginal players. Their role will probably be limited to identifying some good stocks and sticking with them and waiting for an occasional public issue and trying to make a 'quick buck'. Where does the process lead the ordinary Indian saver? Will he be content to be left with low return investments?

With the increasing involvement of foreign portfolio investments, the boundaries between the local and foreign enterprises are getting blurred. The way we look at corporations may need to change. Some of the Indian companies can be called Indian only because they are managed by Indians. They are already majority-owned by foreign investors. How much is this situation different from an Indian heading a subsidiary of a British company? – Is the nationality of the managers more relevant or the ownership which gives control? Does it matter if a person who is, Indian by birth or is born to non-resident Indians, sets up his head quarters in the UK or the US, and owns/manages Indian companies as part of his global operations? Should one consider such companies Indian?

Take the case of Infosys. Technically, 100 per cent of the company can be owned by foreign institutional investors. Already about half of Infosys' shares are owned abroad. The fruit of the enterprise, distributed in the form of dividend, goes mostly to the international investors. This applies even more in the cases of HDFC and ICICI Bank. But for the overall limits on foreign portfolio investments in individual companies, FIIs would have probably held larger shares in these companies than at present. So far, the foreign investors have not meddled with the incumbent managements in Indian companies. A day might come when Infosys might pass into the hands of anyone, Indian or foreign. On the other hand, we have examples where, in the name of NRI/OCB investment, huge stakes are held by global Indian promoters. They work for their own narrow interests and not for any individual shareholder, either Indian or foreign. The wealth they accumulate is displayed globally and the press treats them with wonderment. It is immaterial if the companies under their charge languish locally.

India has built-up huge foreign exchange reserves over the past few years, mainly due to capital flows and services income.

India has built-up huge foreign exchange reserves over the past few years, mainly due to capital flows and services income. During 2003–04 they increased from US$ 75 billion to US$ 112 billion. India has also been liberalising capital outflows simultaneously. Indian MFs and high net worth Individuals are now allowed to invest in other countries. Indian companies can invest more freely abroad. Indians can remit up to US$ 1,00,000 abroad per year towards education, employment abroad, emigration, medical treatment, and maintenance of overseas relatives. Foreign companies can raise funds in India in the form of Indian Depository Receipts (IDRs). Obviously, these steps are in the direction of moving towards full capital account convertibility. To that extent, 'attracting' foreign capital through portfolio investment for domestic investment purposes can no longer be the overriding criteria. This leads to the question: Are the markets for investors or, are the investors for the markets?

...these steps are in the direction of moving towards full capital account convertibility.

Banking Sector

Hari Om Verma

A survey of the banking sector and its performance must focus on the functional as well as the developmental objectives of the sector. Statistical indicators like trends in branch expansion, growth of deposits, and ratios of profits to assets are useful only to a limited extent. It is vital to have a broad view of the linkages of the sector with other sectors of the economy over the recent years. Global Trust Bank (GTB) has failed to meet its obligations to its depositors. This has happened in a situation in which we are made to believe that there exists a surveillance and monitoring system, which could prevent such eventualities. The sensitivity of this system to set the corrective measures in motion well in time is certainly suspect. The official *Economic Survey* which was placed before the Lok Sabha in the first week of July 2004 had noted that this bank had a capital to risk-weighted asset ratio (CRAR) that was untenable at the end of financial year 2002–03.

The *Survey* states:

> At the end-March, 2003, capital to risk-weighted asset ratio (CRAR) for PSBs stood at 12.6 per cent, higher than 11.8 per cent as at the end of March, 2002. All the PSBs had a CRAR above the stipulated minimum of 9 per cent in 2002-03. Of the 27 PSBs as many as 26 banks had CRAR exceeding 10 per cent. In the case of 30 private sector banks operating in India, *only two banks, viz, Centurion Bank with CRAR of just 2.0 per cent and Global Trust Bank with zero CRAR were below the minimum requirement of 9 per cent.* (Italics added)

Fifteen months later, the GTB had to be salvaged by merging it with a public sector bank. But this case reflects our banking system in a poor light especially the surveillance mechanism and the legitimacy of its existence. This also puts a question mark on the cacophony about the ubiquitous efficiency of the private sector.

Interest Rate Policy

Soft interest-rate regime has continued to persist for some years. A persistently downward trend in the interest rates can be seen from Table 1.

It is important to note that inflation rate based on wholesale price index has risen to 5.5 per cent during 2003–04. As a consequence, it can be inferred that real interest rates on deposits as well as those on CDs with Scheduled Commercial Banks (SCBs) have become negative. Negative real interests are sure to adversely affect the savings mobilisation and the Gross Domestic Saving (GDS). The rate of GDS has been stagnating around 22 to 24 per cent of GDP for more than fifteen years. The low interest rate regime is a clear-cut instance of state-sponsored transfer of income from the relatively poor household sector to the rich and concentrated corporate sector. It meets all the tests of perverse redistribution of income.

Negative real interests are sure to adversely affect the savings mobilisation and the Gross Domestic Saving (GDS). The rate of GDS has been stagnating around 22 to 24 per cent of GDP for more than fifteen years.

Table 1
Trends in Interest Rates 2002–2004

Category	*29 March 2002*	*28 March 2003*	*26 March 2004*
Prime lending rate (PLR)	11.00–12.00	10.75–11.50	10.25–11.00
Deposit rate (>one year)	7.50–8.50	5.25–6.25	5.00–5.50
CDs by SCBs	5.00–10.03	5.00–7.10	3.87–5.16

Source: Economic Survey 2003–04

It is instructive to note that fall in interest rate has not lead to a more than proportionate increase in the demand for credit. This is borne out by the fact that the share of income of the SCBs from interest has remained constant despite the fall in interest rates. The advisability of soft interest-rate regime in which the rate of saving mobilisation needs to be stepped-up and in which the demand for bank credit is not very highly elastic is questionable.

Non-performing Assets of the Banking Sector

Yet another symptom of deep-rooted malaise of the banking sector in India is the persistence of the problem of NPAs. Although figures of gross and net NPAs for 2002–03 are somewhat lower than that of the preceding year, it can by no means imply a trend of falling NPAs. Table 2 shows the changes in gross and net NPAs of the different categories of banks between 1999–2003.

Table 2 shows that not only is the overall decline in NPAs marginal, there is a slight increase of gross NPAs for both the private sector and foreign banks. One may not expect a significant impact of the Securitisation and Reconstruction of Financial Assets and Enforcement of Security

Interest (SARFAEST) Act, 2002 but the additional edifice added to the banking structure in India may become another burden unless it serves the purpose for which it has been brought into existence. It is yet to be seen to what extent do securitisation and reconstruction companies facilitate in the process of recovery of NPAs.

While the overall targets for priority sector lending have been achieved, there are significant shortfalls in meeting the targets assigned for agriculture and for the weaker sections of society.

Primary Sector Lending

One of the important developmental functions of the banking sector is providing funds to the priority sectors like small-scale industry, agriculture, exports, etc. Targets are fixed for the domestic as well as foreign banks for primary sector lending. Of their net credit, the domestic and foreign banks are expected to lend 40 percent and 32 per cent, respectively, to the priority sectors.

While the overall targets for priority sector lending have been achieved, there are significant shortfalls in meeting the targets assigned for agriculture and for the weaker sections of society. Even for the Public Sector banks, the advances to the agriculture sector fell short of the target of 18 per cent of the net bank credit.

The banking sector has failed to evolve credit-products, which suit the requirement of the agricultural sector.

There has been a steady increase of institutional credit to the agricultural sector. In the year 2002–03, it was around Rs.70,800 crore. In the year 2003–04, it is anticipated to rise to Rs. 80,000 crore. Almost 65 per cent of this credit is short-term credit meant for cultivation activities. It is well known that the distribution of such loans cannot but be highly skewed. The total credit available is also highly inadequate. Given the fact that more than 19 crore hectares are brought under cultivation, the average short-term credit made available through institutional sources comes to only Rs. 2,800 per hectare.

The banking sector has failed to evolve credit-products, which suit the requirement of the agricultural sector. The lending and recovery mechanism of the

Table 2
Non-performing Assets of the Scheduled Commercial Banks

Category	*Gross NPAs (Rs.000 crore)*				*Net NPAs (Rs.000 crore)*			
	1999–2000	*2000–01*	*2001–02*	*2002–03*	*1999–2000*	*2000–01*	*2001–02*	*2002–03*
All Scheduled Commercial Banks	60.41	70.86	30.07	35.55	63.74	68.72	32.46	32.76
(a) Public Sector Banks	53.03	56.47	26.19	27.96	54.67	54.09	27.98	24.96
(b) Private Sector Banks	4.76	11.66	3.03	6.68	5.96	11.80	3.70	6.88
(c) Foreign Banks	2.61	2.73	0.86	0.92	3.11	2.83	0.79	0.92

Source: Economic Survey 2003–04.

banking sector varies very little from the much-maligned moneylender. A recent report about a farmer committing suicide because his land was sold surreptitiously by the co-operative bank from which he had taken a loan for purchase of a tractor is evidence enough of the banks being no different from the moneylenders. The large spate of suicides by farmers in several states bears testimony to the harassments to which farmers are exposed while borrowing from the modern-day moneylenders. It appears, priority sector lending in general and that to the agriculture sector in particular is being considered as an unwarranted burden by the banking sector. Banks that have amassed huge NPAs over the years are very meticulous in recovering from the farmers. It is nobody's case that farmers loans should be written off, but there is a very strong need for considering rescheduling of recovery in consultation with the whole host of institutions that came into existence for facilitating the flow of credit to the farming sector. From NABARD at the apex to all others, the regional rural banks have failed to evolve even one product, which could suit the needs of the farming sector.

The Kisan credit card scheme has apparently become popular with some farmers. A total of more than 413 lakh Kisan cards cannot, however, be construed to be an index of the easy accessibility of credit to the faming sector as such.

Banks that have amassed huge NPAs over the years are very meticulous in recovering from the farmers.

Overall Outlook

The banking system in India has not tended to spearhead a movement for modernising the organisation of either the industry or the business. It has played the role of imitating the banking products evolved by banks in the developed industrial world. As elsewhere in the Indian polity, the absence of accountability at any level of decision making and an environment in which self-praise is deemed as a virtue has engulfed the banking sector from RBI downwards. Failure of GTB or a spate of suicides by the farmers be damned, the banking sector, including the apex institutions, are in a self-congratulatory mood. And that does not augur well for the banking sectors role in attaining heights that it can and needs to.

The banking system in India has not tended to spearhead a movement for modernising the organisation of either the industry or the business. It has played the role of imitating the banking products evolved by banks in the developed industrial world.

Tea Industry

Vaskar Nandy

The nearly five-year old crisis in the Indian tea industry has been a story of the misery of the hundreds of workers and members of their families, who have lived without potable water or medical care and died of starvation. In fact, they have been bereft of all human rights. The Interim Report of the Indian People's Tribunal (2004), headed by Justice (Retired) Hosbet Suresh, has revealed the apathy, even callousness, of both the Union and the West Bengal governments towards this calamity.

In the fiscal year 1999–2000, prices of tea collapsed in all the auctions, in the north as well as south. They have more or less remained in that state despite odd bouts of minor recoveries in 2003–04. Importantly, the prices are still far below the pre-crisis levels. During the worst days of the crisis, prices of some varieties of CTC tea, the overwhelming bulk of Indian tea, went below Rs. 50 per kg in auctions in North India. The South Indian CTC varieties fetched even lower prices. The most curious aspect of this situation was that while the auction story was one of collapse, the retail prices tea in the domestic market were never threatened and continued on a steady climb throughout the crisis. The retail prices were more than double the auction prices.[1]

This glaring contradiction between the retail and auction prices requires more than just the kind of superficial analysis and mystification offered by the mercenary press that is ever beholden to the 'big boys' at Unilever and Tata for huge advertising revenues from a bewildering variety of products. These corporate giants own and control many tea estates and they are major tea producers in India. Together they account for almost 60 per cent of the domestic retail tea trade (with Unilever having a 40 per cent market share and the Tata Tea 20 per cent). The duo also dominates the tea exports.

Unilever, the biggest player in exports of tea from India, retaliated by withdrawing from the auctions, and the markets collapsed. The crisis was short-lived as the government panicked and slashed the declared minimum export price. Unilever returned to the auctions in triumph. *'Starting up, reviving and collapsing the markets are all well within the powers of Unilever'.*

The collapse of tea prices at the auctions should be studied keeping in mind that the last such collapse occurred in the second half of the eighties and that was not as severe or protracted as the present one.

The auction prices were rising continuously from the early to the middle 1980s. The government decided to set a minimum export price for tea. The intention of this policy decision was to curb manipulation of the export price by the multinationals, such as Hindustan Lever (HLL), a subsidiary of Unilever. Unilever, the biggest player in exports of tea from India, retaliated by withdrawing from the auctions, and the markets collapsed. The crisis was short-lived as the government panicked and slashed the declared minimum export price. Unilever returned to the auctions in triumph. *'Starting up, reviving and collapsing the markets are all well within the powers of Unilever'*.[2]

1. A look at the *Tea Digest* transmitted on the Tea Board's website will confirm this indisputable fact.
2. 'Unilever has huge market power. For example in the mid '80s, when the Indian tea prices started to rise, Unilever and other corporations acted to bring it down by temporarily boycotting Indian tea. When the Indian government tried to set a minimum export price, the TNCs collectively withdrew from the market forcing the Indian government to retreat, and slash the price', *Corporate Watch*, Issue 9, Autumn 1999. http://www.corporatewatch.org.uk/magazine/issue9/cw9cm2.html

Apart from being the biggest player in both the domestic retail market and exports, Unilever is also well placed with regard to sourcing tea. It not only has access to its own tea estates, it has a close cooperation with important foreign (British) concerns such as Magor, the British family firm that controlled the largest tea producing company in the world (Williamson Magor) until the very recent developments in that company. These two factors give Unilever very strong controlling powers over tea prices in India. The collapse of tea prices in the 1980s and their recovery are brutal illustrations of that fact. Some of the latest developments also illustrate this power of Unilever.

With Unilever enjoying such a power over tea prices in India, the question naturally arose as to whether that power was at work during the latest collapse of prices at the auctions. To look for a market influencing power beyond the simple supply-demand equations is certainly called for in a situation where the contradiction between the behaviour of auction and retail prices was so outrageous. It is, however, difficult to prove that Unilever and the other multinationals, probably Tata Tea in cahoots with the Tata's Tetley interests, were, separately or in collusion, the first movers in the collapse of the tea markets. The CPI (M) mouthpiece, *People's Democracy*, reports that small planters in the South 'concede [that collapsed prices at the auctions] are manipulated by big players in the market, like Hindustan Lever (HLL) and Tata Tetley.' (Chopra 2003) Be that as it may, it is clear that the collapsed, low volume markets were not inimical to Unilever's interests. If those interests had been breached, it had the powers to revive the auctions. It did not do so for more than three years. So, while it may not be absolutely clear as to who actually pushed the markets into collapse initially, Unilever, with the possible help of the other big players, certainly made sure that the prices continued to remain depressed. Unilever alone sells, domestically and abroad, nearly forty-five per cent of India's total tea production. It owns Carrit Moran, the second largest tea auctioneers in India. Naturally, it also has tremendous clout over the other auctioneers. Unilever alone could have started up the price discovery mechanisms of the auctions and ensured high volumes. The responsibility for the long-term depressed state of the tea auctions should therefore be laid squarely at the doors of Unilever and the other big players.

What had Unilever to gain from this undermining of the auction process? Making a killing in the short run could be one reason for doing this. As we shall see, Unilever is into an estate-buying spree in India and it may not be in its long-term interest to keep the auctions depressed protractedly. Was Unilever playing for some other stakes? Were Unilever and some of the other foreign tea companies again playing hardball, as in the 1980s, with the government to wrest concessions on vital issues such as the allowable limit on foreign holdings in Indian tea companies and the restructuring of capital-labour relations in tea?

Were Unilever and some of the other foreign tea companies again playing hardball, as in the 1980s, with the government to wrest concessions on vital issues such as the allowable limit on foreign holdings in Indian tea companies and the restructuring of capital-labour relations in tea?

In order to find answers to that question, we will have to make a small detour into the nature and present policies of Unilever. Unilever is a global giant in two fields—personal and fabric care care products and foods and beverages. It is the the biggest player in the global retail tea market. In the mid-1990s, the company faced a crisis of profitability. It restructured its command post in Europe by splitting that into two, one located in England and the other in Holland. Of the nearly 1,600 brands it was selling at the time (1996) and the hundreds of subsidiaries it operated, the company sold or disposed of otherwise more than half of those. These did not include any tea brands, such as Brooke Bond or Lipton, or tea subsidiaries, such as Assam Brooks. The subsidiaries that were ousted had failed the company's test of profitability. All subsidiary whose profits were below the company's average profits were cast out of the company's fold. The new headquarter in London, which was concerned with tea among other things, decentralised all powers to the subsidiaries except those of monitoring the profits. The subsidiaries were to be judged on the principle of maximisation of profits.

Centralisation of capital and greater control over the sources of the product to be marketed are time-tested procedures in capitalism to deliver higher profits, and Unilever has always used such procedures quite effectively. In fact, the formation of Unilever was precisely the combination of capital centralisation and greater control over resources. By the 1930s, Lever Brothers, established in 1885, was a very large seller of soap. There was a much smaller Dutch player at the time, Margarine Unie, which was big in the margarine business. Tallow and oil seeds are the common raw materials for both soap and margarine. Lever Brothers achieved both centralisation of capital and elimination of the rival's source of raw material by merging the margarine producer into itself and becoming Unilever (1930). Its profits soared.[3]

With the mandate for greater profits coming from London in the late 1990s, Unilever and its subsidiaries in India, with other sterling interests in tea such as the Lawrie group in tow, began to pressure the government in 1999 to lift all restrictions on foreign ownership of tea companies. That was just prior to the collapse of tea prices at auctions. Their demand was to change the law and rules on foreign holdings allowable in the tea industry at that time and they tried to force the government to concede 100 per cent foreign ownership of tea companies. Lined up behind Unilever were nearly all the big British players in tea, including the big importing companies such as Twinnings, May, Orimi, and Van Rees. (*The Economic Times* 2004) The Assam Company (Duncan Mcneil), AFT, and Warren Tea, who have controlling sterling holdings in Indian tea companies, are already making their moves towards 100 per cent foreign holding in those.

Not waiting for the government to raise foreign investments in tea beyond the then limit of 51 per cent for new investments and 76 per cent for the companies that were affected by the FERA rules in the late 1970s, Unilever made the move to acquire Rossell Industries in December 1999. It did so through two of its non-Indian subsidiaries, Unilevers Overseas Holdings BV Netherlands and Jokai Tea Holdings, UK, and a wholly owned subsidiary of HLL. By June 2000, Unilever was well advanced in the process of acquiring Rossell with more then 70 per cent of the company in the bag, even as it was waiting for the government to 'liberalise the provision(s)' on foreign holdings and get the clearance from the Foreign Investment Promotion Board (FIPB).[4] (*The Hindu* 2000) By December 2001, Unilever had acquired 95.88 per cent of Rossell's equity.[5] There was still no approval from the government or the FIPB. According to *News Insight*,

> Ever since January 2000, pressure has been mounting on the Union government to relax the FDI norms in the plantation companies so as to facilitate the complete takeover of Rossell industries by Unilever. (*News Insight* 2002)

By trying to buy up Magor's sterling holdings in its Indian tea companies then though it now owns them 100 per cent, Unilever would appear to be eliminating any relative independence that Magor might have enjoyed theoretically and ensuring total control over a major source.

The concerted move by various sterling tea companies is best illustrated by what has happened at Williamson Magor, which was the biggest tea company in the world for many years. In April 2001, *Business Standard* reported that sterling holders in the company, led by the privately owned Magor group of the UK, were making strong moves by the early 2000 to separate their interests from the Khaitans, their Indian, junior partner. Khaitan and Magor were poised to part ways by the end of

3. The data on the history of Unilever comes from two pages of the web magazine *Corporate Watch*:1. http://www.corporatewatch.org.uk/profiles/food_supermarkets/unilever/Unilever-profile.rtf; and, *Corporate Watch*, Issue 9, Autumn 1999.
4. The source for the December 1999 data is *News Insight*, 5 April 2002, published on the net magazine, Newsinsight.net.
5. Investment Research Information Services Ltd. on their website myiris, 'Rossell Industries Limited'.

April, 2001. In May 2001, Philip Magor, the head of the Magor group, issued the statement that his company 'has had a very close and productive relationship for years with HLL's parent Unilever' amidst speculation that Unilever was about to acquire his sterling holdings in its Indian tea company. What Magor does not state is that the 'close and productive relationship' that his company has with Unilever is because it is beholden to the latter for packaging and global market distribution of its tea. By trying to buy up Magor's sterling holdings in its Indian tea companies then though it now owns them 100 per cent, Unilever would appear to be eliminating any relative independence that Magor might have enjoyed theoretically and ensuring total control over a major source. After parting with the Magor group, the Khaitans are also selling out their tea business and HLL is negotiating with them. The other substantial equity holders, mentioned earlier, appear to be preparing to make similar moves. They are merely waiting for the government's reaction.

The present holdings of Unilever in India tea companies, including HLL and other subsidiaries such as Carritt Moran, alone or in concert, or merged with Magor interests, represent a huge increase in tea sources for Unilever. And it has been accompanied with further centralisation of capital. It has been a near-perfect response to a profit maximising strategy in tea.

The United Progressive Alliance (UPA) government's response to this onslaught from the foreign capital has been at par with the NDA government's spineless capitulation to the dictates of the international multilateral institutions.

The situation before Unilever began its moves to acquire complete control of its Indian tea companies and expand the number of those companies was what the government in the seventies agreed to. Then, under the Foreign Exchange Regulation Act (FERA) regimefully foreign-owned tea companies had to divest 24 per cent of their shares to Indians. Any foreign company wishing to make fresh investment in tea during that regime were to be allowed up to 51 per cent holding. By February 2000, FIPB had cleared the way to raise the 51 per cent figure to 74 per cent. This was designed to allow Unilever to legally hold up to 74 per cent of Rossell's shares. (ENS Economic Bureau 2000) By July 2002, in another bout of capitulation to Unilever, the government produced a new foreign direct investment (FDI) policy where 100 per cent FDI would be allowed in tea provided the foreign investors would dilute 26 per cent stake after five years. But that did not satisfy either Unilever or the other sterling shareholders. The five-year provision 'is likely to be a deterrent to any immediate investment flows. Industry sources feel any prospective foreign investor will read the dilution clause very closely before committing funds,' commented *The Economic Times*.[6] By the beginning of 2004, the government had shed all its inhibitions and announced that 100 per cent foreign holdings in tea would be allowed without any need for dilution in the future.

By the beginning of 2004, the government had shed all its inhibitions and announced that 100 per cent foreign holdings in tea would be allowed without any need for dilution in the future.

Having looked at Unilever's new profit maximisation strategy, as it pertains to Indian tea, it is time to look at the chronological parallels between Unilever's relentless pressure on the government on the FDI issue and the developments at the auctions. Prices collapsed in the late 1999–2000. Unilever's pressure on the government regarding FDI limit in tea companies began almost simultaneously. Just before the tea market collapse, Unilever had already begun its buying of Rossell Industries. The crisis at the auctions did not ease until the final capitulation of the government. The parallel and simultaneous occurence of the FDI battle and the persistent depression of prices at the auctions cannot conceivably have been the result of any coincidence, especially when we remember the precedent of the 1980s.

The auction prices have improved now, but they are still far below the 1999 prices and way below the international prices.

6. teauction.com, 'Foreign tea companies may wait before investing in India', *The Economic Times*.

Unilever's power over the Indian tea market has been illustrated again in 2004. The Tea Marketing Control Orders (2003) of the government had incorporated several recommendations of the Ferguson Report that suggested various measures, highly inadequate in our opinion, to check the manipulation of the tea auction procedures. That angered the small buyers and brokers at the Kolkata, Guwahati and Siliguri tea auctions. They struck work and those auctions had no floor-trading for more than ten days. Who came to the rescue of the government and resuscitated trading? And, why? It were our old 'philanthropists' at Unilever and with Tata Tea. Their buyers walked into the auction floors with big shopping lists. Just as in the 1980s, Unilever showed that it could turn the tap on if it so wishes.

The auction prices have improved now, but they are still far below the 1999 prices and way below the international prices. Why are the taps not turned on full? Clearly, Unilever and the other big players have not finished with their agenda. Maximising profitability does not depend only on centralising capital and achieving optimal sourcing. These are a part of the continuous struggle between various fractions of capital. Even more than these struggles, what is involved in maximising profits is the restructuring of capital-labour relations in the favour of capital. The whole manipulated crisis in the Indian tea industry had this as one of its prime objectives. Unilever boss Niall Fitz Gerald is feared for the ruthlessness with which he can slash wages, lay off employees and close down operations.

The closing down or abandonment of some gardens, all owned by *bania* (trading) capital, which played its own games in the space created by Unilever, set the longest benchmark for capital-labour relations. Flout all labour and other laws pertaining to the tea gardens, and misappropriate the employee's contributions to the provident fund (PF), life insurance, electricity, etc. That was the benchmark. While not closing down or abandoning the gardens, the big listed companies also began to force down wages, bonuses, and remunerations. Some of them, such as Duncan Agro-Industries, began misappropriating workers' PF money. The final twist of the knife has come in the form of a charter of demands from the Consultative Committee of Planters' Associations (CCPA) to the unions: no rations, no social safety net whatsoever, greater work load at less cash wages, lay offs, etc. As on the FDI issue, or on the functioning of the auctions, here too Unilever is showing the way.

One just cannot refrain from quoting what the delegates from some of the central trade unions and other mass organisations, organised by the Centre for Education and Communication (CEC), found on visiting a Unilever garden:

> The Hindustan Lever Ltd [the biggest Indian subsidiary of Unilever], one of the main culprits in the auction manipulation, has actually tried to show others the way forward as they see it. In the Srikundra estate this company owns in Tamilnadu, the management served notice to the workers, reducing their wages ... At the same time, they increased the quota of hand plucking, from 25 kg to 27.5 kg per day, 41.5 kg for shear plucking and 110 kg for mechanical harvesting. And, if pluckers fail to meet these increased quotas, they are penalised ....
>
> What horrible results this kind of approach leads to, came clearly across to us when weeping women workers reported how their arms ached and stomachs hurt by using these machines for plucking. They also told us how, when they complained to the plantation owners and management about these problems, they were advised to have the uterus removed in order to work better! It is strange that while the machines that destroy the workers' bodies are tolerated, the employers even suggest that the body be operated upon to meet the needs of the machines. Such harmful mechanisation has to be stopped at once. And when they sought to get leave during menstruation, the supervisors shamed women by harassing them sexually: 'How do we know you are having periods? Show us and we will believe it'. (*People's Democracy* 2003)

At the level of the estates and the industry, the tea unions, ravaged by corruption and mafia control in North India, are mostly bereft of the power of resistance to capital's drive for the maximisation of profits.

Here we should note the pioneering work of Unilever in its profit-maximising drive—the concentration of capital by increasing productivity through the introduction of machinery.

The NDA government was overenthusiastic about labour law reform. The incumbent Prime Minister Manmohan Singh's instincts are not very far from that. The UPA is supposed to be bound by the common minimum programme (CMP) that promises a human face to the reforms. Those bindings are not very secure, especially when we observe that in accepting the Sabyasachi Sen Committee's report the 'Left' government in West Bengalis already quite amenable to some of the demands of the tea lobby. Unilever and the other multinationals, in conjunction with our home grown big boys, are using the strength of the international multilateral institutions and they could easily tear up the bindings of the CMP, especially when there are well known bandicoots in the Congress barn that would love to gnaw at the ropes. At the level of the estates and the industry, the tea unions, ravaged by corruption and mafia control in North India, are mostly bereft of the power of resistance to capital's drive for the maximisation of profits. History will tell whether Unilever completes the whole of its present agenda – centralisation of capital, control over sources of productsand the restructuring of labour-capital relations. Fitz Gerald of Unilever should be running the next London marathon quite at ease with himself.

One more issue needs to be addressed. The 1998 Tea Marketing Control Order (TMCO) allowed unlimited sales outside the auctions. This was a convenient tool to keep volumes low at the auctions and prices depressed. TMCO 2003 has gone back to the earlier formula, limiting off-auction sales to only 25 per cent. Why did the government take so long to change the order? Was it pressure from the NDA's small owner (bania) constituency to be given the chance to asset-strip its gardens through off- garden black market sales before clearing out through sale or abandonment?, In the 1980s, Unilever did not need a new TMCO to squeeze the markets and it did not need it now. The 1998 TMCO was the NDA's helping hand towards its own constituency. It certainly needed help. Even Tata Tea, the giant among Indian owners, has reportedly been selling all its Indian tea gardens. From production and trading, Tata is moving towards only trading, leaving Unilever to control its sources, and all it surveys, as it wishes.

Tata is moving towards only trading, leaving Unilever to control its sources, and all it surveys, as it wishes.

References

Business Standard. 2001. 'Magors, Khaitans to split by month-end.,' teaauction.net.

Chopra, Suneet. 2003. 'MNCs Ransack an Industry The Case of Tea,' *People's Democracy,* http://pd.cpim.org/2003/0525/05252003_suneet.htm.

ENS Economic Bureau. 2000. 'FIPB clears 74% FDI in plantation,' New Delhi, 8 February.

News Insight. 2002. 5 April. As published on the net magazine, Newsinsight.net.

People's Democracy. 2003. 25 May. http://pd.cpim.org/2003/0525/05252003.

The Economic Times. 2004. 29 June, reproduced in, http:/www.teauction,com/news.asp? newsid + 530.

The Hindu. 2000. 'Levers Plan Major update of Rossel Tea Estate', 3 July. As quoted on http:www.thehindubusinessline.com/businessline/2000/07/03/stories/070352ya.htm quoting.

The Indian People's Tribunal on Human Rights and the Environment. 2004. *The Interim Report.* Jalpaiguri: Swadhikar.

The Urban Sector

T.M. Thomas

The official *Economic Survey* is supposed to review economic activities over the last year in a brief yet comprehensive manner. Intrinsic to such a task is the notion of continuity. The government schemes discussed in one *Survey* must not disappear in the next year's Survey. Yet, often exactly this happens. For instance, four programmes that were discussed in the 2002–03 Survey do not find mention in the 2003–04 *Survey*, and there is no explanation for that.[1]

The latest official *Economic Survey* does pay greater attention to the problems of urban infrastructure than the previous one—as many as twenty-two paragraphs are devoted to this subject as compared with just seven. And what is more important, the latest official Survey seems to be more candid about the real problems of the sector, as will be apparent from the following excerpts:

> International experience suggests that without reforms in the institutional framework for urban infrastructure, central or state level government funds directed into the urban sector will not have the expected economic and social returns. On the contrary, the urban sector could make larger fiscal claims when faced with acute problems of infrastructure or poverty, and thus exacerbate India's fiscal problem.
>
> What then are these institutional reforms? We can identify them as follows:
>
> - The strengthening of the Urban Local Bodies (ULBs) as provided under the 74th Amendment to the Constitution.
> - The strengthening and further diversification of community structures so that the people right down to grass-roots level have representative bodies through which they can intervene in social and economic activity. (GOI 2004)

There cannot be any disagreement over the official *Survey*'s emphasis on enhancing the capabilities of the ULBs.

> The task is not easy, not the least because the ULBs do not have the wherewithal to imbibe the concepts and capabilities needed for their responsibilities. These will need to be built up, and legislative and institutional arrangements to achieve this task will have to be made. That the ULBs are not yet in a condition to take on all their responsibilities is no argument against making the necessary transition. On the other hand, the challenge lies in building up the ULBs, because without that there will be neither accountability nor sustained development in the urban sector. (GOI 2004)

Again, there can be no doubt that the official *Survey* is correct in its basically positive assessment of the Swarn Jayanti Shahari Rojgar Yojana (SJSRY), an employment generation scheme initiated by the United Front government in 1997, which relies upon community participation and self-help-groups.

...four programmes that were discussed in the 2002–03 *Survey* do not find mention in the 2003–04 *Survey*, and there is no explanation for that.

> ... two basic requirements of any programme of poverty alleviation ... [are] ... community involvement and empowerment, and employment generation. Evaluation studies show that the progress of the scheme has not been remarkable, but that is no reason to give up

1. The programmes which have disappeared are, 'Pradhan Mantri Gramodaya Yojana (Gramin Awas)', 'Pradhan Mantri Gramodaya Yojana (Rural Drinking Water)', the 'Jai Prakash Rozgar Guarantee Yojana' and the 'Annapurna' scheme. One is left wondering whether these schemes were just paper projects—new names given to existing activity, designed to woo the electorate.

the scheme itself. What is needed, instead, is to take corrective measures and improve implementation. (GOI 2004)

There cannot be any serious dispute over the *Survey*'s suggestions for improvement.

- The wage employment component should be used only for building assets and infrastructure relating to the urban poor, and not for general municipal works. The requirements should be selected by beneficiaries themselves and implementation should be from such lists of works identified by the beneficiaries.
- The guidelines need to be simplified and made more concise, removing all ambiguities and contradictions.
- The component of vocational training should be revamped and the quality of training improved;
- Community organisers and project coordinators should be appointed wherever they are not present, and the persons must be qualified in social work. The role of NGOs in projects should be strengthened. The community structures created under the scheme should be fully involved in the activities under the scheme, including selection and implementation of works, thrift and credit groups, group economic activities, etc. These community structures should be encouraged to fulfil their role as pressure groups for highlighting issues relating to their upliftment.
- Monitoring of the project at both the Central and State levels should be strengthened.

The problem arises over the next few steps in the argument. The official *Survey* emphasises the adoption of appropriate user charges as the key to strengthening of ULBs, which alone, it is argued, will make urban infrastructural projects bankable and pave the way to the mobilisation of the necessary resources. The *Survey* then notes that 'improvements in tax revenues and user charges are likely to be most acceptable in the context of concurrent improvement in the institutions of service delivery'. This means that there is a 'chicken and egg' problem here—without more revenue urban infrastructure cannot be improved; but then, people would not be willing to pay more unless infrastructure services improve. The official *Survey* goes on to set out its solution to this problem in form of the 'Urban Reforms Incentive Fund' and the 'City Challenge Fund'. The cash-strapped state governments are to be told that they can avail of these funds only if they sign up a Memorandum of Agreement with the central government promising to introduce a package of 'reforms'. (GOI 2004)

...while much is made of 'poverty alleviation and employment generation programmes', the total central government spending on these programmes (in the urban sector) has been minuscule. It was just Rs. 333 crore in 2003–04, which has been modestly increased to Rs. 384 crores in the 2004–05 budget.

What is one to make of this diagnosis and this remedy? The truth is that given India's socio-economic situation, despite all the rhetoric about 'reforms with a human face' and safeguarding the interests of the poor, the elite have much more influence over actual programme implementation than the middle or poor sections. Hence, while much is made of 'poverty alleviation and employment generation programmes', the total central government spending on these programmes (in the urban sector) has been minuscule. It was just Rs. 333 crore in 2003–04, which has been modestly increased to Rs. 384 crores in the 2004–05 budget. It may be contrasted with a huge outlay on metro rail in Delhi, costing Rs. 300 crore per kilometre for the underground section. On the other hand, the entire edifice of urban infrastructure—the transport system, the water supply and sewerage systems, and the electric supply system—all are run in such a way that the poor pay much more per unit of urban services than the rich. Official documents like the Tenth Five Year Plan (Chapter on 'Civic Amenities in Urban Areas') testify to this reality. Thus, the failure to collect appropriate user

...the failure to collect appropriate user charges is really a failure to tax the richer urban groups.

charges is really a failure to tax the richer urban groups. And consequently, it can be argued, if a state government, in order to get access central funds, promises to levy property taxes on the rich urban residents or collect full costs of providing water and electricity from the rich urban users, one should not condemn such conditional loans.

The problem, if it exists, will lie in the details of the conditions. The conditions which a state government has to agree to for accessing the 'Urban Reforms Incentive Fund' are as follows:

- Repeal of the Urban Land Ceiling and Regulation Act (ULCRA)
- Rationalisation of Stamp Duty, in phases, to bring it down to no more than 5 per cent by the end of the Tenth Five Year Plan
- Reform of rent control laws to remove rent control on lease prospectively
- Introduction of computerised registration
- Reform of property tax so that it may become a major source of funds for ULBs
- Levy of reasonable user charges with full cost of operation and maintenance collected by the end of the Tenth Five Year Plan
- Introduction of the double entry system of accounting.

Further, it is stated that, 'the Empowered Committee under the Chairmanship of Secretary (Urban Employment and Poverty Alleviation) has been authorised to add more areas of urban reforms in the second and subsequent phases of reforms.' (GOI 2004)

What are the possible objections to this list of conditions? It seems that the problem areas are:

- the repeal of the ULCRA
- the basic principle of allowing conditions to be set by functionaries of the central government on matters which fall in the state list.

As far as the virtue of diluting or scrapping the ULCRA is concerned, it is yet to be established that it has led to any fundamental easing of the land market or improvement in the access of the poor to land in the states where this Act has been repealed. Therefore, it is highly arbitrary to insist that repealing ULCRA should be a condition for accessing central funds.

The more acute problem is that many state governments are opposed to handing over one of the areas of their control to the centre. The solution here lies in the centre agreeing to allow the conditions to be decided after consultations with the state governments. Provided the central government shows flexibility in its approach these are not intractable problems.

As far as the virtue of diluting or scrapping the ULCRA is concerned, it is yet to be established that it has led to any fundamental easing of the land market or improvement in the access of the poor to land in the states where this Act has been repealed.

Again, there cannot be any dispute with the way the official *Economic Survey* deals with the problem of non-availability of credit.

> There is, in general, despondency among agencies responsible for programmes such as SJSRY with regard to availability of credit. There is a feeling that the increased emphasis on the viability of banks and reduction of non-performing assets (NPAs) is beginning to affect the availability of credit for the urban self-employed. This would be an unfortunate development. There is an urgent need to restore the banking sector's role in providing credit support to the urban informal sector, especially the self-employed urban poor. As the Task Force on Employment Opportunities noted, banks can meet the credit needs of the informal sector by financing self-help groups which provide microcredit for informal sector activities. The concept of micro-finance essentially rests on the premise that (a) self-employment/ enterprise formation is a viable alternative means of alleviating poverty, (b) lack of access to capital assets/ credit acts as a constraint on existing and potential micro-enterprises and (c) the poor are capable of saving despite their low level of income. (GOI 2004)

On the whole, the basic theoretical arguments put forward in the official Survey are correct. But what about implementation?

The new government at the centre has been at pains to argue that more than one-third of the current financial year has already gone by and it would be foolhardy to go in for ill-thought out changes at this stage. The implication is that we should be patient enough to wait for the next year's *Economic Survey* and Budget before we come to any conclusions about the direction and effect of the new government's economic policies.

Yet it is possible to pick out a few significant markers, or, to use the language of the stock markets, 'triggers'.

What could be the key indicators of government urban sector policy? We can highlight a few:

- What will be the central government's response to the state governments' demands that the conditionalities attached to the 'Urban Reforms Incentive Fund' be modified?
- Will the new central government continue with the previous government's tendency to proliferate schemes and creating multiple implementing machineries working at cross-purposes in an un-coordinated way?
- Will the new central government rely on the very difficult but inescapable task of building up community structures and capabilities as was envisaged under the original Swarn Jayanti Shahari Rojgar Yojana (SJSRY) or will it go for the kind of structure that has been used for the 'Valmiki Ambedkar Awas Yojana' (VAMBAY), a scheme instituted by the previous (NDA) government, and which has, for all practical purposes, replaced the SJSRY.[2]
- Will there be a greater transparency in the approach? Will the central government in next year's *Economic Survey* give more precise details of the rules, procedures, and financing of schemes such as VAMBAY?
- Will the next year's budget be candid enough to announce which schemes are being wound up and why? Or, will a few more schemes be started in the name of the prime minister—essentially old wine in new bottles?
- Will we go back to the old model of highly centralised functioning rather than go forward to a more participative community-oriented, capability-enhancing approach, difficult though that may be?

The new government at the centre has been at pains to argue that more than one-third of the current financial year has already gone by and it would be foolhardy to go in for ill-thought out changes at this stage. The implication is that we should be patient enough to wait for the next year's *Economic Survey* and Budget before we come to any conclusions about the direction and effect of the new government's economic policies.

In essence, let us wait for another few months. The next *Economic Survey* and next central government budget will tell us where the new central government intends to take the country.

Reference

Government of India (GOI). 2004. *Economic Survey 2003–04*. New Delhi: Ministry of Finance.

2. Budget documents indicate that expenditure under SJSRY has stagnated or declined while that under VAMBAY has increased sharply. In 1998–99 the expenditure under SJSRY was Rs. 162 crore, which fell to Rs. 95 crores in 2003–04. On the other hand, the VAMBAY scheme which started as late as October 2002, and makes no serious effort at community involvement, involves an annual expenditure of around Rs. 250 crore.

Health

Alpana Sagar and *Imrana Qadeer*

The government's priority in the healthcare sector, according to the *Economic Survey 2003–2004*, is to achieve an improvement in healthcare services in the country, with a special focus on the underserved and underprivileged segments of the population. It is believed that this objective can be achieved if the investment in healthcare is increased from the present 0.9 per cent of the Gross Domestic Product (GDP) to 2 per cent by 2010. The second point of attention for reducing imbalances in healthcare services is reorganisation and restructuring of services at the primary, secondary and tertiary levels. This is needed to provide healthcare services not only locally, but also to improve referral services. In addition, accountability of healthcare providers is to be ensured through appropriate delegation of powers to Panchayati Raj institutions. Another important commitment is the need for horizontal integration of all aspects of the vertical disease programmes. The *Economic Survey* also emphasises the Tenth Plan proposal for provision of essential primary healthcare, emergency life-saving services, free services under the National Disease Control Programmes for all individuals and essential healthcare services to people below the poverty line (GOI 2004).

The question we would like to address is—will it be possible to provide quality healthcare and to reach the poorest of the poor through such measures, or do we need to develop a paradigmatic shift in our approach towards healthcare?

...while an increase in the healthcare budget is a welcome proposal in these days of cutbacks in the social sector, we need to explore whether merely increasing the budget for healthcare to the proposed levels can by itself change the health status of the people.

Increasing Investment in Healthcare

The Bhore Committee had suggested in 1946 that investment in healthcare be at least 15 per cent of the total annual expenditure (GOI 1946). Presently the government budget for healthcare is nowhere near that. It is, in fact, closer to 3–4 per cent of annual outlays. However, while an increase in the healthcare budget is a welcome proposal in these days of cutbacks in the social sector, we need to explore whether merely increasing the budget for healthcare to the proposed levels can by itself change the health status of the people.

The survey states that larger investments in healthcare would be needed as 'the technology required for tackling resistant infections and non-communicable diseases are (sic) expensive' (GOI 2004). For the past two years, we have been investing 0.9 per cent of our GDP in healthcare and family welfare. There is no doubt that investment in healthcare needs to be increased, but should it be for the high-tech healthcare that in the long run will only help us to diagnose and treat certain communicable and non communicable diseases, or do we need to improve the overall functioning of the healthcare services in the country? This is a critical issue to be addressed and would require an epidemiological assessment of the causes of mortality and the service infrastructure in the healthcare sector. Only then should a choice of technology be made.

Even today, more than 50 per cent of deaths are due to communicable diseases.

Epidemiological Assessment of Causes of Mortality

Even today, more than 50 per cent of deaths are due to communicable diseases. Among communicable diseases the commonest are diarrhoea, fevers, and respiratory infections (GOI 2000). About 20 per cent of deaths are among children below four

Table 1
Infant Mortality by Sex and Place of Residence

Rural			Urban		
Male	*Female*	*Total*	*Male*	*Female*	*Total*
70	74	72	41	44	42

Source: *SRS 2003.*

years of age, and of those, 75 per cent deaths are among children of 0–1 years of age. Among children below five years, particularly infants, we find that mortality is more among girls than among boys, more in rural areas than urban areas and more among the deprived sections of society (Tables 1 and 2).

It is extremely important that we keep in mind the fact that most of the deaths occur among children under five years of age. The fact that social groups and gender bias are significant predictors of mortality is reflected in a statement of the Planning Commission, which points out that anaemia and under-nutrition are contributory factors in over 50 per cent of deaths among under five-year olds (Planning Commission: 2000).

An examination of the causes of death among infants reveals that about 35 per cent of mortality in infancy is caused by premature births and low weight of babies at birth; the latter is a more common cause. Many babies are born with low weight at birth usually due to under-nutrition of their mothers. Acute respiratory infections (ARI)—mainly pneumonias—are responsible for a quarter of deaths among the infants and diarrhoea accounts for 6 per cent of deaths among them. If we examine the causality of these problems, we find that most of these are linked to poor environmental conditions such as lack of sanitation, non-availability of safe drinking water, and poverty.

Diagnosis and treatment of these infections does not require high-tech facilities. Low birth weight of infants is due to poverty and consequent under-nutrition of the mother. Prevention of deaths of these infants requires improving nutritional levels of the mother. Improving nutrition does not require expensive medical technology. What it does require however is employment, reasonable wages, and access to food. As far as diarrhoea is concerned, one of the first steps in preventing it is safe drinking water and sanitation. In treatment of ARI, careful observation of children with respiratory problems, helps in early diagnosis. Though antibiotics are needed to treat ARI and diarrhoea, if these are given judiciously, expensive fourth-generation medication is not needed. It is in fact unregulated misuse of antibiotics which is the root cause of the problem of the body's resistance to antibiotics. What is needed here is a rational drug policy, and not high-tech investigations or expensive treatment.

Similarly, of the deaths among children of 1–4 years of age, 22 per cent of deaths occur due to respiratory infections, 20 per cent due to diarrhoea, and 9 per cent because of anaemia (All data on mortality is computed from Survey of Causes of Death 1998). Here again, we see that sanitation, safe water, and nutrition are as important as the basic effective healthcare services, with referral services available if needed, to prevent untimely deaths. Newspapers have reported death of about 9,000

...of the deaths among children of 1–4 years of age, 22 per cent of deaths occur due to respiratory infections, 20 per cent due to diarrhoea, and 9 per cent because of anaemia...

Table 2
IMR and Under Five Mortality by Place of Residence and Social Groups

	Rural		Urban	
Social Groups	*(IMR)*	*(Under 5 years)*	*(IMR)*	*(Under 5 Years)*
Scheduled Caste	88.1	127.3	60.4	84.0
Scheduled Tribe	86.9	131.4	57.6	79.6
Others	69.3	93.1	43.5	57.0

Source: NFHS -2

tribal children of below the age of six years due to malnutrition in fifteen districts of Maharashtra—one of India's most prosperous states—over the past year, with about 1,000 of them dying in the past two months (*Times of India* 2004). These reports merely re-emphasise the fact that under-nutrition and poverty are important contributors to mortality.

Further data computed from *Survey of Causes of Death 1998* reveals that of women in the reproductive age group, almost 30 per cent die of communicable diseases (fevers, diarrhoeas, respiratory infections), 7 per cent of burns, about 9 per cent of maternal causes, 4 per cent of anaemia, and about 11 per cent commit suicide. In such a situation, it is being shortsighted and un-epidemiological to concentrate mainly on high-tech investments and to ignore the basic issues of nutrition, sanitation, safe water, and easy accessibility to quality healthcare services besides the need to decrease structural inequalities. We would like to argue, therefore, that a need for high-tech medical services is not as high a priority in bringing down mortality as employment, nutrition, sanitation, safe water, and structural changes are.

Among adults, suicide, homicide, and accidents are gaining ground as causes of death. Here again, the causes are not medical but rooted in the social and economic structures. The recent spate of suicides among farmers in Andhra Pradesh due to the crises in agricultural economy, which are leading to unmanageable debt point to this fact. An important issue here is that when we talk of the diseases resulting from life styles, we tend to think of the optional life styles of the middle class that lead to cardiovascular diseases, hypertension and such ailments. However, some life styles are forced on people due to poverty and we rarely consider the diseases these can give rise to. For example, prevention of cancer or coronary artery disease[1] that arise due to occupations, under-nutrition, or stress are not amenable to individual effort or high-technology but would require an overall change in the larger living and working conditions. Thus, while it is important to emphasise preventive care, prevention will involve much broader social changes.

Significance of Allocation of Resources

The above facts demonstrate the importance of inter-sectoral planning, yet it does not detract from the importance of either reorganising the healthcare services or the need to increase investment in them. However, not only is the amount of investment important, but the allocation of the budget among the departments is also important. Presently, in the budget for the Department of Health and Family Welfare, the Department of Health (including public health) gets 32 per cent of the total allocation, the Indian systems of medicine get less than 3 per cent, and the Family Welfare Department bags the balance 65 per cent (GOI 2004). What is even more noteworthy is that of the budget of the Family Welfare Department, 20 per cent is for contraceptive services, 20 per cent for the polio eradication programme, while about 13 per cent is for the reproductive and child health programme. Significantly, the prevalence of Acute Flaccid Paralysis is only 1.6 per thousand people (Varghese et al 1997) and its elimination is a myth, as critics of this programme have pointed out (Sathyamala and Mittal 2004). Yet, in absolute terms, the polio eradication programme has been allocated Rs. 1,186.40 crores while Malaria, Kala Azar, Filaria, TB, Leprosy, and AIDS control programmes together get only Rs 731.45 crores. The causes of mortality do not justify such a skewed allocation of resources. Rather, they emphasise the importance of diverse policies in the areas of agriculture, employment, and minimum wages, as well as the negative consequences of cutbacks in spending on the social sector in general and healthcare in particular.

...of women in the reproductive age group, almost 30 per cent die of communicable diseases (fevers, diarrhoeas, respiratory infections), 7 per cent of burns, about 9 per cent of maternal causes, 4 per cent of anaemia, and about 11 per cent commit suicide.

1. Studies today point to the possibility of foetal under-nutrition as being a significant risk factor in developing myocardial infarctions in later life (Godfrey and Barker, 2001).

Table 3
Health Services Infrastructure

	Existing	Required	Shortfall
Primary Health Centres			
1 per 20–30000 population	22975	32711	32%
Sub Centres			
1 per 3–5000 population	137271	196266	31%
Community Health Centres			
1 per lakh population	2935	9813	68%

Source: Population 1999—9813.2 lakhs. Computed from HII 1999(GOI 2002).

Reorganising Healthcare Services

The *Economic Survey* is far from lucid in its suggestions for reorganising and restructuring healthcare services. The data computed from Health Information of India 1999 reveals a shortfall in both healthcare institutions and personnel in the rural areas.

Among rural healthcare institutions, the shortfall for primary healthcare centres is 30 per cent, for sub centres it is 30 per cent, and for community healthcare centres it is 68 per cent (Table 3).

There is a shocking shortfall of specialists in healthcare institutions at present—paediatricians 85 per cent, physicians 80 per cent, gynaecologists 73 per cent, and surgeons 72 per cent. However, there is at least one doctor per primary healthcare centre, at least on paper. At the sub-centres, there is a shortfall of 47 per cent for male multipurpose workers (MPWs), and 16 per cent for female workers such as the auxiliary nurse midwives (ANMs) The shortfall of pharmacists and lab technicians is 23 per cent and 50 per cent, respectively.

Investment is needed indeed—not for high-tech services alone—but also for provision of the basic infrastructure and personnel. Not only do we need to expand infrastructure, especially where first referral units, that is community health centres are concerned, but also to ensure that a full complement of personnel is actually present in these institutions. Only then can one start talking of providing even basic services.

The present ethos of consumerism and the need to keep up with the peers among doctors is a basic reason why many doctors prefer to work in the private sector instead of the public sector. Having to work in a backward area is considered a 'punishment' and rural postings are nothing short of 'suffering' that is 'cured' by

Table 4
Health Services Personnel in the Existing Infrastructure

Post	Required	In Place	Shortfall
Community Health Centre			
Paediatrician	2935	453	85%
Physician	2935	585	80%
Gynaecologist	2935	771	73%
Surgeon	2935	809	72%
Primary Health Centre			
Doctor	22975/29702	25506	14%
Sub Centre			
Male MPW	137271	73327	47%
ANM	160246	134086	16%
Community Health Centre + Primary Health Centre			
Pharmacist	25910	21077	23%
Lab technician	25910	12709	50%

Source: Computed from HII 1999 (GOI 2002).

There is a shocking shortfall of specialists in healthcare institutions at present—paediatricians 85 per cent, physicians 80 per cent, gynaecologists 73 per cent, and surgeons 72 per cent.

seeking transfers. This might account for the lack of specialists at community health centres, the first referral units. It is also noteworthy that there is a nearly 50 per cent shortfall of male multipurpose workers (MPWs) and lab technicians at a time when we are talking of reducing mortality due to malaria by 50 per cent by 2010. A lack of male workers would affect not only malaria, but most other programmes being run by primary health centres such as the leprosy elimination programme and diseases surveillance. In the face of such a lack of infrastructure, it would be interesting to know what 'reorganisation' the *Economic Survey* is talking about. It seems that reorganisation would include the private sector and the voluntary sector as well as the public sector. What need to be discussed in this context are the mechanisms the government is putting in place to ensure that the private sector serves the poor. It is often emphasised that the poor access the private sector for out patient department (OPD) care, but this is never linked to the conscious and planned withdrawal of the public sector from healthcare services. It is also ignored that the poor access the public sector for in-patient care more often that the OPDs. It is in this situation that we read of corporate hospitals like Escorts and Apollo consistently denying services to the poor, in whose name they have received heavy subsidies from the government. While these hospitals have hit the headlines, the vast numbers of smaller private institutions are not even theoretically accountable to the poor. Thus, unless the private sector is regulated and controlled, how will the poor be assured of free access to these hospitals? Additionally, even if the private sector takes responsibility for curative care, what part will they play in the national disease control programmes? Studies have shown that the therapeutic practices of private practitioners leave a lot to be desired (Phadke et al 1995), and it is imperative that drug therapy be standardised. It is significant that neither the *Economic Survey*, nor any other policy statement considers these important issues of responsible public-private partnership.

...we read of corporate hospitals like Escorts and Apollo consistently denying services to the poor, in whose name they have received heavy subsidies from the government.

Studies have shown that the therapeutic practices of private practitioners leave a lot to be desired, and it is imperative that drug therapy be standardised.

The *Survey* also considers the issue of accountability of public healthcare institutions. There are two issues involved here. First, there is not much point in talking of accountability of healthcare providers to Panchayats when the providers are not there most of the time. The field work of an ongoing project by the Centre of Social Medicine and Community Health, Jawaharlal Nehru University, India, has shown that Panchayat members are not even able to make accountable the paramedical personnel, whose unions resist any disciplinary action, let alone the medical personnel! Thus, if medical and paramedical personnel have to become accountable to the Panchayati Raj Institutions, not only will the Panchayati Raj Institutions need more power, but the disregard shown by the medical system to panchayats will also have to be tackled. Secondly, it is unethical that the issue of accountability is raised only for the 'public healthcare providers' and not for the private ones. The private providers, if not made accountable to the people they are supposed to serve, will create an unequal partnership, which is profitable for them alone.

...Panchayat members are not even able to make accountable the paramedical personnel, whose unions resist any disciplinary action, let alone the medical personnel!

The present suggestion of horizontal integration of vertical programmes can only be viable once the structures and personnel are in place. Without these, services such as treatment for opportunistic infections of AIDS patients through public healthcare infrastructure cannot be successful. Providing adequate structures has to be the initial step before one can even talk of integration. However, we also find that while on one hand the survey talks of integration, on the other, it claims success for the vertical programmes. If the success of vertical programmes such as DOTS and polio eradication is genuine, then where is the rationale for proposing horizontal integration at all levels? Integration needs to be at the conceptual level as well as at the structural level. However, once again, neither the plans nor the policy documents discuss this.

As a part of reorganisation, it is essential that the doctors' attitude improves, and healthcare services at all levels become more patient-friendly. The issue of re-orientation of medical education has been raised recurrently and it is time it was taken up seriously.

New Distortions of Primary Healthcare

The concept of comprehensive primary healthcare was overtaken by that of selective primary healthcare, which at least talked of certain health problems and the need for three levels of care. Even this did not last long and was reduced to primary level care. Today in the name of going back to the expanded notion of the earlier concept, there is talk of essential primary healthcare and essential healthcare. A review of these concepts shows that in the Alma Ata document, primary healthcare was seen as essential healthcare. The Ninth Five Year Plan also defined essential healthcare as the basic minimum healthcare. It is only now that the World Health Organisation (WHO) has shifted its position to redefine the content of essential healthcare as a 'paradigm shift towards integrated preventive healthcare, promoting financial systems and policies that support prevention in healthcare, equipping patients with the needed information, motivation, and skills in prevention and self-management, making prevention an element of every healthcare interaction' (WHO 2002). Similarly, the National AIDS Control Organisation (NACO) too emphasises hygiene, immunisation, and individual prevention through increased awareness and promotes its provision through public private-partnerships with the assumption that private practitioners are meeting a significant proportion of healthcare needs of the people (NACO 2003). This reveals a trend towards shifting responsibility to individuals and private practitioners and undermining the importance of the secondary and tertiary care in primary healthcare, thus finding a way for the State to abdicate its responsibility.

Essential primary healthcare, as it is being redefined today, is contrary to the concept of primary healthcare, which involves the concept of 'intersectorality' and the need for the understanding of healthcare services as a complex system. The present effort is to reduce the concept of essential primary healthcare to primary level care, and to place the responsibility for their health squarely on the people!

This reveals a trend towards shifting responsibility to individuals and private practitioners and undermining the importance of the secondary and tertiary care in primary healthcare, thus finding a way for the State to abdicate its responsibility.

Conclusion

The *Economic Survey*, therefore, seems to be moving in the direction of technocentricity instead of rational therapeutics—a Frankenstein of an unregulated private sector, and a decimated set of services, which inevitably force people to find their own solutions. Those who cannot afford the prescribed solutions are then held responsible for being unable to prevent ill health. In such a situation, the dream of good health for underprivileged Indians will remain just that, and the majority of Indians will continue to be deprived of healthcare and medical services.

References

Godfrey, K.M. and D.J. Barker. 2001. 'Fetal Programming and Adult Health' in *Public Health Nutrition*. April, 4(2B): 611–24.

Government of India (GOI). 2004a. *Economic Survey 2003–2004*. 'Ministry of Finance and Company Affairs, Economic Division.

Government of India. 1946. *Report of the Health Survey and Development Committee*, Vol. IV (Bhore Committee). Manager of Publications. Delhi.

Government of India. 2000. *Survey of Causes of Death, 1998, Rural*. Delhi: Office of the Registrar General, Vital Statistics Division.

Government of India. 2002. *Health Information of India, 1999*. Delhi: Central Bureau of Health Intelligence, DGHS.

Government of India. 2003. *SRS Bulletin*. New Delhi: Sample Registration System, Registrar General, India, Vital Statistics Division.

Government of India. 2004b. *Expenditure Budget 2004–2005*, Vol. 2, Delhi: Ministry of Finance.

International Institute for Population Sciences and ORC Macro. 2000. *National Family Health Survey. (NFHS–2), 1998–1999.* Mumbai, India.

National Aids Control Organisation (NACO). 2003. www.naco.nic.in/nacp/public.html accessed on 29 July 2004.

Phadke, A., P. Mane, A. Fernandes, L. Sharda and A. Jesani. 1995. *A Study of Supply and Use of Pharmaceuticals in Satara District.* Pune: Foundation for Research in Community Health.

Planning Commission. 2000. http://planningcommission.nic.in/aboutus/committee/strgrp/stgp_fmlywel/sgfw_ch6.pdf.

Sathyamala C. and O. Mittal. 2004. 'Global Polio Eradication Initiative (GPEI) in India—A Cause for Concern,' presented at a workshop 'Questioning Prevailing Paradigms in Public Health: Putting People Centre Stage' at the World Social Forum, Mumbai.

Times of India. 2004. '1,000 Children Dead in Two Months,' 6 July: 1, col. 2–5.

Varghese, M., I. Qadeer and D. Mohan. 1997. 'Paralytic poliomyelitis in a rural area of north India,' in *The National Medical Journal of India,* 10(1).

WHO. 2002. WHO Integrating prevention into health care.htm

Education

Kumaresh Chakravarty

Even the World Bank is now emphasising the urgent need for imparting elementary education for all as a part of economic reforms. Since education is the first condition for creation of 'human capital', improvements in labour productivity cannot be ensured without universal education, at least up to the elementary stage. But with large sections of the masses living in poverty or near-poverty, this cannot be achieved without widespread and effective intervention by the state. Welfare economists of neo-liberal persuasion also argue that education is one of the instruments for reducing economic and other disparities.

There is another way of evaluating the necessity for education, especially in developing societies. While education is a source of acquisition of prevalent skills, it is also the foundation for developing new knowledge and skills through work experience. Knowledge becomes the prime productive force when it opens the door for developing new technologies, and new technologies, in turn, call for acquisition of new skills by the workforce.

Universal elementary education alone is not enough to form a base for creation of knowledge. Unless a high and rising proportion of the workforce receives education at higher levels also, generation of new knowledge remains confined to a tiny segment. This restricts creative potential of a society and retards its scientific and ideological progress. It also perpetuates uneven access to theorised knowledge in the domains of science and technology. Developed countries' monopoly of intellectual property rights is a product of such uneven access to theoretical knowledge. Astronomy specific to space research, bio-technology, hardware for information storing and processing, and the ever-renewing mass destruction weaponry are the leading areas where such disparity in knowledge is most visible. Developing countries remain unequal partners in the international fora like the World Trade Organisation (WTO) on the one hand, and they lose a good part of their scientific and technical manpower to developed countries on the other.

Unless a high and rising proportion of the workforce receives education at higher levels also, generation of new knowledge remains confined to a tiny segment.

The actual meaning and implication of such singular emphasis on elementary education, often at the cost of education at post-elementary levels, should be examined with reference to the second of the two aforesaid ways of recognising the importance of education. The World Bank's approach to education is essentially exclusivist. It suggests, for example, higher state expenditure on elementary education, but advises gradual withdrawal of state support (subsidy) to other segments of the formal education system. The Government of India on its part has been persistently encouraging privatisation of higher education, which several expert committees have recommended as a desirable policy. Privatisation of all branches of higher education, professional education in particular, has been a fast growing process. In the sphere of non-professional education, increasing expenditure cut has been a consistent programme, especially since the early nineties, when economic reforms were officially inaugurated. Particularly alarming is the severe contraction of whatever research opportunities that were made available during the sixties and seventies through state-funded centres of research and advanced studies. The Council of Scientific and Industrial Research (CSIR) has now been asked to generate funds by selling technological innovations to the private corporate sector. In sum, higher education

...higher education and research are being increasingly handed over to the private sector for earning profit.

and research are being increasingly handed over to the private sector for earning profit. Profit-seekers, on the other hand, are not the best patrons of fundamental theoretical research. They would rather import technology to the extent their resources would allow.

Elementary Education

Nothing that has been said above, however, reduces the importance of elementary education. Even elementary education—basic reading, writing, and computing—imparts some tools for everyday survival. Elementary education is divided into primary (for age-group 6–11) and upper primary/middle (age-group 11–14) levels. Since primary schools are more numerous and are located closer to their students homes than the middle level schools, universal primary education (UPE) should be easier to achieve. The 93rd amendment to the Constitution however, takes up universal elementary education (UEE) as the new 'fundamental right' of children. We therefore, emphasise UEE and examine the progress made here.

What Drop-Out Figures do not Reveal

Dropping out of students has perhaps been the most difficult problem, especially at the primary level. Drop-out rates have seemingly declined over the decades, but short period data show significant fluctuations. What is actually alarming is that the number of drop-outs and those who have never been enrolled in a school has been rising.

A simple numerical exercise may be useful here. Official enrolment figures show that primary enrolments went up 1.22 per cent between 1991–92 and 2001–02, while growth rate in the population in the age-group 6–11 was almost 1.8 per cent. Clearly, the number of those not enrolled in schools will keep on rising so long as the enrolment growth rate remains below the growth rate of the school-age population.

Every year more children get added to the stock of the education-deprived. And the stock will continue to rise cumulatively so long as the drop-out rate remains even half of the lowest achieved so far. By a rough estimate, this stock, in the 6–14 age group, accumulated up to more than 75 million during the 1990–91 to 2001–02 period. In 2000–01 alone, the number of children in this age group who were out of school was 35.56 million while their estimated population was 192 million and their enrolment in classes I–VIII was 156.66 million. The situation in some states was much worse than what the all-India aggregate indicates (See Table 1). The *Economic Survey* is silent about whether or how such a process of increasing left-outs can be dealt with.

How bright then are the prospects of realising UEE in the near future? The answer mainly depends on one's anticipation about the prospect of full enrolment and elimination of drop-out, and the realisable level of project-specific state funding and its growth. For the second condition, raising public expenditure on education to six per cent of GDP is not enough. The official estimate of additional expenditure required for implementing UEE (Table 2) shows that by 2007–08, this addition alone will cost 1.32 per cent of GDP. It is quite likely that the growth rate of GDP assumed in the estimate is unduly ambitious, in which case the addition will cost

What is actually alarming is that the number of drop-outs and those who have never been enrolled in a school has been rising.

Table 1
Expenditure on Education as Per Cent of GDP

	Rs. Crore at 1993–94 prices			*% of GDP*		
Year	*Private*	*Public*	*Total*	*Private*	*Public*	*Total*
1993–94	10092	25484	35576	1.29	3.26	4.55
1996–97	12020	31637	43657	1.24	3.26	4.50
1997–98	13526	33713	47239	1.33	3.31	4.64
1998–99	14605	38408	53013	1.35	3.54	4.89
1999–00	16303	41487	57790	1.38	3.65	5.03
2000–01	18129	45554	63683	1.51	3.80	5.31

Table 2
Additional Expenditure for UEE

(Rs Crore)

Year	*Recurring*	*Non-Recurring*	*Total*	*As % of GDP*
1998–99	100	–	100	0.007
1999–2000	1500	2000	3500	0.24
2000–01	4000	3000	7000	0.46
2001–02	6000	4000	10000	0.62
2002–03	8500	4000	12500	0.73
2003–04	10000	4000	14000	0.78
2004–05	13000	4000	17000	0.90
2005–06	16000	4000	20000	1.01
2006–07	20000	4000	24000	1.16
2007–08	27250	1572	28872	1.32

Source: *A Profile of Basic Education*, National Institute of Educational Planning and Aministration.

more than 1.32 per cent of GDP. Total recurring public expenditure on education in 2000–01, based on National Accounts Statistics, was 3.8 per cent of GDP at 1993–94 prices (Table3). An additional 1.32 per cent will take the figure to 5.12 per cent. So, whether the residual 0.88 per cent will be sufficient even for maintaining the recurring expenditure on other sectors of education is a big question. In any case, the estimated sum of Rs. 14,000 crore for 2003–04 does not seem to have been provided for in the central budget.

Complete prevention of dropping-out appears to be an impossible task under the present policy dispensation. An elaborate analysis of the reasons for the high drop-out rate is not possible here. But, to put some of the essential conditions for it in a simplified way, it calls for the following:

1. Elimination of poverty via employment and income growth for the poor;
2. Imparting greater relevance to education through change in content; and
3. Improving the present infrastructure including the student-teacher ratio.

Experience so far has conclusively shown that predominance of market mechanism raises an insurmountable roadblock in the path of poverty elimination.

Secondary and Higher Education

A reading of the *Economic Survey* always indicates that the central government has stopped considering these two sectors as of any importance. The *Survey* does not devote more than a few sentences to these, and some information is merely repeated in the subsequent Surveys. Some of the highlights of an implicit policy for these sectors are:

Table 3
Out-of-School Children, 2000–01 for Select States

(Age: 6 to 14 Years)

State	*Population (6–14)*	*Enrolled*	*Out-of School*	*Out as per cent of Total Children*
Andhra Pradesh	14.20	11.73	2.5	21.12
Bihar	21.57	13.12	8.45	39.17
Haryana	4.07	2.94	1.13	27.85
Madhya Pradesh	16.08	14.59	1.50	9.26
Punjab	4.22	3.10	1.12	26.58
Uttar Pradesh	35.07	19.13	15.94	45.45
India	192.00	156.66	35.36	18.41

Note: Number in Million.
Source: Answer to Question in Rajya Sabha, March 10, 2003.

Complete prevention of dropping-out appears to be an impossible task under the present policy dispensation.

1. The Open University system, with its increasing popularity has been a great advance in terms of numbers with access to higher education.
2. A hike in university fees, along with contributions from industry, private individuals, etc. in the constitution of funds/trusts like the Bharat Shiksha Kosh is also necessary.
3. Vocationalisation is being and will be preferred as a part of the curriculum for creating greater employability.

The first two items clearly indicate the rising dependence of secondary and higher education on private funding, the latter in particular, while the third is a routine repetition of what was stated in the New Education Policy, 1986 (partly modified later). Vocationalisation as an umbrella term may mean many things under different configurations of technology, demand for specific skills, and probable sources of demand generation. When it becomes an official faith, it loses serious relevance, but it keeps guiding reform of curricula in educational institutions. The New Education Policy, for example, said that a student should 'be able to graduate with modules pertaining to political theory, public administration, mathematics and word processing'. In terms of employability, the idea seems to have been guided by the understanding that word-processing jobs are available in abundance. Word processing can be substituted here by many other skills such as draughtsmanship, boiler attendance or lath operation skills. What is never examined is that the gap between supply of and demand for specific skills is miserably wide today with the exception of a few new skills related mainly to information and communication technologies.

...the gap between supply of and demand for specific skills is miserably wide today with the exception of a few new skills related mainly to information and communication technologies.

As regards source of funds for education, the *Survey* is silent about a fast-spreading new trend, especially in urban areas—private investment in secondary education (which often includes upper primary education in the same institution) and technical/professional education. Even low-income parents send their children to high-cost private schools, which are preposterously called 'public schools'. The perception is that education through such institutions gives students easier access to jobs, even higher-paying jobs.

Conclusion

In sum, except for the preference for increasing privatisation, the only area where the government seems to have some semblance of a policy is the recent adoption of UEE as a priority. Developments related to imparting of education indicate a clear trend against a scientific and democratic education system. Student-teacher ratio is rising at all levels of education. Libraries are suffering due to inadequate funds. Availability of specialised journals required for higher study and research is declining. Examination system has become almost completely out of sync with the desirable inseparability of instruction and evaluation. Finally, access to higher education is increasingly contracting. Thus, howsoever much it sounds an exaggeration, it is time to examine whether India's education system is not already in a structural crisis.

Developments related to imparting of education indicate a clear trend against a scientific and democratic education system. Student-teacher ratio is rising at all levels of education. Libraries are suffering due to inadequate funds.

Social Exclusion

Vivek Kumar

Global capital seeks to complete its agenda of universal coverage by means of imposition of the Structural Adjustment Programme (SAP) on the countries in which the process of capitalist transformation was aborted or remained incomplete. Among the votaries of global capitalism, there has emerged a non-orthodox school, which is realistic enough to recognise the sub-optimal and exclusionary character of an unrestrained and unregulated global capitalism. As shown in the first chapter of this Survey, the Indian experience with the SAP has strengthened the exclusionary character of development brought about by global capitalism. In this article we discuss and specify some crucial aspects of the process of social exclusion and its outcomes in India over the last few years. Social exclusion, on the basis of age, gender, and class, as fostered by globalisation and capitalism, is present in most of the societies of the world, and Indian society is no exception. But in the Indian society, the Dalitsalso face social exclusion because of their caste. Because of their unique location in the social structure, the Dalits, who constitute more than 16 per cent of the Indian population and are divided into 1,091 castes, have been facing this exclusion for ages, which was legitimised on the basis of Dharma (faith) and Karma (fate). The economic developmental programmes of together with the processes like modernisation, westernisation, and now globalisation, have all failed to ameliorate their socio-economic condition. In fact, they seem to have reinforced social exclusion by topping it off with economic exclusion and discrimination against the rural, agricultural, petty production and informal sectors.

The exclusion of the Dalits is evident not only in the social and interactional pattern in everyday life, but also in the secular spaces as well, where it is proclaimed that the interaction between individuals takes place on universalistic principles. Their scant presence, in public institutions like the bureaucracy, judiciary, public sector enterprises, banking, educational institutions, and institutions of higher learning, even after 57 years of Independence, demonstrates that they are not treated at par with others. The same is the case in the private sector, specially in industry, services, and the media, where there is no reservation. As 80 per cent of the Dalits still live in the rural areas, they face discrimination of the worst kind. Their colonies are still outside the main villages and they are kept out side the normal interaction pattern of the society. Further, the restricted freedom of occupation, landlessness, high incidences of poverty and unemployment, denial of access to health and education services have made them cumulatively discriminated against and deprived.

The exclusion of the Dalits is evident not only in the social and interactional pattern in everyday life, but also in the secular spaces as well, where it is proclaimed that the interaction between individuals takes place on universalistic principles.

Added to these types of deprivation is the continuation of caste-based discrimination, such as the practice of untouchability and the committing of various types of atrocities, which testify to the fact that the life for Dalits is overwhelmingly 'disfigured' in contemporary India. For instance, from 1981 to 2000, the Dalits suffered 3,57,945 cases of atrocity or discrimination; that means 22,371 cases per year, or approximately 617 cases per day. The exclusion of the Dalits becomes more problematic when the institutions, which are supposed to be the protectors, become the oppressors. The police and the other administrative institutions at the local level often act with hostility towards them. That is why most of the policies launched for their upliftment have been utter failures—whether it is distribution of *Patta* land,

The exclusion of the Dalits becomes more problematic when the institutions, which are supposed to be the protectors, become the oppressors.

distribution of food grains from the Public Distribution System shops, or distribution of houses under Indira Awas Yojana. That is why in 1999–2000, after nine Five-Year Plans, about 36.25 per cent of the Dalits were languishing below the poverty line in the rural areas and 38.47 per cent in the urban areas, and about the same percentage are unemployed.

The Dalits had faith in and hope from the political institutions, where their representation is quite substantial. From the Panchayat Raj institutions, state legislative assemblies to Parliament, their representation has been around 14 per cent (Table 1). Yet they have not been able to raise their issues, let alone initiate inclusive policies. Time and again it has been reported that the Dalit *Sarpanch* (village headman) was not allowed to unfurl the national flag or take a decision. Most of the decisions for the development of a Dalit colony go unheeded or the facilities intended for the Dalit colonies are diverted to the colonies of the dominant castes. Similarly, the Dalit members of the legislative assemblies and Parliament complain that they are not allowed to raise their issues in the respective houses and if they do so on their own, then the party leaders get upset with them and they are penalised by denial of an opportunity to seek re-election. That ensures that the Dalit representatives do not develop an independent 'clout'. It is worth mentioning here that, under Article 338 of the Indian Constitution, the Scheduled Castes and Scheduled Tribes Commission submits, annually, a report on the status of SCs and STs. But many Dalit parliamentarians have revealed that Parliament hardly gets any time to discuss it and even if it does, it does so very casually. Hence, we see that even after half a century of political democracy, the Dalit issues have been excluded from coming to the centre stage in various political and policy fora.

But many Dalit parliamentarians have revealed that Parliament hardly gets any time to discuss it and even if it does, it does so very casually. Hence,, we see that even after half a century of political democracy, the Dalit issues have been excluded from coming to the centre stage in various political and policy fora.

Children and Women

Apart from the Dalits, India's children and women, have been the worst sufferers of this deeply embedded culture of exclusion. Further, among women and children, we can easily detect that the Dalit children and women are further marginalised. Children, who are considered the 'future of the nation' need special mention here, as they have been deprived of their right to health, education, livelihood, and development. The denial of health facilities to the infants in general and the Dalits infants in particular, can be proved by the high mortality rate existing in India. (Table 2) As the state withdraws from its responsibility for public healthcare, and leaves the masses to the market forces, the situation will became even worse.

Table 1
Scheduled Caste Participation in the Political Institutions

Panchayat Raj Institution (2001)				*State Legislative Assemblies (2000)*	*Lok Sabha 2004*
Gram Panchayats	*Panchayat Samitis*	*Zilla Parishads*	*Total PRIs*		
367941 (14.3)	18546 (14.4)	1822 (13.5)	388309 (14.3)	562 (13.8)	79 (14.5)

Source: Election Commission, New Delhi; Department of Rural Development, Government of India, New Delhi.

Table 2
Infant Mortality — 1998–1999

S.No.	*Indicators*	*Scheduled Caste*	*Others*
1.	Infant Mortality	83.00 (88.0)	61.8 (69)
2.	Child Mortality	39.5	22.2
3.	Mortality under Five	119	82

Note: The data in bracket account for the infant mortality in rural areas.
Source: National Family Health Survey 1998–1999.

As children cannot unite and protest against the injustice meted out to them, their plight usually goes unheeded. Education can work as an independent variable for social change. But quality public school education, equally accessible to everyone, has never been India's priority. Primary education at the public school level has remained low-priority since the market leaders and their political representatives have not been enthusiastic about educating the children of deprived sections like farmers, poor and marginalised workers, artisans, and the Dalits. These sections of people were expected to follow their family vocation and remain cheap sources of manpower. The public schools were also neglected because the well-to-do among these sections sent their children to the exclusive and costly private schools. India spends only about 1.9 per cent of its Gross Domestic Product on primary and elementary education. And because of lack of adequate funds and misguided approach to the content and relevance of education for the disadvantaged and deprived sections, there has been a dearth of adequate infrastructure for running public schools for these sections.

Gone are the days when it was argued that the poor and the Dalits do not want to send their children to schools. A recent Public Report on Basic Education in India (PROBE) survey (1999) found that nearly 98 per cent of the rural parents believe that it is important to send their children to school. The PROBE survey also belied the myth that education was free in the government schools. In the northern states, the study pointed out, the annual direct cost of sending a child to a government school was Rs. 366; in Maharashtra it was Rs. 385; in Rajasthan Rs. 810; and in Karnataka it was Rs. 1,200. These amounts are spent on stationary, transport, and uniform. Now, it is a moot question that when 50 per cent of the Dalits and approximately 23 per cent of the general masses are still under the official poverty line, can they afford to send their children to the schools? And we all know what the government's definition of the poverty line in India is. It is clear that the planning and delivery of social services, grossly inadequate though they are, also happen to be exclusionary, as far as the poor and the Dalits are concerned.

The Education Policy of 1968 focussed on the common school system for children, irrespective of the socio-economic and other differences. But the policy has never been implemented by the government and today we have different types of schooling for the different sections of society. According to PROBE, the poor and disadvantaged go to the public schools; the middle-class, and those in the lower socio-economic ladder, go to private schools that are either aided or unaided, recognised or unrecognised; the rich go to the high-fee-charging private schools; the elite to schools offering international certification. The monthly education cost of one such child would easily exceed the annual earnings of about five families of labourers, as the current daily wage rate is around Rs. 60–70, and work availability rarely exceeds 180 days per annum. Therefore, we observe that education, which is considered to be a social leveller, is itself accentuating social inequality in the society. The most significant impact of these policies has been a high rate of dropouts, particularly from the Dalit communities. (Table 3)

In the northern states, the study pointed out, the annual direct cost of sending a child to a government school was Rs.366; in Maharashtra it was Rs. 385; in Rajasthan Rs. 810; and in Karnataka it was Rs. 1,200.

The Indian state has to realise that for nation building primary education is essential, especially for the poorer sections, and needs immediate remedial measures, including a massive infusion of funds.

...education, which is considered to be a social leveller, is itself accentuating social inequality in the society.

Table 3

Drop-out Rate of Scheduled Caste and Total Population

Year/standard	*1998–99 Standard (I-V)*	*1998–99 Standard(I-VIII)*	*1998–99 Standard(I-X)*
SCs	44.27	63.58	76.63
Total Popu.	39.74	56.82	67.44

Source: Department of Educator, Ministry of Human Resource Development.

The lack of education facilities forces poor children into the labyrinth of poorly paid jobs in harsh working conditions. A rough estimate of child labour in India suggests that there are about 60 million child labourers in India, forced to work for mere survival and about 40 per cent of them are from the Dalit communities. A casual look will tells us that the Dalit children constitute more than 80 per cent of the child labour in the carpet, match stick, and crackers industries and in domestic labour.

A significant point to be noted here is that the social scientists and social activists discuss the hazardous working conditions for children only in , the mines, carpet, cracker, and glass industries. The children working in houses, , *dhabas* and hotels, or in the agricultural work are not considered for this purpose. Though the Dalit children are involved in all these types of labour, what is most detrimental to their chances of a decent life is the initiation into the hereditary labour at a tender age. Yet, few have ever tried to probe this issue.

The tanning, colouring, and preparing of leather for manufacture,, lifting dead animals, cleaning human excreta, cleaning soiled clothes, butchery, collection and sale of toddy, are a few hereditary jobs generally persued by the Dalit children. The irony is that the researchers and activists do not discuss these jobs and their impact on the Dalit children. Nor has the state formulated an alternative programme for such children. It is ironic that when the Dalit children are involved in their hereditary occupations, there is no law to stop them, but as soon as they try to leave the hereditary occupations and take up alternative occupations, their parents are liable to penalisation.

Women too have been victims of the expanding process of social and economic exclusion, in the Indian society. The lower status of women in Indian society is evident from the low literacy rate among them, 54.2 per cent, and the declining sex ratio, which according to the 2001 census, is 933 women per thousand men. Besides this, women in general, and the Dalit women in particular, suffer from the lack of healthcare facilities and a secured and dignified life. Maternal mortality is defined by the World Health Organisation (WHO) as the death of a woman while 'pregnant or within 42 days of termination (by delivery, miscarriage or abortion) of pregnancy, from any cause related to or aggravated by pregnancy or its management, but not from accidental or incidental causes'. India has the highest number of maternal deaths in the world. Every five minutes a woman dies from complications related to pregnancy and childbirth, adding up to around 136,000 such deaths every year. The primary reason for such large number of maternal fatalities is the non-availability of healthcare facilities. In India, over two-thirds of women give birth at home—nearly 85 per cent in rural areas, and 95 per cent in the remote areas. Often, even the minimum facility that of a trained midwife, is not available to the mothers. According to an estimate, only 40 midwives are available per 100,000 women in India, forget about access to skilled medical care or manned and equipped healthcare facilities.

The lower status of women in Indian society is evident from the low literacy rate among them, 54.2 per cent, and the declining sex ratio, which according to the 2001 census, is 933 women per thousand men.

...only 40 midwives are available per 100,000 women in India, forget about access to skilled medical care or manned and equipped healthcare facilities.

While women in general are a mistreated lot in India, the Dalit women n are even more exploited and excluded. . They are triply discriminated against: first, on the basis of their gender, second, on the basis of their caste, and then on account of their economic class. Their exploitation emanates from their structural position in Indian society. Yet, the State has not succeeded in protecting them from subjugation, suppression, and exploitation. No doubt a Dalit woman faces problems similar to those faced by women in general, but as 50 per cent of the Dalits still live below the poverty line and 80 to 85 per cent of them live in rural areas and most of them discriminated against on the basis of their caste, their problems more complex. For instance, a rape is a heinous crime against any woman, but the rape of a Dalit women is often treated as qualitatively different and is generally unconsciously or consciously ignored by the government and academicians. The rape that occurred in the village Bhomaatola in Seoni district of Madhya Pradesh is case in point. In that village, three woman of a Mahar family

Table 4
Depicting Rape Cases on Dalit Women in Different Years

Year	*1991*	*1992*	*1993*	*1994*	*1995*	*1996*	*1997*	*1999*	*2000*	*2001*
No. Rapes	784	849	837	–	837	949	1002	1000	1083	1136

Source: National Commission for Scheduled Castes and Scheduled Tribes Report 1991–2000, New Delhi & *Crime in India 2001*, National Crime Records Bureau Ministry of Home Affairs, New Delhi.

were dragged from one corner of the village to the other and gang-raped by 16 men of the dominant Gowli community of the village. The worst part of the story is that it was a collective decision of the Gowli community in which elders and youth all participated to teach a lesson to the Mahars because one Mahar boy had eloped with a Gowli girl (*Frontline,* 13 August 2004). Hence it is evident the gang rape of a Dalit woman cannot be seen just as a crime against a woman. It has much wider social ramifications. That is why we have to take a special note of the rape of the Dalit women, as the cases of such communal rapes are on the rise. Nationally, 1,136 cases of rape of Dalit women were reported in the year 2001 compared to 1,083 cases in 2000, an increase of 21.5 per cent. Uttar Pradesh accounted for the largest number of such cases—412 or 31.3 per cent of all the reported cases. (Table 4)

Nationally, 1,136 cases of rape of Dalit women were reported in the year 2001 compared to 1,083 cases in 2000, an increase of 21.5 per cent. Uttar Pradesh accounted for the largest number of such cases—412 or 31.3 per cent of all the reported cases.

Conclusions

The central and the state governments are not making targeted plans to uplift the Dalits, children and women. Instead, they are going ahead with their markets and corporate sector friendly policies, with the inevitable worsening of the all-round socio-economic exclusion and disempowerment of the masses.. There have been no serious efforts or purposive policies or schemes for the development of these mistreated groups especially in the wake of the increasing withdrawal of the State from different social sectors. As a result of privatisation and disinvestment in the economic sector, the Dalits have been left in the lurch. The present union government and its allies have mooted an idea of dialogue with economic institutions, political parties, and private sector entrepreneurs for reservation in the private sector in their Common Minimum Programme for governance. One can confidently say that it is a big farce. These programmes just do not fit in with the logic or thrust of the Structural Adjustment Programme. When the government has not been able to fulfil the reservation for the Dalits enshrined in the constitution in half a century, then who will assure about a reservation policy which is not yet born? Moreover, if the government is really committed for the upliftment of the Dalits through reservation, then they should declare reservation first in those sectors that are still under its control and where reservation has not yet been implemented, such as judiciary, army, boards of the public sector enterprises.

Media

Sanjay Kapoor

It was in the month of February this year when I was attending a function in a foreign mission that I experienced the tyranny of the mass media. It was just around this time that one of the magazines had conducted an opinion poll about the prospects of different political parties in the forthcoming elections and relative popularity of different leaders. The poll had indicated that the ruling National Democratic Alliance was on a roll and it would win seats in excess of 320 seats in the Lok Sabha if the elections were to be held then. Similarly, the then Prime Minister Atal Behari Vajpayee was shown to be far superior in ratings then any of the opposition leaders.

During the function some senior diplomats and foreign correspondents finding a local journalist began to ask about the likely prospects of the ruling coalition in the forthcoming elections. I told them that the National Democratic Alliance was unlikely to return to power as they were loosing the southern states quite badly. I also wondered in front of my sceptical hosts about how the coalition can beat the anti-incumbency factor in different parts of the country. Finding my views strange, my hosts politely made light of my radical suggestions by describing me as 'anti-BJP'. 'These surveys cannot be wrong. And yes India shining campaign would help the BJP', they explained to their guests.

It was at this juncture I came to know about the import of these opinion polls and what the spin doctors of the Bharatiya Janata Party were trying to do: using mass media to practice a kind of fascism that had not been practised before. In some ways, this high voltage multi-crore media campaign was meant to snuff out dissent—even in social gatherings—and bring in a touch of inevitability about the return of the BJP to power. It was also meant to convey to those foreign contractors and businessmen who were dealing with the government that they should not pause in their negotiations as the elections were close by after all it was clear that they were returning to power. They were quick to provide these opinion polls as an evidence that there would be no change in Delhi. 'The India shining campaign and the sterling performance of Vajpayee would ensure our return', the BJP leaders were known to tell every one.

In this larger game of the BJP, the media—both the visual and the print—became a willing tool. All the top newspapers and channels, beneficiaries of the government's largesse during the India shining campaign, were co-opted to create a chimera about the impending triumph of the BJP.

In this larger game of the BJP, the media—both the visual and the print—became a willing tool. All the top newspapers and channels, beneficiaries of the government's largesse during the India shining campaign, were co-opted to create a chimera about the impending triumph of the BJP.

Besides the enormous money power at their disposal, the BJP bosses also sought to build their credibility in the eyes of the masses about why they were coming back. They gave the example of their successes in Rajasthan, Madhya Pradesh and Chattisgarh to prove how good their skills at running a good election campaign were. These electoral triumphs also gave them an opportunity to package leaders like Pramod Mahajan and Arun Jetley's as 'rain makers'—people who are endowed with the magical quality to create rain even when the elements suggest otherwise.

The BJP went about building a climate of opinion in its favour quite astutely. Even though they were more concerned about the visual medium, they knew that it were the newspapers and their editorial pages that provided a road map to the television channels to follow.

They sought to give primacy to the India shining campaign as well as the big things that the government was doing in United States of America and in Pakistan. The test series and one day international with Pakistan was seen as the crowing glory of the Vajpayee's regime. Newspapers and their editorial writers gushed unceasingly at the triumph of the Vajpayee government and how he was redefining the politics of this region. For quite a while, every newspaper or news channel, was virtually eating out of the hands of the omnipotent Prime Minister's office. There was not a single contrary noise emanating from the media. And if there was, then it did not count. During the run up to the elections, BJP and its variegated achievements seemed to have overwhelmed the media.

After glowing pieces in the editorial pages, newspapers and channels began to expand on the need for the people bringing back the BJP, after all so much work had to be completed. They pointed out the golden quadrilateral of the railway network and the speedy privatisation of public sector enterprises. There were other aspects of the economic reforms that needed the presence of a BJP led government. In the realm of diplomacy, compelling arguments were proffered to show how India would slip in the global pecking order if the BJP was prevented from coming back to power. The efforts of the Congress and the left parties to stop the BJP were contemptuously dismissed. 'Their campaign cannot just take off. They will run out resources by the time the elections take place,' reasoned media professionals.

After soaking up Rs. 300 crore worth of advertising in a space of a few months, Indian media had become a stakeholder in the re-election of BJP government. Vajpayee for them was the 'king of good times'.

This growing incestuous relationship between the ruling party and the media began to reveal itself in different ways. Television newsrooms are full of horror stories about how political experts who sported anti-BJP views were either not called or not given space. Even independent minded reporters who could give a contrary picture about the party were either sidelined or their reports pruned to take out all the 'juice' from it. One anchor of a prominent television channel was told by the Editor to stop being critical of some top BJP personalities.

Similarly, newspapers too were subjected to similar manipulations. Most of the reports that were carried did not indicate what was happening on the ground. And least of all, if it had any thing to do with the BJP or it's allies doing badly in any of their states. In many prominent newspapers, friendly special correspondents were parked so that reports loaded in favour of the government and the party found greater space. Secular minded reporters were slowly marginalised.

Needless to say most of the editors submitted to not so gentle pressures of the BJP bosses. Some news channels were forced to follow the BJP's political line as their expansion plans were kept hanging by the government. Most media heads did not object to these exertions, as such an approach brought rich financial dividends to them as well as their organisations. A study of the advertisements that the newspapers and channels received from the government would indicate what proximity to the powers that be does to the fortunes of news organisations. The growing affluence had a multiplier affect all over the media world and regional players, too, play the same tune.

BJP's other clever devise—which on hindsight boomeranged—was to sell the mood of the nation through opinion polls to newspapers. First the opinion was repeated ad nauseum on 24X7 news channels and later the same report was carried in the newspapers. There were very few reports by special correspondents of daily newspapers. Most of the newspapers were now reporting the television surveys.

The strategists of the BJP thought that this would work for them. Study by media researchers showed that the news channels gave almost 90 percent of the television time to BJP leaders.

After soaking up Rs. 300 crore worth of advertising in a space of a few months, Indian media had become a stakeholder in the re-election of BJP government. Vajpayee for them was the 'king of good times'.

This mood reached its crescendo during the staggered election campaign when the channels were first doing their opinion polls and later topping it with exit polls. What was worse was that nearly all the channels were projecting the outcome of the elections after the first round of polling. And a majority of the channels only brought to the fore the inevitability of the BJP's return to power.

So simplistic were some of these surveys—many of them conducted by the favourites of the Sangh Parivar—that they did not even take cognisance of the winds of change blowing in Andhra Pradesh or Tamil nadu. There could be a reason for this. At least two surveys were based on the same raw material. Only the conclusions were slightly different. Due to this reason, every one got the polls wrong. Right till the end of the third round, an impression was leavened that the BJP led coalition would come to power. But this did not happen.

Every one was surprised except the people of the poor states of Uttar Pradesh, Bihar, Andhra Pradesh etc. they voted with their hands and their feet and proved the spin doctors of the BJP so far off the mark.

It is alright for the party to go wrong in its assessment. But the bigger question is: why was the media surprised by the outcome? Quite clearly, some of the editors began to believe in the chimera that they created for raising the morale of the BJP leaders. They began to nurse ambitions that if the party came back then some of them would go places: may become ambassadors, etc. after retirement. The other reason was that many of the reporters and editors got too close to the BJP and NDA leaders. Many times it seemed like a mutual admiration club. Is it any surprising that the media lost the battle quite like the BJP?

...some of the editors began to believe in the chimera that they created for raising the morale of the BJP leaders.

Is it any surprising that the media lost the battle quite like the BJP?

The Grand Alliance of Fundamentalisms

Vasanthi Raman

In the following essay we attempt to understand the linkages between the current day resurgence of Hindu rightwing ideologies, the mobilisation of women under its aegis and the neo-liberal paradigm. While these linkages are complex, this is an attempt to sketch the broad trends that we believe are significant for the understanding of the present situation.

The Decades of 1980s and 1990s

The decades of the 1980s and 1990s have been significant for the country. These decades marked a departure from the political consensus of the post-independent years. It signalled the end of a consensus among the principal political parties of the centre and left regarding the nation-building project. Three significant developments marked the period. The decision to take the first World Bank-IMF loan, the Ayodhya issue that marked the shift to the centre stage of Indian politics of the forces of Hindutva (the ideology of Hindu nationhood) and the decision to implement the recommendations of the Mandal Commission. These developments have had a far-reaching influence on Indian politics. The World Bank-IMF loan marked the beginning of India's full integration into the world capitalist system, with no holds barred. While in the sphere of the economy, it was the reign of the so-called free market, ideologically and politically, this meant the beginning of an overt communalisation of the state and simultaneously the inauguration of what has been termed 'identity politics'. The contradictions of the development paradigm became apparent and visible.

While we focus on the political and social processes that characterised this period, the economic support base for the new policies was indeed already in existence. The preconditions for the change of course, as it were, have multiple causes. One major reason has been the sluggish growth of the home market beginning from the onset of the crisis period in the mid-1960s. Different groups of business houses responded differently depending on the extent they had either benefited under the previous regime with some being more enthusiastic than others. However, it became evident that there was a significant section of big business which supported the opening of the economy, the elimination of anti-monopoly legislation and a reduced role for the state sector. But the shift in policy also threw the entire society into turmoil. (Mazumdar 2004: 25–26)

...there was a significant section of big business which supported the opening of the economy, the elimination of anti-monopoly legislation and a reduced role for the state sector.

The 1990s saw the inauguration of the present phase of communal violence with the destruction of the Babri Masjid, an event that can be considered a watershed in the life of post-independence India. This signalled the entry of the politics of Hindutva onto the centre-stage of Indian politics. In a sense, the communalisation of not merely the state but also of civil society had now reached a climax. Certain features mark this phase:

...the destruction of the Babri Masjid, an event that can be considered a watershed in the life of post-independence India. The signalled the entry of the politics of Hindutva onto the centre-stage of Indian politics.

* Another version of this chapter has been published in *Revolutionary Democracy,* September, 2004, titled 'Communalism, the Neo-Liberal Project and Women'. Grateful thanks to Vijay Singh for painstakingly reading through my first draft and suggesting necessary changes; also to Indrani Majumdar, Centre for Women's Development Studies, for comments and suggestions; the free-wheeling discussions that I have had with her have always been very useful.

1. One significant feature is that the ideology of Hindutva once again resurfaced with ferocity unknown before. With it the whole contestation between two visions of India—the pluralistic, composite one which embraced all identities and an exclusivist one of a Hindu nation—is once again thrown open.
2. It is not accidental that the coming onto the centre stage of the forces of Hindutva has been accompanied by an accentuated thrust towards globalisation and the adoption of structural adjustment policies and the neo-liberal paradigm. Although one does not wish to posit a uni-dimensional relationship between the forces of globalised capitalism and that of Hindutva, one can hazard a hypothesis. Given the complex, segmented, heterogeneous and pluralistic nature of Indian society wherein marginalisation of the oppressed and subaltern groups have more or less proceeded along the lines of traditional social hierarchies, the forces of Hindutva represent status-quoist forces leading to a convergence of agendas.
3. Another significant feature—the othering and demonisation of Islam (not merely of Muslims) has to be analysed in the Indian context but also in the context of ideological barrage from the West, with Huntington's thesis of the 'the clash of civilisations' providing the latest 'historical' ammunition. As some scholars have pointed out, Indian Islam is older than American Christianity and European Protestantism and yet the depiction of Islam as foreign is an integral part of the Hindutva project. The same can be said of Christianity, though the targeting of Muslims and Islam is central to the ideological-political plank of Hindutva. (Ludden 1996)
4. This phase has also witnessed the heightened mobilisation of women by the forces of Hindutva as discussed later in this essay.

The transition of women from being weak victims to strong subjects is part of the mobilisation of gender in the overall project of the creation of a Hindu state. Corresponding to this and in a sense very much a part of this is the othering of Muslim women and men by denying them subjecthood and agency and portraying them as weak and passive victims requiring them to be rescued from the Muslim community, particularly the Muslim men.

The Collapse of the Nehruvian Consensus and the Beginning of the Neo-Liberal Project

Trying to draw the linkages between the above-mentioned processes is complicated and difficult. One can only broadly sketch certain trends that are indicative of the present situation.

Structural Adjustment Programme

The simultaneous jettisoning of the paradigm of the Welfare State and the adoption of the neo-liberal paradigm has serious implications for the lives of the majority of Indian citizens.

The introduction of the structural adjustment programmes since the nineties has meant drastic changes in the overall development paradigm. Politically, the most significant factor has been the jettisoning of the State as a major actor in socio-economic development and as an important agent mandated by the Constitution responsible for the welfare of the citizens. The simultaneous jettisoning of the paradigm of the Welfare State and the adoption of the neo-liberal paradigm has serious implications for the lives of the majority of Indian citizens. The abdication by the state of its responsibilities in the social sector, specifically health, education and provision of food security, compounded by economic policies which have exacerbated unemployment in the formal sector, increased insecurity of employment even in the informal sector, the collapse of traditional subsistence agriculture and intensified commercialisation of agriculture, the precarious situation of the artisans, particularly the weavers, the predatory commercialisation of coastal fishing, affecting the lives of millions of fisher folk leading to increased insecurity for the people—has intensified polarisation and exacerbated further the existing fault lines in Indian society. What is significant is that the divides based on class, caste, region, religion and gender have intensified. In short, the whole project of building a welfare state and ushering development with the state playing a major role in it has been abandoned and a whole new regime of the neo-liberal paradigm with its logic has been put in place. For the mass of Indians, their whole world is changing for the worse.

Nation-building in the Nehruvian Era

It is important to note the difference between the old regime and the new one. The post-colonial state in the first three decades after independence was still guided by the consensus of the national liberation struggle and continued to an extent to function as an arbiter between different classes. However, in actual operation, this consensus was flawed particularly when it came to struggles of workers and peasants or challenges to the state. The 1950s and 1960s has been characterised as the era of 'optimistic nation-building' and the state's legitimacy as the central political authority determining the future of the country and the nation-state. In this post-colonial consensus evolved among the ruling classes and elites, economic development was to play a central role in consolidating the nation and binding the diversities based on caste, region, language and even class together. Needless to say, there were many flaws in this consensus since the consensus itself was an amalgam of conflicting interests and ideologies some of which had their origins in the anti-colonial struggle.

One important element of this consensus was the notion of a secular republic, a state committed to equality for all citizens, regardless of caste, creed and gender, and the modern notion of citizenship of a modern, territorial nation-state. The Indian Constitution is one result of this consensus, a consensus which was a bitterly contested one formulated as it was in the immediate aftermath of the Partition of the country, compounded by the presence of diverse and conflicting interest groups and world-views. The consequence of this was a situation wherein while the state itself was committed to democratic values and secularism (defined as equal treatment of all religions and not as separation of the state from religion), the existing social structures were riven with contradictions based on caste, class, region, religion, gender etc. And development policies only partially addressed this chasm between constitutionally mandated social objectives and the reality of a deeply hierarchical and segmented society. In fact, if anything, development policies at times only exacerbated those very contradictions they were supposed to resolve. And so substantive equality remained a mirage for the vast majority of Indian citizens, particularly those who were at the lower rungs of the traditional social hierarchy. A scholar analysing the post-independence state writes:

> The Nehruvian high-mindedness and the powerful sense of moral legitimacy that it engendered was an important factor, rendering invisible the unequal benefits that development brought to different classes, castes and regional groups. (Deshpande 2003: 145)

...development policies at times only exacerbated those very contradictions they were supposed to resolve. And so substantive equality remained a mirage for the vast majority of Indian citizens.

The economic policies followed in agriculture were not based on the mass of the poor peasantry and the landless and therefore led to a steady marginalisation of these sections. Over the decades immediately after independence, the proportion of agricultural labourers increased while the proportion of cultivators declined. The process of differentiation and pauperisation intensified with the Green Revolution, vastly restricting the home market. The policies of state-led industrialisation could have taken social roots only if the home market expanded. Thus, the industrialisation that was initiated in the first two decades after independence had a very narrow social base and the collapse of the Nehruvian paradigm was almost a foregone conclusion.

The Social Base of the Indian State

There is another very important dimension that has often escaped scholarly and political scrutiny. The Indian state is not merely the Constitution; there are the personnel of the state, the administration, police, judiciary etc. The state continued to be dominated by personnel belonging to the upper castes and upper classes or at least the upper sections of the middle class. The struggle for equality of the lower castes, particularly the Scheduled Castes (SCs) and Scheduled Tribes (STs), has been an arduous one.

The dominance of the upper castes in administration, education and the upper echelons of the government continued. Despite reservation in education and jobs for SCs and STs, the Report of the Commissioner for Scheduled Castes and Scheduled Tribes over several years reiterate about the backlog in the fulfilment of the quotas for these groups in education and administration. Even now most of the Class III and Class IV posts in Government are filled largely by people from the Scheduled Castes and Tribes with them having a really meagre presence in the Class I and II posts. A study by Santosh Goyal (1990a, 1990b) on the social background of Indian Administrative Service (IAS) officers and top corporate executives in the private and public sectors shows the dominance of upper castes in these fields. There is similarly enough data to show that the presence of minorities, particularly Muslims (India's largest minority), in government and administration leaves much to be desired. It has been pointed out that the grand narrative of national development has nurtured an elite that overwhelmingly consists of Hindu upper-caste males, especially Brahmins.

However, categories such as caste, class, religion, region and language and gender are so finely and closely intermeshed that mere Constitutional guarantees, while necessary, are not sufficient to address the multiple sources of deprivation of the mass of Indians. Data of the NSSO for monthly per capita expenditure (MPCE) for 1999–2000 reveal that more than half of the ST population are below the poverty line with the SCs constituting about 43 per cent and the Other Backward Classes (OBCs) about 34 per cent. The residual category of Hindus (which we assume to be upper castes) have only 17 per cent below the poverty line. The data show that that the Hindu upper castes are over-represented in the topmost MPCE in both the rural and urban areas constituting 59 per cent of this class (Rs. 1,925 or more) in urban areas and about 40 per cent of this class (Rs.950 or more) in the rural areas even though they constitute only about 18 per cent of the rural and 27 per cent of the urban population. (Deshpande 2004: 146)

...categories such as caste, class, religion, region and language and gender are so finely and closely intermeshed that mere Constitutional guarantees, while necessary, are not sufficient to address the multiple sources of deprivation of the mass of Indians.

While certainly more complex indices need to be used to elaborate the social processes whereby certain castes and classes and regions have benefited from the development paradigm while others have either been left out of it or have borne the burden of it, there is enough to indicate the polarising impact of such a paradigm. Sensitive interventions are called for at the regional/local levels since most of the castes and communities are largely localised or regionalised. Interestingly, there has been a movement over the last two to three decades in building inter-regional and even pan-Indian alliances of caste groups, which roughly occupy comparable positions in the social hierarchy with a view to build pressure groups to claim a share of the social cake. The example of the dalits and the OBCs comes readily to mind. However, the social vision of the administrative personnel is crucial in dealing with the social and political dynamics of this society to bring about a democratisation of the society. To our mind, the failure of the project of building a democratic society can be traced to this inability and/or unwillingness and even opposition on the part of the personnel at the higher echelons of the administration to address the real sources of conflict. One might even argue that even ushering a democratic social order would have meant a radical restructuring of the social order involving genuine land reforms with land to the tiller and other radical redistributive measures. Certain measures like the Zamindari Abolition Act and the various Tenancy Acts brought certain significant changes in social relations; however, even these measures were stymied by the generally lackadaisical approach of the administration.

It would not be too sweeping a generalisation to state that perhaps historically the options of the Third World ruling classes, including India, were narrow and perhaps even non-existent. The option for a sustained and self-reliant development would have necessarily meant basing the strategy on the mass of the peasantry and delinking from imperialism and imperialist sponsored policies with radical social and political implications. This option was indeed not available for the Indian ruling classes for obvious reasons.

While polarisation is inherent in any development paradigm within the bourgeois-liberal framework what is only recently being recognised is that this polarisation has heightened and exacerbated the multiple and criss-crossing cleavages and fault lines of Indian society.

While polarisation is inherent in any development paradigm within the bourgeois-liberal framework what is only recently being recognised is that this polarisation has heightened and exacerbated the multiple and criss-crossing cleavages and fault lines of Indian society.

Continuities and Disjunctures

What marks the difference, to our mind, between the pre-SAP period and the subsequent one is the transformation in the nature, perspective and balance of social forces of the state leading to far-reaching changes in the society and polity. At the international level, the hegemony of the International Monetary Fund (IMF) and the World Bank (WB) and the neo-liberal paradigm effected drastic changes. The crucial difference that marks the earlier consensus and recent regimes is the abandonment of even the commitment on the part of the political class to principles of democracy and the commitment to the welfare of the weaker sections.

It is not fortuitous that this shift in the balance of forces is part of a world-wide process wherein there has been a shift to the Right which has been accompanied by:

(a) the deep structural crisis of capitalism beginning in the seventies after a thirty-year period of boom;

(b) the collapse of the welfare state and a jettisoning of the nation-building project among the ruling classes of the third world, and

(c) the defeat of the attempts to chart out an alternative course of forms of state socialism in the Soviet Union and eastern Europe.

What are the changes that have taken place? For one, this is an era where capital has penetrated every aspect of life across the globe leaving almost no aspect of the lives of people untouched; thus the reign of capital is complete. While the universalising tendencies of capital has been accompanied by a de-territorialisation leading to a certain 'disembedding of social relations' (Deshpande 2003), there has also been a counter-process that has led to a conscious cultivation of specificity. This is an assertion of particularistic identities based on ethnicity, religion and language. At a time when identities whether of the group or of the individual are in a state of flux, boundaries are getting blurred and there is talk of a borderless world, when the nation state is itself being refashioned to suit the requirements of global capitalist imperialism, the flip side is the resurgence of the search for identity. While the quest for the millennium among the dominated and the marginalised whether among nations or peoples takes particularly agonising forms of revivalism, the 'beneficiaries' also re-invent the golden past in the attempt to further bolster their hegemony. Many facets of the globalisation process have been subjected to scholarly scrutiny; but there is one dimension that needs to be emphasised—it is the defeat of the forces of national liberation, of the socialist and democratic forces on a world scale that has occasioned the rise of the forces of right reaction, which now speak the language of exclusionary identities. The growth of ideologies based on religion, race and ethnicities find the most fertile soil in the peripheries of the world imperialist system, i.e. in countries of the Third World, where the imperialist onslaught has got the upper hand over forces of national liberation and radical social transformation. One might even add that there is a conscious attempt to cynically foster precisely such tendencies and forces. Samir Amin draws attention to an important aspect of capitalist globalisation:

> Capitalist globalisation does not homogenise the world but, on the contrary organises it on the basis of ever stronger and more pronounced hierarchies. The peoples which are its victims are thereby deprived of active and equal participation in the shaping of the world. By encouraging culturalist responses, globalisation strategies make as much use as they can of diversity inherited from the past. At the same time, however, capitalist globalisation imposes on the dominated some of the 'specificities' that characterise its dominant centres. (Amin 2004: 191)

While the most irrational and backward-looking ideologies seem to have nested in the Third World, the manifestations of this worldwide shift to the right in the metropolitan countries have been very different. As one Marxist scholar has pithily put it:

> It is one of the ironies of ideological production in our time that precisely in the historical moment when capitalism has finally penetrated the farthest reaches not only of economic but also cultural production itself, across the globe, we witness the rise of an ideology, culturalism, ... which shifts the locus of determination from the field of political economy to that of culture. (Ahmad 2004: 94)

But it would be useful to remember that imperialism in another time also displayed analogous and seemingly contradictory tendencies. When analysing the processes of imperialist penetration in the colonies, Mao Zedong referred to the contradictory processes of retention and erosion: while imperialism erodes the old social relations it also simultaneously retains those elements and aspects of the social relations of the colony that help to sustain its rule. Thus the feudal classes, mercantile classes and other such dominant classes in the colonies most often constituted the social bulwark of colonial rule. Thus imperialism became internalised. While British colonial rule was getting established and western liberal-bourgeois concepts and norms were being propagated, simultaneously, Orientalist scholarship and discourse was also in the process of inventing India.

...the feudal classes, mercantile classes and other such dominant classes in the colonies most often constituted the social bulwark of colonial rule.

As far as the Indian situation goes, while the above-mentioned contradictory processes are operative, one can hazard a hypothesis that given the complex, segmented, heterogeneous and pluralistic nature of Indian society wherein the marginalisation of the oppressed and subaltern groups has more or less proceeded along the lines of traditional social hierarchies, the forces of Hindutva represent status-quoist and retrogressive forces with a modern garb thus leading to the convergence of the agendas of globalisation and Hindutva.

The Hindu Right and the Middle Class

There is a resurgence of a virulent form of social Darwinism wherein any form of protective measures for the welfare of the weaker sections are under attack either under the guise of downsizing the state or in the form of policies that directly affect the livelihoods of the vast majority of Indians. This has been accompanied by the increasing significance and centrality of the middle class, which constitutes the social base for Hindutva. The numerical strength of the middle class has been estimated between 50 to 200 million. The numbers would vary depending on the definitions employed and ranging from the schoolteacher and the clerk in the *moffusil* to the well-paid professionals in the metropoles. However, here we are particularly referring to the upper echelons of the middle classes who are crucial in opinion-moulding and who constitute an extremely significant support base for those who rule. There

There is a resurgence of a virulent form of social Darwinism wherein any form of protective measures for the welfare of the weaker sections are under attack either under the guise of downsizing the state or in the form of policies that directly affect the livelihoods of the vast majority of Indians.

have been important changes in the character of the middle class over the last five decades.

This class has been one of the beneficiaries of the Nehruvian development paradigm; the expansion of the state/public sector, the increasing proportion of the tertiary sector in the economy all have contributed substantially to making this class an important actor on the national stage. It was this class that provided the ideological support base for the development paradigm. But the recent changes in the development paradigm have intensified the differentiation of the middle classes, with the upper rungs turning to the ideology of neo-liberalism with alacrity. As one scholar has put it: '...the nation is no longer the canvas for their dreams and aspirations.' (Deshpande 2003: 148)

The ideologies that the middle class espouses today is a strange and anachronistic amalgam of the most retrogressive forms of cultural nationalism and revivalism and the most hedonistic forms of consumerism. The change that we have alluded to earlier can be traced in the metamorphosis of the middle class from a certain nebulous commitment to equality, democracy and secularism to being the most active spokespersons of the most aggressive forms of social Darwinism, where the welfare of the least privileged—the bottom 30 per cent—can be dispensed with and perhaps even necessary for being part of the global order.

Demographic Fundamentalism

An important though only partially recognised element of the emerging social Darwinism is the rise to prominence of what has been termed 'demographic fundamentalism'.[1] There are two elements of this phenomenon that need to be emphasised. The first one refers to the crucial significance that numbers assumed in the discourse of the Hindu revivalists right from the latter part of the nineteenth century with the Census contributing to a freezing of identities. The twenties and the thirties of the last century witnessed the resurgence of the politics of the Census in the armoury of Hindu political mobilisation. In northern India, there was a series of popular writings and pamphlets on this issue, which highlighted the conversion of lower caste Hindus to the fold of Islam and Christianity along with the alleged rising numbers of Muslims due to the prevalence of polygyny and proselytisation. (Gupta 2001: 222–30 and 2004: 4302–04) An important element of these popular writings was the attempt to wean the Hindu lower caste women away from those Muslim occupational groups (like vegetable sellers, bangle sellers etc.) with whom they had regular everyday contact along with dissuading these women from frequenting *dargah*s and shrines, thus fracturing shared spaces between the two communities. (Gupta 2001: 269–81) Needless to say, various statements of Census Commissioners (in 1891 and 1921) on the issue provided grist to the mill of Hindu publicists. (Gupta 2004: 4303) Thus the highly charged clarion call on the plight of the 'Dying Hindus' became an integral part of the campaign of Hindu publicists. One of the consequences of this was the movement of Shuddhi where there was a concerted attempt to reconvert those who had converted to either Islam or Christianity. The attempts at conversion were not so much designed to educate the new converts to the tenets of Hindu religion as to make them jettison those practices which were considered 'Islamic' like circumcision. (Sikand and Katju 1994: 2214–19) The entire issue of numbers was also linked to the position of women within Hindu society, particularly the position of widows. Thus the repressed sexuality of widows, the perceived promiscuity of Muslim men resulting in high fertility of Muslims,

The ideologies that the middle class espouses today is a strange and anachronistic amalgam of the most retrogressive forms of cultural nationalism and revivalism and the most hedonistic forms of consumerism.

1. This term was first used by Prof. Vina Mazumdar, Centre for Women's Development Studies, to describe the fundamentalism associated with population control policies at the cost of the girl child. However, I have extended the use of the term to incorporate the use of demographics to further communalism.

the alleged proselytisation of Muslims and Christians and of course, the need to qualify for the benefits of political representation, all combined together to form a highly potent and explosive weapon to further polarise and communalise the situation.

The campaign against Muslim fertility rates has been a constant in the repertoire of the Sangh Parivar. However, the Government of India's decision to release the religion-wise data of the Census of 2001, initially rather selectively (by excluding to mention that the figures for the Muslims do not take into account Kashmir and Assam) could have contributed to further polarising the society along communal lines and targeting a community which has already been battered by a regime of riots. But official clarifications helped to restore the balance. Census data shows, in fact, that the growth rate among the Muslims has shown a decelerating trend over the last decade both at the national level and in most states. (Premi 2004: 4298)

The second element of 'demographic fundamentalism' is the issue of population. Population policy has always been an integral element of the development paradigm since the early years since independence. There has been assumption shared by all sections of policy makers across the political spectrum that bringing down growth rates of the population was crucial if development has to be accessible to all. But the population policies in the first three and more decades after independence was pursued under the reigning slogan 'development is the best contraceptive' popularised by Karan Singh. However, the beginnings of a coercive approach was dramatically and brutally evident with the campaign of forcible sterilisation during the Emergency period. This directly contributed to the downfall of the Congress and Indira Gandhi and had to be subsequently abandoned.

An overt and more concerted shift in approach surfaced in the nineties, with population control being substituted for a more integrated health policy which would address the issue of the high Infant Mortality Rates (IMR), the rising Maternal Mortality Rates and other social development indicators. The recent policy measures of introducing disincentives and the two-child norm in some states, which would disqualify local self-government representatives from contesting elections, has affected the poor and marginalised groups in the rural and urban areas. And it is precisely the poor who tend to have more children since they are the only social insurance in a situation of extreme insecurity characterised by unacceptably high infant mortality rates (IMRs), generally poor access to health care exacerbated by the recent policies of cuts in the health budget and privatisation of healthcare, and shrinking livelihood options.

Census data shows, in fact, that the growth rate among the Muslims has shown a decelerating trend over the last decade both at the national level and in most states.

Even an incentive-based approach, innocuous as it may sound, effectively functions against the girl child in a society where son-preference is the norm.

If one were to view the current measures against the serious decline in child sex ratios in the 0–6 age group over the last decade along with the rising instances of female foeticide resulting in a legal measure, the PNDT Act, then the direct implications of such incentives and the two-child norm for the survival of the girl child are indeed ominous and obvious. Even an incentive-based approach, innocuous as it may sound, effectively functions against the girl child in a society where son-preference is the norm. The social and political implications of the current policy thrust need to be analysed in the context of the declining child sex ratios. That the child sex ratios have declined in almost all the states except Kerala, Mizoram, Tripura and Sikkim seems to indicate:

(a) the trend towards masculinisation of CSRs is the result of policies which have gestated over the last fifty-odd years and

(b) that the particular development paradigm pursued since independence has not only not benefited women and girls but in fact they have been the victims of this paradigm.

Again, if one were to look at the religion-wise child sex ratios, it is Christians and Muslims (964 and 950) followed by Buddhists (942) who fare better than Hindus with a child sex ratio of 925, which is the lower than the national ratio at 927. Jains and the Sikhs fare poorly with 870 and 786, respectively. A detailed and thorough analysis of this is beyond the scope of this essay. Yet it is necessary to note the various factors that impinge on this, i.e. socio-economic status, education, minority group status, age distribution, the prevalence of lack of widow remarriage etc. (Basu 2004: 4294–96) Basu points out that a higher growth rate of Muslims in India does not automatically imply unbridled Muslim fertility but instead suggests lower mortality rates. This could imply that Muslims seem to ensure the health and survival of their children, particularly their daughters, better than Hindus.

If one were to disaggregate the impact of these measures on the poor marginalised groups of dalits, tribals, Muslims and women and juxtapose these against the existing inequities of access and prevalent social indicators, the picture is indeed serious. The People's Tribunal on Coercive Population Policies and the Two-Child Norm has voiced its concerns on the matter. (*The Hindu* 2004a: 10 & 2004b: 13) The grave implications of the recent measures targeting 209 'high fertility districts' should not be lost since these are also districts with poor social development indicators.

While the recent initiatives for a strong population policy have been of exogenous origin, the unwritten consensus among the middle classes on the issue of population is widespread and often blurs political boundaries. The issue of population has the potentiality of promoting a seemingly 'progressive' consensus among the educated middle classes; those who oppose it could very easily be stigmatised as backward-looking and apologists for India's backwardness.

The fact that the social Darwinism of the neo-liberal vintage with its origin in the metropole has found ready allies in the social Darwinism of the desi variety with strong Hindu overtones from an earlier time and with deeper roots in our own not very distant past is something that should not be forgotten.

The fact that the social Darwinism of the neo-liberal vintage with its origin in the metropole has found ready allies in the social Darwinism of the desi variety with strong Hindu overtones from an earlier time and with deeper roots in our own not very distant past is something that should not be forgotten.

Support Base of Hindutva

The crucial support for Hindutva comes not merely from sadhus and sanyasis or from the moffusil middle class supposedly steeped in some form of little tradition Hinduism or even from the cosmopolitan professionals located in the big urban centres. Critical support comes from the big business houses (the extravaganzas on public events like the Republic day organised by the Modi government in Gujarat were financed lavishly by groups like Reliance and Essar among others) and from the Non Resident Indians (NRIs) in the US, UK and Europe, from the dominant sections of the Indian diaspora. Recent revelations from Britain prove the link between British-based 'charity' organisations and the funding of the most rabid and murderous organisations of the Sangh Parivar. In fact, there is now even a reference to the Export and Funding of the Hatred Industry. Our purpose here is not to underestimate the communalisation of what has been called civil society, but to underline the culpability of the state and those in power and the dramatic shift in the balance of social and political forces in favour of both Hindutva and the neo-liberal paradigm. There are many other aspects of the developing situation that are part of an integral whole: the steady and insidious communalisation of both the state machinery and also the various institutions, the skilful social engineering by the organisations of the Sangh Parivar in dealing with the fault lines of Indian society and specially in dealing with the different social actors—whether it is the tribals, the dalits, the OBC groups, the women and various regional-level contradictions.

The thrust of the Hindutva strategy is to divide classes, castes, groups and communities and to posit 'cultural nationalism' to counter economic nationalism. In this sense, the Hindutva strategy gels perfectly with the needs of imperialist capitalism. Hindutva is par excellence the ideology of inequality and hierarchy.

Hindutva and Women

One of the features of the 1990s has been the heightened mobilisation of women by the forces of Hindutva. There has been a fair degree of analysis on this subject but highlighting some features of the situation may not be out of place.

There was an upsurge in the women's movement in the late 1970s and 1980s which was broadly democratic and secular. The women's movement that arose on the crest of the wider political upsurge shared the broad consensus of a nationalist, secular and democratic framework even while focussing on the specific nature of women's oppression. However, there were diversities, differences and regional specificities within the movement. However, the dominant language of the women's movement was one of a universalist claim to citizenship, to equal participation in society and polity, unsullied by particularities of caste, religion, ethnicity and other such 'primordialisms'. (Raman 2001)

However, the Supreme Court judgement on the Shah Bano case and the controversial *obiter dicta* of Justice Chandrachud raising the issue of the Uniform Civil Code (UCC) contributed to polarising further a highly communalised situation, with the mass of Muslims, both men and women ranged against the judgment. It is important to understand the decisive nature of the polarisation that ensued in the wake of the Shah Bano judgement. In the past, similar judgements granting maintenance to Muslim women under section 125 of the Cr.P.C. did not evoke the opposition that the Shah Bano case did among the Muslim community. It contributed to fuelling the sense of being besieged among the Muslims. The Muslim Women's Bill further complicated the situation by providing the Hindu right-wing forces an opportunity to further communalise the issue. When the slogan of the Uniform Civil Code was taken over by the right wing Hindutva forces, the mainstream women's movement was forced to reflect on the changed situation and altered balance of forces.[2]

The Muslim Women's Bill further complicated the situation by providing the Hindu right-wing forces an opportunity to further communalise the issue.

The Shah Bano judgement came at a time when the entire mainstream of the women's movement was speaking in one voice demanding a uniform civil code. But, by 1996, there were wide divergences of opinion on the question of a common set of laws for all women. This change was not merely confined to women's groups alone but also encompassed the political parties (with the exception of the BJP and the Shiv Sena), which voiced their opposition to a uniform civil code. The shifts in positions reveals the attempts of various groups and organisations at coming to terms with the changed political scenario, characterised by the dominance of Hindu right wing forces. The most notable change has occurred in the position of the All India Democratic Women's Association (AIDWA), which voiced its opposition to the 'fundamentalist' demand for a uniform civil code in the mid-nineties. What is

2. The Indian Constitution recognises and sanctions various systems of personal laws based on religion and customary laws based on customary practices. These deal with issues of inheritance, rights to property, marriage, divorce, maintenance and guardianship of minors, adoption etc. This constitutional sanction to these various personal and customary laws arose out of the need to acknowledge and give recognition to the diversity and plurality of Indian society. However, the Directive Principles of State Policy also state that the State should endeavour to bring about a Uniform Civil Code which would govern all citizens regardless of religion, caste and creed. But the question of the Uniform Civil Code has always been a somewhat knotty issue since this invariably arouses fears that the identity and culture of the minorities may be swamped in the name of a common code which, it is feared would be a majoritarian Hindu code. The Shah Bano case was one instance of a Muslim woman, who went to court demanding maintenance under the civil law in the early eighties. But the Supreme Court judgement while granting maintenance was also accompanied by an *obiter dicta* which strongly recommended the need for a Uniform Civil Code. The judgement came at a time when the social and political atmosphere of the country had become highly communalised and polarised with the vast majority of the Muslim community, both men and women, rallying against the judgement. (See Raman 2001)

significant about AIDWA's position is the recognition that gender justice and the fulfilment of constitutional guarantees of equality need not necessarily be linked to an umbrella legislation and that in fact such legislation might actually be counter-productive. (Karat 1995)

We highlight the change in the perspective of the mainstream women's organisations because the question of the UCC brought to the fore a whole series of questions regarding the nature of the social processes and the consequent differential political articulation among women in general and women's organisations in particular. To reiterate a point mentioned earlier, the ensconcement of the upper-caste, educated middle classes in the structures of government and administration meant that women from these sections became much more visible in these areas; these women were the first generation beneficiaries of the developmental paradigm. Conversely, women (and men) from the subaltern groups and classes were, by and large marginalised by the developmental process. That these groups are Scheduled Castes, Scheduled Tribes and Other Backward Classes and minority groups (particularly Muslims) cannot be underemphasised. The neo-liberal paradigm has only sharpened the polarising thrust inherent in the developmental paradigm pursued so far with the cushion of the welfare state being finally abandoned in the nineties. The pursuit of this paradigm has heightened traditional social and economic differences of caste, class, religion, region and ethnicity, and women have only got more and not less embedded in their groups leading to a greater differentiation among them. This also accounts for the differential political articulation among women. The divergent responses on the Mandal Commission and the Uniform Civil Code testify to this.

The overall economic and social situation that obtains is one wherein as a result of loss of jobs in the organised sector women have also suffered. The policy of a ban on recruitment has led to a loss of at least 45,000 jobs held by women in the banking sector alone and an estimated one lakh jobs in the Central Government services. The employment growth rate for women is very low at less than two per cent while the mass of women in the rural areas have to deal with a situation where they get work for hardly 45 days in many parts of India. Agricultural policies implemented as part of the WTO agreement have led to a severe crisis of agriculture leading to a large number of suicides. Out of the 9,000 farmers who were driven to suicides, at least one-third were women. This period has also seen a massive onslaught on food security; while food grains either rotted in the godowns or were exported at very low prices, people starved; and women and girl children were the worst affected.

The destruction of the Babri Masjid saw the above-mentioned processes coming to fruition with the Hindutva forces' political strategies to mobilise women for furthering the project of a Hindu Rashtra. The change can be seen in the response of the middle classes, both men and women, to the victims of communal violence. While the first three-four decades saw sections of the Hindu middle classes coming to the fore in restoring communal harmony after riots and heading peace committees, the nineties witnessed the phenomenon of upper caste Hindu women not only actively encouraging riotous acts but also participating in looting the properties and valuables of the Muslim community.

In the decade of the 1990s, the coming on to the centre stage of Indian politics of Hindutva forces spurred significant work on the role of gender in politicised religion. Some of the scholars (Sarkar and Butalia: 1995) referred to the disturbing prominence of the Hindu right and its successful mobilisation of women in furthering the project of Hindutva in the 1980s and the 1990s. Many of the scholars/analysts have drawn attention to the fact that this large-scale mobilisation of women behind movements and organisations with professed anti-feminist and anti-democratic agendas could not be dismissed as an instance of 'false-consciousness' but that there

The overall economic and social situation that obtains is one wherein as a result of loss of jobs in the organised sector women have also suffered.

was an informed consent and agency in this participation. In fact, it has also been pointed out that this mobilisation has actually been 'empowering' to the extent that it provides a legitimate avenue for breaking the confines of domesticity and stepping into the public sphere, although this has not meant nor was intended to lead to a redefinition of women's roles either in the domestic or in the public sphere. However, the significant question is: what are the implications of the 'empowerment' of Hindu women under the banner of Hindutva for Muslim women when this mobilisation is directed against both men and women?

Gujarat 2002

There are certain features of the Gujarat situation that need to be reiterated so that the situation of women and their responses to it can be contextualised.

The scale of ethnic cleansing that occurred in Gujarat is enormous and giving figures somehow seems to take away from the enormity of the crime that was perpetrated.

There have been many reports of what transpired in Gujarat during the night of the long knives. Women's groups, civil liberties groups, trade unions independent citizens groups, the many reports in the print media, documentary film makers, all have testified to the horror of what happened. And as Tanika Sarkar has put it:

> What is new about Gujarat can best be exemplified in what happened to Muslim women and children on the days of the long knives. Not just their killings, not just the sadism that effected their killings, but the large symbolic purpose behind the deaths sums up the nature of ethnic cleansing, the shape of Hindu Rashtra. (Sarkar 2003: 153)

...Gujarat did not occur in a vacuum nor was it some irrational madness that had seized the mobs. Gujarat has been in the offing for a long time. It has been in the offing because of the economic developments of the last two decades and more when lakhs of textile workers have been rendered jobless with the closure of the mills, the pauperisation that ensued with the collapse of the social infrastructure that accompanied it and heightened insecurities among those affected;

For one, Gujarat did not occur in a vacuum nor was it some irrational madness that had seized the mobs. Gujarat has been in the offing for a long time. It has been in the offing because of the economic developments of the last two decades and more when lakhs of textile workers have been rendered jobless with the closure of the mills, the pauperisation that ensued with the collapse of the social infrastructure that accompanied it and heightened insecurities among those affected; it has been in the offing because of the planned manner in which the Hindutva forces engaged in the 'social engineering' towards the creation of Hindu Rashtra.

The pattern of violence and the targeting of Muslim owned properties including those with names that could not be identified as Muslim show long and careful planning. There were house checks under the guise of data collection just prior to the violence. Mosques and dargahs were destroyed.

An integral part of the social engineering was the careful planting of many members of the Sangh Parivar in the administration. There was a total surrender of the state machinery to the Hindutva forces with some honourable and courageous exceptions.

The much touted economic development of the state has really meant jobless growth. Jan Breman (2003: 367–76) refers to the close linkages between what has happened in Gujarat as a resurgence of social Darwinism. The changing political economy, the altered balance of social forces with the traditional working classes seriously eroded numerically and reduced to pauperised informal sector workers and corresponding to this the rise of a wealthy middle class which constitutes the base of Hindutva has contributed to Gujarat 2002.

As one writer has put it:

> The key element in the recent atrocities is the new role of the prosperous, educated middle class. In the past, the middle class has halted communal violence, as members of state bureaucracy, police and business community. Now it organises communal cleansing with the efficiency of a business project.' (Choudhury 2003: 259–364)

The active acquiescence and in many cases participation of women in the Hindutva project and the victimisation of the large masses of Muslim women are two sides of the same coin.

Gujarat has rather ironically demonstrated the success of 'agency' and 'empowerment' of Hindu women under the banner of Hindutva in rather macabre ways. The women of Gujarat were divided into Hindu women who were the agents and the Muslim women who were the vulnerable victims. Needless to say, there have been not a few courageous men and women from among the Hindus, many courageous Adivasis and Dalits who risked their lives and sometimes paid with their lives for saving Muslims. But their attempts could not withstand the tornado of hatred that had been carefully nurtured over the last few decades. Then there were the examples of large numbers of well-to-do, middle class Hindu Gujarati women who were active participants in large scale looting of Muslim shops and godowns apart from showing a callous disregard for the thousands of Muslim women who were raped and children who were burnt and killed in the most heartless manner.

Gujarat has rather ironically demonstrated the success of 'agency' and 'empowerment' of Hindu women under the banner of Hindutva in rather macabre ways. The women of Gujarat were divided into Hindu women who were the agents and the Muslim women who were the vulnerable victims.

Concluding Remarks

Two agendas have converged: the neo-liberal paradigm with its thrust on integration into an essentially unequal world capitalist-imperialist system, an important element of which is to dispense with the bottom 30 per cent of society, and the agenda of Hindutva which has no place for the diversities and pluralities of India and certainly not for *shudras*, *ati-shudras*, Muslims and women.

The general elections of May 2004 have given a decisive verdict against both the impact of the new polices and the communalisation of social and political processes. While the Bharatiya Janata Party and the National Democratic Front led by it has been defeated and the Congress-led United Progressive Alliance has come to power at the Centre, we believe that the basic analysis still holds. The change of regime is a reprieve for the people and opens up avenues for the assertion of people's movements to attempt to change course and alter the balance of forces. The new government will have to take bold steps to retain the people's confidence. Given that the coalition partners have different and even divergent perceptions of the country's future, the manner in which these are played out keeping in mind the popular mandate will depend on how skilfully these are handled.

The change of regime is a reprieve for the people and opens up avenues for the assertion of people's movements to attempt to change course and alter the balance of forces.

References

Ahmad, A. 2004. *On Communalism and Globalisation*. New Delhi: Three Essays Collective.

Amin, S. 2004. *Obsolescent Capitalism*. Delhi: Rainbow Publishers.

Basu, A. 2004. The Squabble that Never Ends : Religion and Fertility, *Economic and Political Weekly*, September 25: 4294–96.

Breman, J. 2003. 'Communal Upheaval as a Resurgence of Social Darwinism', in C. Krishna (ed.), *Fascism in India, Faces, Fangs and Facts*. Delhi: Manak Publications.

Choudhury, K. 2003. 'Hindutva's Foreign Hand and the Middle Class', in C. Krishna (ed.), *Fascism in India, Faces, Fangs and Facts*. Delhi: Manak Publications.

Deshpande, S. 2003. *Contemporary India*. New Delhi: Viking.

Gupta, C. 2001. *Sexuality, Obscenity, Community: Women, Muslim and the Hindu Public in Colonial India*. Delhi: *Permanent Black*.

——— 2004. 'Censuses, Communalism, Gender and Identity—A Historical Perspective'. *Economic and Political Weekly*, September 25: 4302–04.

Karat, B. 1995. 'Uniformity vs. Equality: The Concept of Uniform Civil Code', *Frontline*, November 4 –17: 12(13).

Ludden, D. (ed). 1996. *Making India Hindu*. New Delhi: Oxford University Press.

Mazumdar, I. 2004. *Emergent Contradictions—Globalisation and Women Workers in India* (mimeo). New Delhi: Centre for Women's Development Studies.

Premi, N. 2004. 'Religion in India—A Demographic Perspective'. *Economic and Political Weekly*, September 25: 4297–4302.

Raman, V. 2001. 'The Women's Question in Contemporary Indian Politics', *Asian Journal of Women's Studies*, Ehwa Women's University, Korea, 7(2): 39–71.

Sarkar, T. 2003. 'The Semiotics of Terror: Muslim Children and Women in Hindu Rashtra', in C. Krishna (ed.), *Fascism in India, Faces, Fangs and Facts*. Delhi: Manak Publications.

——— and U. Butalia (eds). 1995. *Women and the Hindu Right*. New Delhi: Kali for Women.

Sikand, Y. and Katju, M. 1994. Mass Conversion to Hinduism among Indian Muslims. *Economic and Political Weekly*, August 20.

Social Movements

Prakash Louis

The effects of liberalisation, privatisation and globalisation (LPG) in the developing countries are increasingly becoming apparent. The current trends demonstrate that these processes disadvantage the poor and advantage the already well-off. It is obvious that those who encourage globalisation are the rich who benefit from it and those who oppose it are the poor who lose because of it. Globalisation today means liberalisation, privatisation, and structural adjustment (LPS), according to the formula of the World Bank (WB), International Monetary Fund (IMF), and World Trade Organisation (WTO). The growing opposition is a response to the manner in which globalisation is proceeding and to its ill effects on the poor, and not to globalisation per se. There are also some among the rich who oppose it. But they do so out of a sense of justice that the proponents of globalisation say is misplaced. 'Globalisation is a fact today and it is also a fact that it is indiscriminately eating into the lives of people. It is a mindless imposition of policies irrespective of conditions obtaining in each country. The world is caught in a debt trap...' (*Janata* 2004: 6) If these words had been spoken by an activist, they could be discounted. But, they happen to be the words of K.R. Narayanan, the former President of India, at the Asian Social Forum (ASF) held in Hyderabad in January 2003.

Two parallel streams can be identified in the development discourse. On the one hand, there are the proponents of liberalisation and privatisation who insist on structural adjustment programmes, which base their entire operation on the premise that the common good will follow in the long run without in fact making any provisions for the new problems the majority of the population is forced into. They seek elimination of the legislative barriers that protect workers in order to create incentives for private investment. They exempt the powerful groups from taxes and environmental obligations and shelter them in order to accelerate the industrialisation process; thus creating an even greater concentration of wealth and economic power. These are part of the economic doctrines that give paramount importance to macroeconomic variables such as growth and inflation, with no attention to income distribution, job security, food security, environmental degradation, people's rights or justice.

It has been argued by many social scientists and members of people's movements that, on one hand, market forces are engaged in a global transformation for their own benefit, while, on the other, the collective action groups and people's movements have tried to address the debilitating and devastating effects of LPS. Most of these protest movements are planned and sporadic, localised and broad-based, sectoral and multifaceted, national and international. In this paper, an attempt is made to examine the various social movements and protests against the structural adjustment programmes and other globalisation processes. Due to lack of space, the innumerable protests, resistances, and movements are not highlighted here. The nature, structure, form, and outcome of some of these protests and people's movements discussed here are only representative in nature.

'Globalisation is a fact today and it is also a fact that it is indiscriminately eating into the lives of people. ... The world is caught in a debt trap...'

There are different understandings of social movements. For our discussion, social movements are collective social actions aimed at either demanding a change or resisting change in any or total realms of social life. They propose and pursue particular objectives, which in turn generate conflicts and tensions. Social movements are the outcome of the existing social structure and they, in turn, affect these structures. Thus, social movements leave their footprints on the social structures that bred them. Careful sociological examinations of the various unfolding social movements suggest the diversity of the demands, the intensity of dissent, and the direction these movements take. They also call for a serious analysis of the interconnectedness of the various issues that give rise to social movements. (Louis 2002: 30)

At the outset, it needs to be stated that the resistances, protests, and social movements that are generated to counter LPS have some specificity about them. While they counter the global forces that are the proponents and beneficiaries of these realities, these social movements also challenge the national or local forces, which collaborate with global forces to initiate and benefit from the anti-people development paradigm. Expectedly, there is no uniformity among them with regard to organisational procedures, leadership, or resources to mobilise the victims of globalisation for resistances and protests.

Impact of Structural Adjustment Programme

It is expedient here to examine some of the impacts of structural adjustment programmes (SAPs) on the common citizens of a country, especially on the marginalised segments of society. The SAPs have demanded reduction in subsidy for agricultural inputs, which in turn has pushed up the prices of food grains—not just in the open market but also in the public distribution system (PDS). The rising fuel and freight costs have led to further decline in the purchasing capacity of the common people. Moreover, loss of jobs, loss of security available to those in jobs, and the non-availability of new employment opportunities are directly affecting the interest of the workers. Above all the SAPs, in the name of fiscal constraint, are affecting public expenditure in all sectors, especially the social sector.

...the SAPs, in the name of fiscal constraint, are affecting public expenditure in all sectors, especially the social sector.

It has been repeatedly demonstrated that the government is slowly and steadily abdicating its responsibility towards its citizens by withdrawing or reducing its share and role in the social sector, particularly in food security, education, and health. This move has direct consequences for the excluded and marginalised segments of society. Simultaneously, the policies and programmes that benefit the privileged are being adopted. For example, the Indian Institute of Technology (IIT) alumni have proposed to set up a $1 billion (Rs. 4.5 crore) fund to privatise five IITs in the country. (*Asian Age*, 13 December1999: 1) IITs are among the most subsidised higher education institutions. Moreover, almost all the students who pass out from these institutions go abroad and settle there and thus there is no return to the contribution made by public funds. This is just one instance of how SAPs encourage interventions that ultimately benefit only the rich and the powerful.

The labour and employment fronts have also been subjected to serious crises by the reforms introduced in 1991. The aggregate employment elasticity of output fell from 0.52 during 1983–94 to 0.16 during 1994–2000. This phenomenon raises some crucial questions. Why is the government doing nothing about it? Why, in the past five years, have budgetary allocations for all employment schemes been so low? Why has the government not put more resources and energy into ensuring that small enterprises, which employ most of the people in the country,have access to capital and basic infrastructure so that they can be viable? Part of the answer is that the central government is so limited by constraints of its own making—financial liberalisation and a dependence on the shifting priorities of international investors—that it simply cannot take the more obvious measures such as directly increasing employment through more public work. (Ghosh 2004: 17)

...the central government is so limited by constraints of its own making—financial liberalisation and a dependence on the shifting priorities of international investors—that it simply cannot take the more obvious measures such as directly increasing employment through more public work.

There is a historical precedence to the imposition of the SAPs. The international banking system came up with SAPs in response to the debt crises among the Third

World countries., Such programmes were aimed at forcing the Third World countries to pay their debts at the expense of their internal development. The SAPs entailed devaluation of local currency, a sharp rise in interest rates on loans, removal of trade barriers that protected local industries and agriculture, privatisation of public sector enterprises, particularly those involved in transportation, energy, telephones and electricity, deregulation of manufacturing, services, and labour, which meant removal of minimum wage laws, and reduction of subsidies in basic benefits such as food allowances, education, and healthcare for the poor. Accepting such a package was mandatory in order to receive new loans to repay old debts. Each indebted country was directed to focus on exporting commodities to earn international currency to repay debts at the expense of the diversification of agricultural and industrial production for local consumption. (Ralte et.al. 2004)

The SAPs were billed as austerity measures that would cause temporary pain but would soon cause the whole economy to adjust and prosper. The reality was largely the opposite of these rosy predictions—by dismantling trade barriers, local production was devastated. As cheap products of multinational corporations flooded markets of the borrowing countries, their local industries and agriculture declined, in some cases precipitously. Why did the Third World governments accept these conditions that were devastating their economies? They did so basically for three reasons:

1. Although the majority of people were suffering, the wealthy elites, who also controlled the governments, were prospering.
2. Economists in these governments were trained in the same perspectives as those working in institutions like the World Bank and accepted these theories of market neo-liberalism as unquestioned dogma.
3. Any government that resisted the package would be isolated and denied loans and markets. This reality reduced the scope for social intervention by governments that lack political will to address the core concerns of their citizens.

Each indebted country was directed to focus on exporting commodities to earn international currency to repay debts at the expense of the diversification of agricultural and industrial production for local consumption.

...by dismantling trade barriers, local production was devastated. As cheap products of multinational corporations flooded markets of the borrowing countries, their local industries and agriculture declined, in some cases precipitously.

In Defense of Structural Adjustment Programme

The proponents of LPS continue to argue that every reform introduced is an attempt to build market socialism with an indigenous character. They also argue that this is economic reform which would not have impact on other sectors. Others argue that this is a 'reform with human face'.

There are some who strongly defend globalisation and decry anti-globalisation. Jagdish Bhagwati, for instance, argues that anti-globalisation sentiments are more prevalent in the rich countries of the North, while pluralities of policy makers and the public in the poor countries of the South see globalisation as a positive force. This was the finding of the World Economic Forum's (WEF) extensive poll on global public opinion on globalisation, carried out by the Canadian polling firm Environics International, with twenty-five thousand urban respondents in twenty-five countries, and presented at the WEF's annual meeting in New York in early 2002. (Bhagwati 2004: 8) Bhagwati further states that these countries now regret having made the wrong choice.

One also finds that those who defend globalisation contend that only a small minority resist globalisation. According to the polls conducted by the Centre on Policy Attitudes of the University of Maryland, Americans largely tend to see globalisation as somewhat more positive than negative and appear to be growing familiar with the concept. A large majority favours moving with the process of globalisation and only a small minority favours resisting it. (Bhagwati 2004: 10) It is opinion polls of this nature that are utilised by the votaries of globalisation to advance their cause.

Interestingly, the neo-liberal economists have found another ingenious way of explaining away the failure on the employment front and even suggesting that it requires further doses of liberalisation. The mainstream policy response is that even the extensive reforms undertaken so far have been inadequate; they have not addressed some of the more politically difficult areas such as labour market policies and institutions that are impediments to private investment. The argument is that investment has been constrained and employment growth has been insufficient because of rigidities in the labour markets that adversely affect employers' sentiments. (Ghosh 2004: 18)

There are some who argue that civil society is slowly being drawn towards supporting the plans of the global forces. According to them, the biggest votaries of civil society today are none other than the World Bank, US Agency for International Development (USAID), United Nations Development Programme (UNDP), Ford Foundation and other such organisations. The World Bank defines civil society as the whole of the private sector led by non-governmental organisations (NGOs) and to deal with them the Bank has already established an executive wing, called World Bank/NGO Committee. World Bank literature describes global market expansion and growth of civil society as identical. It defines the growth of democracy and 'good governance' in Afro-Asian-Latin American countries in terms of the degree of replacement of the traditional political sphere by civic action. (*Red Star*, January 2003: 7) It is this contention which needs to be seriously addressed by civil society in its response to the global forces.

Protests and Movements against Structural Adjustment Programme

It is these processes which have ignited disappointment and depression among the people and have in turn triggered movements. One can identify some movements that have emerged in the recent past. Women's relation to globalisation works in two ways:

1. Women, especially poor women, are disproportionately affected by globalisation, and
2. Women, or women's groups, are among the important sites of the critique of and resistance to globalisation.

Instead of more and more control over wealth by a small elite in distant centres of power, it calls for a redistribution of power and transfer of control over decision making to the local level.

Women's alternative organisations for survival have become major actors in the movements of resistance to the World Bank and the IMF and the alternative visions of more just, democratic, and ecologically sustainable forms of development. This vision of an alternative way of development demands a major turnaround to the corporation-led globalisation. Instead of more and more control over wealth by a small elite in distant centres of power, it calls for a redistribution of power and transfer of control over decision making to the local level. Instead of disempowering local governments, it calls for re-empowering them, as they are much more democratically elected and reflect local interests. Instead of stripping local people of protection for their agriculture and industry, it calls for local governments to protect the national economy from being overrun by large corporations. (Ralte et.al. 2004: 61)

In India, the Right to Food and Work campaign is also directed at opposing local and global forces that are depriving the poor of food and forcing them to starvation deaths.

History bears testimony to this fact that resistance and protest to LPS were not triggered off or limited to the organised industrial sector. 'The Battle of Seattle' and the World Social Forums (WSFs) are perhaps the best-known expressions of the Global Justice and Solidarity Movement. The movements provoked by neo-liberalism and globalisation began with the 'Food Riots' or 'IMF Riots' in the Third World in the 1980s. This became the first major radical-democratic movement in response to the globalised, networked, and 'informatised' capitalism. It is a radical-democratic movement, in the sense that it represents a response to, against, and beyond the hegemonic globalisation project known as neo-liberalism. It is radically democratic in so far as it seeks out the roots of that project and suggests detailed alternatives. (*Labour*

File. Nov-Dec 2003: 20) In India, the Right to Food and Work campaign is also directed at opposing local and global forces that are depriving the poor of food and forcing them to starvation deaths.

Resistance to globalisation has assumed global importance and is no longer an activity special to the Third World progressives. Within the advanced capitalist countries, a new kind of activism is getting organised on the recognition that globalisation is bad for everyone except the corporate elite; hence the sudden and surprising congregations of large numbers of people in Seattle, Washington, Davos, Prague, and Porto Allegre in a historically unique wave of transnational solidarity. These defensive resistances against the capitalist destructiveness and corporate elite have an analogue in other struggles, which are designed to augment the capacities and cultural capital of the labouring masses by providing them, with or without cooperation from the state, the means of education, vocational training, health and sanitation, instructions in simple sciences and technologies for local use, recovery of local traditions, and thus of an alternative history. These diverse practices give rise to what one might call a 'social left' alongside the older, more recognisable institutions of the 'political left' such as the trade unions, the peasant leagues, and the political party. (Ahmad 2004: 91)

It is also a fact that resistance and revolt against the globalising forces is not a uniform or unifocal phenomenon. In this regard, Aijaz Ahmad wonders how then to conceptualise these complex movements that have

1. Been widespread, involving more people around the globe than ever before, even in the period of restoration.
2. Tended to become local and issue-based, with no shared focus, precisely at the time when capital has gained unprecedented global unity.
3. Worked to reform capitalism, but not to destroy it.
4. Shown two different and parallel movements: those that seek the more traditional kinds of reforms that strengthen the system and others who seek what Andre Gorz called 'non-reformist reforms' that undermine it.

Irrespective of many pitfalls, these people's movements represent various aspirations, sectors, and processes of response to LPS. For instance, the biennial national conference of the Hind Mazdoor Sabha, which was held in Nagpur on February 8-10, heard a strong plea from the president of the conference, Prabhu Narain Singh, for unification of all the organisations of the working class. He stressed that it could not otherwise face up to the united onslaught of a truly united global capital. (*Janata*. 15 February 2004: 3)

Similarly, the fourth bi-annual convention of the National Allaince of People's Movements (NAPM) held in Andhra Pradesh on 22–24 May concluded with the resolve to intensify the nation-wide struggle for the rights of the Dalits, Adivasis, workers, farmers, fishers, women, minorities, and all other marginalised sections and against globalisation, privatisation, and communalism-casteism. The convention called for a new alternative water, forest, and land policy, rejecting forthwith the Interlinking Rivers Project and all such mega-projects of anti-people development. (*Janata*. 6 June 2004: 6)

It is also significant to note that the joint forums that deal with peace between neighbouring countries also take the negative impact of globalisation process seriously and respond to it in their own way.

It is also significant to note that the joint forums that deal with peace between neighbouring countries also take the negative impact of globalisation process seriously and respond to it in their own way. The Joint Convention of the Pakistan India People's Forum for Peace and Democracy stated in their declaration that the people of the world in general and South Asia in particular face new forms of imperialistic globalisation that are today

1. Increasingly aided and abetted by local interests and constituencies.

2. Imposing an iniquitous system on developing countries.
3. Destroying livelihood of the common people.
4. Undermining the political and economic independence of countries.
5. Directing violence against societies with different political parties and social ideals, particularly Muslim people.
6. Terrorising entire countries in the name of fighting terrorism.

The declaration also states that the future of the people of Pakistan and India as independent countries is contingent on permanent peace and harmony, which is also imperative in order to fight the imperialist machination for subjugation and exploitation of the resources and the people of our countries. The declaration affirms that building strong trade and economic cooperation between the two countries and in the entire South Asia to foster independent development is the only way to build substantive resistance against the IMF, World Bank, WTO, and the agents of imperialist globalisation. (*The People's Movement.* March-April 2004: 29)

Another radical approach was undertaken by some of the people's organisations in India. The Forum Against Imperialist Globalisation (FAIG) was formed by people's organisations from various parts of the country in Delhi on 13 October 2001 with a determination to forge unity against imperialist globalisation—the process of exploitative policies unleashed by the imperialist powers and implemented by our rulers, particularly for the last one decade. Sixty-two people's organisations engaged in grass-roots level struggles in different parts of the country came together and undertook various activities to oppose the forces of globalisation. Many state level conventions, rallies, and demonstrations have been organised to continue the struggle. (*People's Resistance.* May-June 2002: 31)

There are also movements for the recovery of traditional methods of farming that rebuild soil and prevent soil erosion as well as air and water pollution. There is an organised resistance to trade rules that seek to deprive local farmers of their traditional knowledge. There is also a connected movement that calls for the shutting down of the World Bank and the IMF, in favour of the international bodies built through people's organisations that represent this alternative vision.

There are also movements for the recovery of traditional methods of farming that rebuild soil and prevent soil erosion as well as air and water pollution. There is an organised resistance to trade rules that seek to deprive local farmers of their traditional knowledge. There is also a connected movement that calls for the shutting down of the World Bank and the IMF, in favour of the international bodies built through people's organisations that represent this alternative vision. The move to form *Pani Panchayats* or 'Water Forums' indicate the resolve of the collective action groups and people's movements to ensure that the common people not only have water for their various needs but they also have access and control over water resources.

One of the most powerful, broad-based open forums which provided a platform for debate on the globalisation process was the WSF. The advocates of globalisation propagate the myth that 'globalisation is a fact of life and it is a natural phenomenon'. They also declare that 'There is no alternative (TINA) to globalisation'. Against these pronouncements, there has been a powerful current to mobilise and organise those who oppose this dominant process. The WSF is one of the major expressions of this collective thrust. In response to the TINA slogan, they state SITA (Socialism is the Alternative). Others state that 'There are Many Alternatives' (TAMA).

The Fourth WSF meet , which took place in Mumbai on 16–21 January 2004, was the continuation of the efforts to comprehend the effects of the globalising forces and search for meaningful alternatives. Right from the initiation of the WSF process, it was kept in mind that though the impetus for organising the WSF emerged from Brazil, the forum should be held in various parts of the world. This was kept in mind since WSF represents the search for global alternatives. Since India has been a country where innumerable and diverse people's movements have emerged to oppose anti-people and anti-human forces, it was considered appropriate to hold the Fourth WSF here in India.

As witnessed by the over a hundred thousand participants, who assembled in Mumabi for the WSF, the protests as well as the search for alternatives were diverse.

It is in Mumbai, more than in Brazil, that the WSF exhibited the plural, diversified, non-confessional, non-governmental, and non-party context that represented the serious search for alternatives. This also exhibited the unity of purpose between the organisations and movements engaged in concrete action at all levels, from the local to the international, to build another world. The vibrant and colourful participation of the tribals and Dalits further demonstrated the ascendance of these marginalised people to the fore of the protest politics. Above all, the fourth WSF also demonstrated that the WSF is a process that encourages its participant organisations and movements to position their actions as issues of planetary citizenship, and to introduce onto the global agenda the change-inducing practices that they are experimenting in building a new world. Thus, the holding of the WSF in Mumbai generated greater enthusiasm to respond to the LPS and search for alternatives at the indigenous level.

Significantly, while the WSF was going on, another mobilisation and organisation under the name of Mumbai Resistance–2004 (MR–2004) against Imperialist Globalisation and War was held in Mumbai, just opposite the venue of the WSF. The objective of this mobilisation was to build a strong worldwide anti-imperialist movement that seeks to take the people of the world, including those attending the WSF, beyond the limits of '*reflective thinking and debate*' towards organised resistance against imperialist globalisation and imperialist wars. It is based on clear and unambiguous premises. The MR-2004 considers itself as a continuation of the militant traditions set in the anti-globalisation and anti-war movements that assumed a new intensity after Seattle. (Louis 2004: 125–40)

Taken together, it can be stated that the new social movements in India and many parts of the Third World and the First World, particularly in the 1980s onwards, have been a blending of serious contemporary issues, aspirations, and principles. They are challenging the conventional developmental model prevalent in the capitalist mode of production and consumption, and they have developed a formidable critique of one or more aspects of the current development project, policy, or paradigm. In the 'negation' were seeds of what an alternative development should be like. The resistance against Silent Valley, Narmada and Tehri dams, the issues emerging out of the Bhopal gas tragedy, the resistance to the multinational and national capitalist forces, the struggles of the tribals, fishers, labourers and peasants, Dalits and other backward classes, the campaign for peace and communal harmony or the new constructive movements for alternatives in water, energy, education, and health etc. have all added dimensions to the struggle. (*The People's Movement*. January-February 2004: 6) The *Raithara Sangha* (Farmer's Organisation) of Karnataka has helped small farmers to implement changes at the farm level and modernise agriculture without falling into the clutches of the loans sharks.

People's movements, collective action groups, and NGOs have been trying to understand the emergence and impact of the LPS as well as the globalisation of economy and polity by the most powerful countries in collaboration with the powerful elite of the developing countries. Their understanding also has resulted in various forms of responses to these issues. What would be the ultimate outcome of these protests, resistances, and movements will be known only in the course of time. But these people's movements have underscored the issues that both the forces of globalisation at local, national, and international levels cannot take the common people for granted. It is here that the role of civil society becomes very crucial as searching for alternative forms of development, participation, governance, and existence would alone pose the formidable challenge to liberalisation, privatisation, and structural adjustment.

...the new social movements in India and many parts of the Third World and the First World, particularly in the 1980s onwards, have been a blending of serious contemporary issues, aspirations, and principles.

References

Ahmad, Aijaz. *A Reflection on our Times: Revolution, Restoration and Resistance*. Hyderabad: Prajasakti Book House.

Asian Age. 1999. 13 December: 1.

Bhagwati, Jagdish. 2004. *In Defense of Globalisation*. New York: Oxford University Press.

Ghosh, Jayati. 2004. 'Employment and the NDA Government'. *Labour File*. January-February: 17.

Janata. 15 February 2004.

Janata. 6 June 2004.

Janata. 20 June 2004.

Labour File. November-December 2003.

Louis, Prakash. 2002. *People Power: The Naxalite Movement in Central Bihar*. New Delhi: Wordsmiths.

Louis, Prakash. 2004. 'World Social Forum: Issues and Perspectives', *Social Action*, April-June.

People's Resistance. May-June 2002.

Ralte, Lalrinawmi et. al. (ed). 2004. *In Waging Peace: Building a World in Which Life Matters*. Delhi: IWIT/ISPCK.

Red Star. January 2003.

The People's Movement. January-February 2004.

The People's Movement. March-April 2004.

The Quest for Equity in Development*

Manmohan Singh

[As for an *alternative policy framework*, in the present circumstances, it appeared to us that we could do no better than to fall back upon a policy package articulated by the Head of the UPA government way back in 1986, who was then the Deputy Chairman of the Planning Commission. —*Ed.*]

The time has come to integrate these programmes, including programmes for social services, into the framework of comprehensive local level planning. Unfortunately, local level planning has yet to take firm roots. As part of strengthening the local level planning capabilities, the technical expertise of the rural development administration at all levels will need to be substantially upgraded. *Too often, there has been a tendency in our country to believe that rural development can be brought about rather cheaply.* This is a mistaken belief. In addition, if various leakages are to be avoided, it is necessary to revive and revitalise the Panchayati Raj institutions as a means of enlisting requisite public cooperation and support for programmes of grassroot development. Furthermore, it must also be appreciated that the pace at which these programmes can be expanded in the future is a function of both financial resources and build-up of administrative capabilities at the grassroots level. It is only on the basis of a sound and elastic public financial system that we can devote increasing volumes of resources simultaneously for productive investment, social services and anti-poverty programmes.

Conclusion

In the preceding analysis, I have tried to highlight the reasons for our limited gains in terms of social justice under planning. This analysis brings out that progress towards poverty eradication can be accelerated by:

(a) a fairly high rate of economic growth maintained over a long period;

(b) a sustained increase in agricultural production;

(c) an expanding public sector with a growing capacity for generation of internal resources; and

(d) a combination of efficiently administered programmes designed specifically to increase incomes and productivity of the poorer sections and to improve their access to basic social services particularly education and health.

Physical controls at strategic points and sound fiscal and monetary policies are no doubt also essential for an orderly management of the economy. However, in view of the inherent administrative constraints, one must not overestimate the redistributive potential of either physical controls or fiscal policies. Indeed past experience shows that an over-extended system of physical controls and a seemingly progressive tax system which cannot be made effective are often counter-productive in terms of their impact on both growth and equity.

As to the future, I remain convinced that even within the overall framework of the existing development strategy for which there is today a broad national consensus, it is possible to make such faster progress towards the removal of poverty in years to come. However, the underlying potential can be realised only if policies and programmes are so oriented as to fulfil the following conditions:

* Excerpted from the Rao Bahadur R.P. Kale Memorial Lecture, delivered by Dr. Manmohan Singh at the Gokhale Institute of Politics and Economics at Pune on 2 June 1986. *Emphasis not in the original.*

(a) We are successful in stabilising the aggregate growth rate of economy at a minimum level of 5 per cent per annum.

(b) Agricultural growth rate is stabilised at close to 3.5 to 4.0 per cent pre annum, there is greater regional balance in agricultural development and particular attention is paid to increasing the productivity of small and marginal farmers.

(c) *The satisfaction of basic human needs is given an over-riding priority in resource allocation* and there is a clearer indication of national priorities so that scarce resources are not diverted to less essential uses.

(d) There is a major reform of the public sector so as to enhance its internal resources generating capacity to finance its future expansion.

(e) The elasticity of the tax system is improved through a rate structure which is realistic and through administrative reforms which induce stricter enforcement and compliance.

(f) Inflationary pressures are kept strictly under control and in particular, through arrangements such as adequate buffer stocks, prices of foodgrains are prevented from rising unduly in years of drought.

(g) The industrial sector is freed of such controls which serve no useful social purpose so that it can grow at an average annual rate of 8 per cent leading to faster growth of public revenues and employment outside agriculture.

(h) The requisite political will is generated to implement sincerely the nationally accepted policies regarding ceilings on land holdings, protection of sharecroppers and consolidation of holdings.

(i) *The various area development and beneficiary oriented programmes are integrated into a consistent package based on detailed analysis of local needs, resource potential and capabilities.* There should be a revamping of the administration of agricultural and rural development programmes, with much greater emphasis being placed on upgradation of technical and managerial skills and improvement of motivation of functionaries at the grassroots level.

(j) The Panchayati Raj institutions and the cooperative movement are revitalised so as to provide effective public support and assistance which are vital for the success of programmes of rural development.

(k) Social services particularly education and health are expanded fast enough to universalise elementary education and to reduce infant mortality rate to no more than 60 per 1,000 live births. *Greater equity in the access to basic social services is essential for progress towards greater equity in development.* Apart from improving the capabilities of the poor to participate in economic processes more effectively, emphasis on education, particularly of girls and on reduction of infant mortality rate, will help to generate a climate conducive to the acceptance of the small family norm, without which a substantial improvement in living standards of the poor may not be possible.

The country has now the necessary administrative, managerial, technical and financial capabilities to soften very considerably the harsh edges of extreme poverty. It has of course to be emphasised that the progress towards a just society is not merely one of providing more income and job opportunities or more equal access to the basic social services.

Determined action will be necessary to reform and refashion our social and economic institutions so that barriers to social mobility and progress rooted in the rigidities of our social structure are removed. We have a long journey ahead of us in our quest for a more equitable society. What is required is that the collective will of the nation is brought to bear on this problem so that we can mobilise all our latent resources for a successful social and economic transformation of Indian society.